CHEATING IS ENCOURAGED

CHEATING IS ENCOURAGED

A HARD-NOSED HISTORY OF THE 1970S RAIDERS

MIKE SIANI
AND
KRISTINE SETTING CLARK

SPORTS
PUBLISHING

Sports Publishing books may be purchased in bulk at special discounts for sales promotion, corporate gifts, fund-raising, or educational purposes. Special editions can also be created to specifications. For details, contact the Special Sales Department, Sports Publishing, 307 West 36th Street, 11th Floor, New York, NY 10018 or sportspubbooks@skyhorsepublishing.com.

Sports Publishing® is a registered trademark of Skyhorse Publishing, Inc.®, a Delaware corporation.

Visit our website at www.sportspubbooks.com.

10 9 8 7 6 5 4 3 2

Library of Congress Cataloging-in-Publication Data is available on file.

Cover design by Tom Lau
Cover photo credit: AP Images

Print ISBN: 978-1-61321-820-4
Ebook ISBN: 978-1-61321-868-6

Printed in the United States of America

This book is dedicated to James Garner, friend, number one Raider fan, and the "original" Maverick.

And to those Oakland Raiders who have departed this world far too soon, but who left an indelible imprint on professional football.

Photo courtesy of LB Archives

The Autumn Wind is a Pirate
Blustering in from sea
With a rollicking song
He sweeps along
Swaggering voicelessly
His face is weather-beaten
He wears a hooded sash
With a silver hat about his head
And a bristling, black mustache.
He growls as he storms the country
A villain big and bold and the trees all shake and quiver and quake as
he robs them of their gold.
The autumn wind is a raider pyre raging just for fun.
He'll knock you round and upside down
and laugh when he's conquered and won.

Born and bred by the Bay in Oakland, California, the Raiders played their own special brand of football. While the defense struck with the hammer of Thor, the offense flew on the wings of Mercury with a succession of rough-and-tumble running backs.

The Oakland Raiders were warriors cut from a different cloth . . . renegades with faces only a mother could love. The banner they fly—the skull and crossbones—is a clue to their personality. Show no mercy, take no prisoners. This is a team that revels in its ominous image.

For over fifty years the specter of Silver and Black has forged a reputation as gatekeepers of an evil empire—a realm where might makes right.

—John Facenda, "The Voice" of NFL Films

CONTENTS

PREFACE

STRAIGHT FROM THE MOUTHS of the legends of the silver and black, a book appropriately entitled *Cheating Is Encouraged* captures the many famous—as well as infamous—stories from the last team to play "outlaw" football. Regardless if you loved them or hated them, the Oakland Raiders of the '70s were an amusing cast of outlaws, misfits, and other anomalies that made up one of the greatest pro football teams of their era.

For the Raiders, it was a time when professional team sports such as football, baseball, and basketball were considered blue-collar forms of entertainment—the NFL leading the pack. It was the Raiders—and Oakland alone—who personified a blue-collar town with their aggressive style of play.

Gridiron characters such as Kenny (Snake) Stabler, Willie Brown, Phil "Foo" Villapiano, Jim "Pops" Otto, Jack "The Assassin" Tatum, Jim Otto, Art Shell, George "The Hit Man" Atkinson, Skip "Dr. Death" Thomas, Fred Biletnikoff, Ted "The Stork" Hendricks, Bob "Boomer" Brown, Daryle "The Mad Bomber" Lamonica, head coaches John Madden and Tom Flores, and many others chronicle the infamous barroom explosions, on- and off-the-field exploits, away game adventures, and party-hard attitudes that are reflected within the team's intimidating and glorified mix of rebels, renegades, and masterminds of the game.

The Raiders roster consisted of a collection of misfits and rebels—some with behavioral issues such as Ben Davidson and John "Tooz" Matuszak, and castoffs like the aging George Blanda and semi-pro player Otis Sistrunk, who were passed over or disregarded by other NFL teams.

To say that this group of degenerates had attitude would be considered a gross understatement. They were the Oakland Raiders, the silver and black, and Al Davis's dream of "Just Win, Baby."

The legacy of the Oakland Raiders has always been "Commitment to Excellence," but the legacy of the team's behavior has always been on the cutting edge. For example:

- When receivers were allowed to use Stickum, Fred Biletnikoff used so much of it that he had to have the other players in the huddle pry his fingers apart.
- Bob Brown got his point across to Willie Brown when he pulled out his gun and riddled his mattress with bullets . . . while Willie was still on it!

Cheating Is Encouraged defines an era that can only be considered as the last glory days of "real football played by real men"; a game where hurt players kept playing and the injury known as turf toe had yet to be defined.

So belly up to the bar, gents, and read about the good ol' days of Raiders football. It is as close as most of us will ever get to sitting in the locker room, opening a few cool ones, and listening to these gridiron greats talk about the famous and infamous legendary wars and warriors of Oakland's glory years.

FIRST HALF: 1970–1974

AL DAVIS
THE DEFIANT OWNER

AL DAVIS WAS ONCE asked how he would like to be remembered. Without hesitation he responded, "If there was anything we've ever done that I am particularly proud of, I would have to say it is the greatness of the Raiders—to take a professional football team and give it a distinct characteristic that is different from all others.

"Commitment to excellence—the greatest players and coaches—the great games we played in—the flame that would burn brightest here is the will to win."

Even as a young boy, Davis had dreams of greatness.

"I had a dream that I someday I would build the finest organization in professional sports. I had a lot of thoughts on how I would do it. I had the inspiration of two great organizations when I was growing up. The Yankees personified to me the size of the players, power, the home run and intimidation and fear. The Dodgers under Branch Rickey were completely different in my mind. They represented speed, they represented development of players, the Dodgers way of playing the game. I always thought that someone intelligent could take all the great qualities of both, put them together, and use them.

As everyone is well aware, Al Davis was known for his creative slogans. We are all familiar with his "Commitment to Excellence" and "Just Win, Baby!" Raiders safety George Atkinson had this to say about Davis.

"Al had more slogans than an ad agency. That was just his thing. He didn't have a marketing group. Those were his phrases that he came up with and believed in."

Davis may have been a walking ad agency, but Matt Millen says that it went way beyond just words. Davis's wardrobe was, in itself, a "marketing opportunity."

"His whole world was pretty black and white when it came to fashion. It was silver and black or white and black and that was it. We were told he was colorblind and that's what we always understood it to be."

Raider executive Mike Lombardi (now with the New England Patriots) once said of Al's strategy, "They were really an advertisement for the Raiders and he really felt like that when they saw him, they needed to see the colors. I think he was so far ahead of his time that he branded a team and he built the framework for the league to understand what branding was all about."

Quarterback Ken Stabler and the rest of the Raiders all knew that Al padded his jackets so he would look bigger, but Al would never admit to it.

"Someone once asked him if he didn't think those padded jackets were out of style.

"'What padded jackets?' Al said. 'I don't wear padded shoulders. Don't need them.'

"We saw him pumping iron in the weight room and eyeing himself in the mirror, trying to build up his deltoid muscles so he could stop wearing those padded jackets that he denied wearing."

Davis also wore baggy pants—which was something he could do nothing about.

"One thing that Al could do nothing about in the weight room was the fact that his pants bagged in the seat," said running back Pete Banaszak. "There was enough fabric hanging there to clothe a midget. But even Al wouldn't wear cheek pads. He looked like a man who had gone to the track and literally lost his ass."

Pete Banaszak used to do a great impersonation of Al Davis. According to Kenny Stabler, he had Davis down to the letter.

"Pete did the greatest imitation of Al Davis, who had a habit of sucking his teeth and admiring his diamond ring. He would stand at practice cupping an elbow at his waist with his other hand at his chin. Then he would suck his teeth, roll his wrist sleeves up, cock his pinkie finger, and admire the ring he had on it bearing a diamond about the size of a shot glass. He was always bareheaded, proud of his pompadour hair that he greased and combed straight back on the sides like Bowzer of Sha Na Na.

"In the locker room, Banaszak would lower his pants around the cheeks of his ass, stuff towels in the shoulders of his jacket, slip the tab from a beer can on his pinkie, soak his hair and comb it straight back on the sides. He never could fashion a pompadour. Then Pete would walk around sucking his teeth, rolling his wrist sleeves, and admiring his ring, he'd say, 'Anybody know who this is?' and guys would crack up.

"One day at practice Pete walked up about five feet behind Al and stood there in the same pose, elbow cupped at is waist, his other hand on his chin. Freddy noticed the scene as those of us on the field huddled up. 'Sneak a peek at Pete standing back of Al,' he said. We all started laughing.

"Al yelled, 'What the hell's wrong with you guys?'

"Then he looked behind him, but Pete quickly turned his back.

"'Nothing, Al,' someone said as we got control of ourselves.

"I called a play and ended it with tooth sucking sounds, and everyone broke the huddle holding their stomach in laughter."

* * *

Davis had met Los Angeles Rams coach Sid Gillman in Atlantic City at a coaching clinic. Gillman had this to say about the future coach.

"I had known Al for quite some time. As a matter of fact, when I used to speak at coaching schools, Al would sit in the front row taking pages and pages of notes and, at the end of the lecture, he would be the first one up to talk to me. At that time Al was looking for a job. I thought he would be a splendid guy for the staff. I hired Al as a backfield coach on a coaching staff that included Chuck Noll. I hired Al for his success both as a coach and as a recruiter, and because he had the knack of telling people what they wanted to hear. He was very persuasive."

Former Chargers quarterback John Hadl remembers the respect that was given Al.

"I think he was a coach that Sid had a lot of respect for. He listened to Al when he had something to say as far as game plans at that time. You knew he was going somewhere. He was a bright guy with his own plan."

"Even though I had the advantage of working with Sid Gillman in San Diego, I still had philosophies of my own that had to be a part of what I was going to do," said Davis.

"We were going to stretch the field vertically. When we came out of the huddle, we weren't looking for first downs. We didn't want to move the chains—we wanted touchdowns. We wanted the big play—the quick strike. It's number one to say that you want to do that, it's number two to say that you have the players to do it, but it's number three to do it—to do it on first down against any football defense that you are playing against. For those cornerbacks who play out there on the corners to know that the Raiders are coming at you on top and they have the speed to do it and they will do it. It's like having the bomb and being willing to drop it. The adage that goes around in professional football is, 'Take what they give you.' That all sounds good to everybody but I always went the other way, 'We're going to take what we want!'

"Next we would have a full defensive makeover complete with a combative nature.

"The defensive theory evolved early on in the '60s.

"**1: Put pressure on the pocket.** This is a psychological game of intimidation and fear. Not cowardly fear—but fear. I think that somewhere within the first five to ten plays in the game that the other team's quarterback must go down and he must go down hard. That alone sets the tempo for a game, and diversification of defense and the utilization of your corners in a bump and run principle. We used to call it 'the press.' We got the idea from John Wooden when he had his great zone press with his basketball teams. They picked you up as soon as you took the ball out and they pressured you. I think it was Don Shula who began to call it the 'bump and run.' So we changed it to the 'bump and run.'"

In January 1963, Al Davis became the youngest coach in AFL history. Raiders then-owner F. Wayne Valley later stated, "We needed someone who wanted to win so badly, he would do anything. Everywhere I went, people told me what a son of a bitch Al Davis was, so I figured he must be doing something right."

Davis immediately began to try to build the Raiders into a championship team—both on the field and in the front office. Many Raiders players and front-office employees were quickly dismissed. Davis was impressed by the black uniforms of the football players at West Point, which he felt made them look larger. He changed the look of the Raiders from black and gold to black and silver to resemble those great Army teams he idolized in the 1940s.

"The coaching staff the year before was 1–13, and we went 10–4; so that was the greatest turnaround. I was the Coach of the Year in professional football.

"The precision of the Black Knights of West Point really impressed me. Their quickness and the explosion with Blanchard and Davis always left an indelible impression with me."

In 1966, the American Football League turned to Davis for leadership. AFL owners, while liking the existing league commissioner, Joe Foxx, had no confidence in his abilities at a time for struggle between the AFL and the NFL. So in early 1966, the leagued voted Davis in as league commissioner. Davis took the job with Valley's agreement, and was hired as a fighter who would win the war against the NFL.

The owners, led by Chiefs owner Lamar Hunt, felt that Davis could put pressure on the NFL and force a favorable settlement.

"We felt that the League had probably gotten to a point where we needed a different level of participation by our leader, and in 1966 a decision was made and Al Davis became the Commissioner of the American Football League."

Michael MacCambridge, author of *America's Game*, saw Davis as a "military mind."

"Davis was somebody who had perhaps read *The Art of War* one too many times, but he was somebody who had a very military mind-set. His idea was that this was a guerilla war."

When AFL star Pete Gogolak jumped to the NFL, it gave Davis the opening to launch a counter attack. Pro Football Hall of Fame Vice President Joe Horrigan talks about Davis's response.

"The NFL fired a shot with a revolver and Al Davis responded with a machine gun. That's exactly what he did. All bets were now off. He began signing NFL players to future contracts with the AFL."

"Al wasted no time," said Michael MacCambridge.

MacCambridge continued: "All the AFL needed to do was sign a few stars and they were going to, as Davis put it, 'bring the NFL to its knees.'" And he did.

John Madden describes Al's strategic plan.

"Al's exit strategy was not a merger. Al's exit strategy was, take them on, become their equals, then become better than them.

"We had about four or five quarterbacks already lined up." said Davis. "Three or four of their other great players had signed and it was a preliminary strike to let them know what is going to happen if they continued this."

"Davis felt that he was undercut because Hunt and Tex Schramm from the Cowboys cut a merger deal behind his back," said David Harris, author of *The League*.

"The last guy they told about the merger was Davis, and when he found out he was really pissed off. Davis said, 'There was no reason that we had to settle for any of the things did. We had them whipped.'"

Davis always said that the generals win the war, but the politicians make the peace.

With that, Davis resigned as AFL commissioner—his interest in being commissioner ceased once there was no war to fight. He wanted to go back to football and he was quite happy to do that and go back to competing with the Raiders and try to win a Super Bowl.

Al was now under the thumb of the NFL and its commissioner, Pete Rozelle.

"Al never talked to us about his differences with Rozelle," said the late John Matuszak. "He might have said something vague once or twice, like 'this guy in New York is giving us a hard time.' But he never mentioned Rozelle by name, and he never bad-mouthed him. But we all knew perfectly well how the league office felt about the Raiders. And we were all affected by the consequences."

Upon returning to the front office, Oakland dominated—posting the most wins in the final three years of the AFL's existence.

In 1969, John Madden became the team's sixth head coach and, under him, the Raiders became one of the most successful franchises in the NFL, winning seven division titles during the 1970s.

"1967 was my first year (as an assistant coach) and it was George Blanda's and Willie Brown's first year as well. Gene Upshaw was our number-one draft choice. We were a really good team and we won the AFL that year and went to Super Bowl II," said Madden.

Scotty Stirling, a Raiders executive from 1964 through 1967, had this to say about those Raiders teams. "I thought that was the beginning of a real dynasty for us. That that team was going to get better and better and we drafted well. I thought the Raiders were going to be in a lot of Super Bowls."

Al Davis had already served as an assistant coach, head coach, general manager, and commissioner of the AFL. In 1972, Davis became the managing general partner in Oakland. Until his death, he was the embodiment of the Raiders. He thrived at being the boss, and always made his presence known.

According to former Raiders front-office exec Mike Lombardi, the organization chart flowed—Al, and then everybody below him. You knew he was there. You could smell him. He wore very distinctive cologne, so you knew he was in the building. He was not shy about what he wanted. Sometimes there was frustration in his expectations of what he wanted, but they were unrealistic at times.

Right from the start you knew that it wasn't just the coaches who were looking at things. It was Al, himself.

George Atkinson, a Raiders safety from 1968 through 1977, talks about Al's presence.

"During the time I played there, Al was on the practice field every Wednesday and Thursday, and his presence was felt."

Daryle Lamonica, the Raiders quarterback from 1967 to 1974, remembers coming to "attention" when Davis walked on the football field.

"We could be sitting on our helmet or maybe not paying attention on the sidelines but as soon as Al Davis walked on to the football field, everyone would come to attention. Al had that ability, and I call that fear and respect. He carried that to every player who has ever played for him."

Al Davis rewarded respect with loyalty. He coined the phrase, "Once a Raider, Always a Raider."

"You look around this organization," said George Atkinson, "and you will see a lot of guys who are still with this organization—who were here in the '60s like myself and Willie Brown."

Willie Brown, cornerback from 1967 through 1978, agreed with Atkinson.

"I think right now we have fifteen to twenty guys who played for him still in the organization."

Al Davis explains his devotion to his team and his organization.

"In 1961, I got a call [at] about five in the morning. It was my brother telling me that my father had died. To this day that is the one thing that stands out in my life that I come back and focus on, because quite frankly I had never really gotten the chance to thank him for all the things he did for me and all the opportunities that he gave me. So I made a vivid memory of that but I also made a promise that I would not hold back to the people that I really do love and let them know while they are living about my respect and appreciation for them."

Willie Brown expresses one way that Davis showed respect for his players and their families.

"When someone passed, he would tell me to go to the service and take this check to the family. This happened many, many, many times. That's just the way he was. He would do things like that."

Former linebacker Matt Millen was selected by the Raiders in the 1980 draft. Matt shares his first hand experience in dealing with the kindness of Al Davis.

"When my dad was eighty he was going to have bypass and how Al found out, I have no idea. He told me to get him on a plane because everything had been set up for him at the Mayo Clinic, and they were going to take care of him. I told him 'Coach, he's eighty. I can't do that. He won't even get into the car with me to go to the doctor.' Al said, 'I'm going to have that doctor fly into your place.'

"Every day after that surgery, he would call me to see how my dad was doing."

"I will also say this," Millen continued. "If, for some reason, he thought that you crossed the line, and you could have been there for thirty-five to forty years, but if you crossed the line on him, it was over."

It's no secret that Al Davis was known for his feuds. Davis had a major feud with Hall of Fame member Marcus Allen, but nine other Hall of Famers requested that Al introduce them for induction into Canton, making Al Davis, by far, the most frequent presenter at the Pro Football Hall of Fame.

When John Madden got *the call* from the Pro Football Hall of Fame that he had been selected as a member of the Class of 2006, the first person he thought of was Al. In his Hall of Fame speech, he touched on the kind of person Al Davis was. Below is an excerpt from that speech.

"Talking about loyalty and what a guy Al Davis was, I said if I had one phone call to make, it would be to Al Davis. I got voted into the

Hall of Fame and I had a phone call to make for a presenter, and I called Al Davis."

In 1969, the thirty-two-year-old Madden was named the coach of the Oakland Raiders. Al knew from the start that he had the right guy for the job.

"He is someone who helped me build this organization into the greatness that it was. We were like kids. We had our dreams. He had a big ego and I had a big ego but we were smart enough to know that we wanted the same thing.

"There was no one between Al and I," said Madden, "so anything that I wanted I didn't have to go to any general manager or anyone. There was just the two of us, and Al Davis never once turned down anything I wanted."

Madden reached 100 wins third-fastest (behind only George Halas and Curly Lambeau) of any coach in NFL history, while leading Oakland to eight playoff berths in ten seasons. Under Madden, the Raiders played in some of the most famous and controversial games of all time: the Immaculate Reception (1972), Sea of Hands (1974), Ghost to the Post (1977), Holy Roller (1978), and Super Bowl XI.

Al Davis loved the underdog. He enjoyed creating opportunities of overlooked players—even at the expense of his own team . . .

In Week 3 of the 1974 season, the Raiders faced the Steelers in Pittsburgh. Al Davis tells the story of how Terry Bradshaw became the first string quarterback—a kindness that would haunt him forever.

"Pittsburgh started Joe Gilliam in the game and we beat them something like 17–0. After the game. Terry Bradshaw came into the Raiders locker room and said to me, 'Can you get me out of here? Can you trade for me?' I told him, 'I love you but I have enough problems. I've got Stabler, I got Blanda, and I still have Lamonica and I can't get you, but let me put in a good word for you.

"Chuck Noll had been a close friend, and one of the dumbest things I had ever done was to tell him, 'Why the hell don't you play Bradshaw and stop playing Gilliam? Bradshaw can win for you.'

"He put Bradshaw back in the lineup and they beat us in the championship game in '74, they beat us in the championship game in '75, and we had our hands full with the Steelers from then on because *good me* raised his hand and suggested that they ought to start Bradshaw."

Unlike other franchises, Davis believed in giving players a fresh start.

"We may take a player in who doesn't have good social habits or has been a failure somewhere else. But it's predicated on bringing them into an environment that can inspire in them the will to do great—and they have done great."

Ted Hendricks, linebacker for the Raiders from 1975–1983, recalls, "There were a lot of retreads with the Raiders and he would get great use out of them.

"Al Davis's always had a plan," said Willie Brown. "How can I use a guy like Billy Cannon? How can I use a guy like Willie Brown? How can I use a guy like John Matuszak? All down the line, he had a plan when he brought those guys in there. Even the bad guys that nobody else wanted ended up coming to the Raiders and becoming great ball players. You can attribute that to Al Davis and how he dealt with people."

Al Davis once said, "When you have to lead men you don't do unto others as you would have others do unto you. You do unto them, in a para-military situation, as they want to be done unto. You have to treat them the way they want to be treated."

Davis was active in civil rights, refusing to allow the Raiders to play in any city where black and white players had to stay in separate living arrangements. He was the first NFL owner to hire a black coach (Art Shell) and a female chief executive (Amy Trask). He was also the second NFL owner to hire a Hispanic coach (Tom Flores).

Al Davis's legacy of equity and fairness has spanned a lifetime where he opened a field of dreams for countless others. It first surfaced when he was a football player at Syracuse over half a century ago. There Davis showed his support for teammate Bernie Custis (1948–1950), a black quarterback in a white man's game.

"As our relationship grew," said Custis, "I came to know Al as someone who lived by a certain code, and this code was to judge every individual by the content of their character and their capabilities, and nothing else. I think that was the code that I detected at that time and had stayed with him throughout the years."

In the 1960s and 1970s, minority players and white players were not always treated equally.

"In certain positions you saw no black players," said George Atkinson. "Most offensive lines had white players. At the quarterback position, there were none."

Guard Gene Upshaw came into the league in 1967.

"We used to say that we could have a convention of black offensive lineman in a phone booth. There just weren't that many of us doing it."

Al Davis took a different approach to drafting players that other clubs overlooked.

"We went into many of the predominant black schools to take a lot of their players. We called it 'an untapped reservoir.' We wanted to win—we wanted the best players. We weren't interested in who they were or where they came from."

Eldridge Dickey was the first black quarterback to be drafted in the first round in 1968 by the Raiders.

"Gosh. That was a huge step for Al Davis. There was so much against him for that. They had gotten tackles and receivers but here you are talking about a position that has orientated that 'a black man cannot lead.' I could see where he was seeing. I could see him see beyond complexion. Al was saying, 'Let it go! You're stifling the growth of the game!'"

By 1989, two thirds of the players in professional football were black, but there had yet to be a black head coach.

Former Steelers defensive back, Steelers assistant coach, and Tampa Bay and Indianapolis Colts head coach Tony Dungy said, "At that time, I just didn't know if owners had looked at black coaches as people they could be comfortable with.

"Al Davis was a legacy of equity and fairness. The visionary efforts of Al Davis were not just in how the game was played but also who would play it."

Brad Pye was a former AFL administrative assistant. He remembers Al Davis as a civil rights maverick.

"A lot of people think of Al Davis as a maverick. He's also been a maverick in opening opportunities for minorities. He was a trailblazer for justice as far as I'm concerned, because he had no color barrier."

Former Vikings head coach Dennis Green had this to say about Al Davis.

"Al opened the game up for the African American athlete."

Consistency wasn't that important to Al Davis. "I've always said it's not important to be consistent. It's important to be right."

In 1989, Davis made Art Shell the first black NFL coach of the modern era.

"I want you to know one thing," said Davis. "I'm not hiring you because you're black. I'm hiring you because I feel you are the best possible candidate for this job at this time."

When the press asked Shell how if felt to be the first minority coach, he responded with, "I wasn't the first minority coach, Tom Flores was."

Ten years earlier, Davis had hired Flores, who was already a part of the Raiders family. As a player he was the first quarterback of the Raiders; as a coach his roster included Jim Plunkett—a number one pick and Heisman Trophy winner who failed in both New England and San Francisco.

Eldridge Dickey felt that only the Raider organization could pump life into Jim Plunkett.

"He was a guy that I watched with New England getting beat to a pulp and all of a sudden he was Super Bowl MVP."

Al Davis called the Super Bowl XV victory "the finest hour in the history of the Oakland Raiders organization." He told the press, "Tom Flores is not just one of the great coaches in our league—he is one of the great coaches of all time. When you have great coaches you get great players and when you have a great organization you tell them just one thing, 'Just Win.'"

The Raiders late announcer, Bill King, had this to say to the Raiders fans.

"The prince, Pete Rozelle, came calling. He had a silver slipper. He tried it on and the only man it fit was Al Davis."

* * *

Raider Rule #1: *Cheating Is Encouraged*. Rule #2: See Rule #1.

Davis's plan was to 'dominate.' "I'm going to dominate if I can, other than maybe life or death, the things that I want. I'm going to dominate them."

Linebacker Phil Villapiano describes the arm pads that were made exclusively for Raiders players.

"We had a guy named George Anderson who was our trainer.* George was an expert in pads—probably most of them illegal. He would take stuff that you make casts from and mold it for me. What I sensed I had was two casts so when I hit somebody like *Boom!* That was my first shot—right to the eye. I could take them down if I hit them just perfect."

Coach Madden didn't know if the pads were illegal or not.

"I'm not sure. Anything that you are wearing has to be checked by the umpire during the pregame warm-ups. Of course, you could not wear it in the pregame warm-up and then put it on for the game. I know that."

"If they were to use the word *devious*, just by itself, it would be annoying for the moment, but when you throw it in there with, *brilliant, genius, winner, devious, ruthless*, cunning . . . no, I'll take it."

—Al Davis

David Harris, author of *The League*, said, "This was Al Davis's character. Clearly this guy was a carnivore from the get-go."

---

* Anderson passed away in 2012.

The Raiders lived to fight—especially Villapiano.

"I just liked to fight. I went to Bowling Green and if I threw a punch they would send me back to New Jersey. When I was with the Raiders and I threw a punch, that was good—as long as it was at the right guy."

San Francisco 49ers head coach, Bill Walsh (1979–1988), saw the Raiders as a group of "misguided" youths.

"One thing they'll do is take a swing at you. If you hit them good, they'll take a swing. There are four or five guys who are demented on that team."

The Raiders were a team of misfits with short fuses and held open season on supposed stars of opposing teams. In the 1975 AFC Conference Championship, George Atkinson knocked Pittsburgh wide receiver Lynn Swann out of the game with a concussion. In a regular season Steelers–Raiders game in 1976, Atkinson hit Swann with a forearm to the head, knocking him out of the opening game of the season and again causing another concussion.

Swann had this to say about Atkinson.

"Both blows were illegally delivered and delivered with malice."

The media and Pittsburgh coach Chuck Noll called Oakland "the criminal element of the NFL."

* * *

Al Davis himself was not liked by the other owners, and his move to Los Angeles was not granted by the NFL.

"The thing that disturbed me most of all was the bad faith in fair dealing. For three years I waited to hear Commissioner Rozelle finally tell us the reason that he wanted to split up this territory amongst the owners. They wanted it for themselves. As far as good faith, there is no question in my mind that I have never got the same treatment that anyone else got in their respective cities from the very beginning."

Tex Schramm was the Cowboys General Manager from 1960 to 1989, but he wasn't exactly a fan of Davis.

"I feel very strongly that he is wrong and that he's doing something treacherous to this league."

Author David Harris described Davis as "never a popular figure," because he was "an abrasive kind of guy." And his insistence on dominating and winning everything tended to rub a lot of people the wrong way.

During game day warm-ups, Al would visit the players of the opposing team. Mike Garrett, Kansas City Chiefs and San Diego Chargers running back (1966–1973) remembers Al's *method of operation.*

"During warm-ups before the game, Al would come around and walk around our team and say things like 'How are you doing today?' 'You're looking sharp.' And you knew that he really didn't mean it. He was coming over to get an edge, and I thought that was pretty crappy."

Mike Shanahan, former head coach of the Los Angeles Raiders from 1988–1989 and then head coach of the Denver Broncos and Washington Redskins, knew how to handle his former boss's escapades.

"During pregame warm-ups, we're on the 10-yard line and going out of the end zone and Al was at the 25-yard line out on the numbers with his hands folded watching our team. The players are complaining that they can't run anything with him out there, and to tell him to get out of the way. I told our quarterback Elvis Grbac to throw a go route and if you happen to get the ball close to that guy in the white outfit over there you won't bother me.

"Elvis throws the ball as hard as he can at Davis's head and at the last second he ducks out of the way and it almost hits him. He looks over at me and sees me waving at him and he flips me off. But after that I never saw Al again on that side of the fifty."

A classic Al Davis story has to do with Harland Svare, who was the coach of the San Diego Chargers. In the old days, one of the rumors you heard about Al was that he would bug the other team's locker room when they came to the Oakland Coliseum. Svare was so spooked by this that he talked himself into believing it. Before a game in Oakland, as his players looked on in disbelief, Svare stared cursing out the light fixture.

"Damn you, Al Davis." Svare screamed at the fixture. "I know you're up there. Damn you."

When the incident was related to Al, he wouldn't even deny it.

"I can tell you one thing." Al said with a shrug. "The damn thing wasn't in the fixture."

Another so-called rumor had to do with the air in the football. Sound familiar? No, it's not "Deflate Gate," but it's similar.

"As players, we used to hear all kinds of things about Al," said Stabler. "Two that stand out the most were that Al used to pump the football up with added helium for our punter Ray Guy, and that he'd water our field extra heavily the night before games against high-powered offenses."

* * *

Most players would know *not* to challenge Al Davis, but there was one player who thought he could get away with it. Matuszak described the unfortunate incident.

"The only time I ever saw a player challenge Al was in 1980, the year we beat the Eagles in the Super Bowl. Late in the season one our starters on offense went down with an injury. When he was just about healed, he told Al he wanted to get back into the starting lineup. Al said no. We had been winning with the lineup we had, and Al had no desire to break up the combination.

"A few days later, we were boarding a plane for a road game. The Raiders had a rule that you couldn't drink on flights to games. This guy was in no mood for rules, not even one of Al's. He had smuggled a bottle of tequila onto the plane and was knocking it off like it was tap water.

"When the plane landed, he staggered up to Al and said something to the effect of 'play me or trade me.' When Al didn't reply, the player started cursing him out—right in front of Mrs. Davis. Everyone was horrified. We'd never seen Al confronted that way. At first we tried dragging our teammate away, but once he started cursing, everyone just backed off. No one wanted to even be near him when he was talking to Al like that. Al never said a word. Not one. He just shot the guy this look I call the 'look of goodbye.' We knew that guy was through as a Raider. He never played another down for us that season. The next year he was released."

During practice, Al Davis always worried about NFL "spies." Fred Biletnikoff remembers one day in particular.

"I remember when Al threw a rock at a plane that flew low over the practice field. He thought it was a spy plane."

* * *

Marie Lombardi, the wife of the great Green Bay Packers coach Vince Lombardi, wrote to Carol Davis, Al's wife after the Raiders' first Super Bowl win.

"Enjoy it now because fame is fleeting. Enjoy it while you can."

Marie's prophecy came to be.

The flame began to flicker. The firing of coaches was approximately once a year. The so-called good and high-priced players that Davis had drafted went bust. Davis began to lose his touch.

Al's health had greatly deteriorated by the time he reached his eighties. He always wanted to be the strength of the organization, but time was not on his side.

In 2011, Davis passed the torch for the final time by hiring Hue Jackson, who called Al Davis "Coach."

"When you can have talks with your boss about the actual x's and o's, that was a first for me. I've never been able to do that with anyone else. That's why I call him Coach, because he can still talk football with me."

On October 8, 2011, Al Davis passed away at the age of eighty-two. The next day Hue Jackson and his Raiders beat the Houston

Texans 25–20 in pure Raiders style on the final play with an Oakland interception in the end zone. At that time, with only ten men on the field, it is said that Al Davis was on the field during that play, and *was* the eleventh man.

JOHN MADDEN
THE CREATIVE COACH

WHEN JOHN MADDEN WAS asked what he considered to be his greatest team, he responded without hesitation.

"To me, the Raiders of the '70s were the greatest team ever. When I went into the Hall of Fame, I had a party and showed old highlight films. I told the players that I'd started believing that thing about how players are bigger, better, faster, stronger now, and the game is better now, but when I look back at how we played it, and the guys who played, I realize that's not true.

"We were better. Football is great now, but that doesn't mean it wasn't great then. The stars then would be stars now. Freddy would be. Stabler would be. Bob Brown would be. Upshaw, Willie Brown, Shell, Otto, Ted Hendricks—they all would be."

Raider's linebacker Monte Johnson described Madden's unique style of dress.

"John kind of looked like an oaf when he would dress. In practice he would wear the same polyester stretch pants, the shoes not tied, no whistle, and a towel hung around the neck. He would chew on the towel, not as a pacifier but as a habit, just because it was there."

Tight end Ted Kwalick said, "I was glad to play for a coach that treated you like a man, not like a kid."

Willie Brown though of Madden as one of the guys—not necessarily as one of the coaches.

Madden liked *all* his players.

"I didn't like just a few of my players. I liked them all. I made a point of talking to every player every day. I'd walk up and down the locker room and talk to them as they'd come in, going into the training room, because I liked them. They were my friends. They're people. When you start thinking, 'How do you treat them?' you're thinking about it too much. You just do what's normal."

Defensive end Pat Toomay was traded to the Raiders via the Tampa Bay Buccaneers, after previously playing for the Dallas Cowboys and Buffalo Bills.

"In the morning he'd be sitting in your locker with a cup of coffee and the paper. 'Hey, did you see this?' This is a coach interested in your opinion about something in the newspaper? Can you imagine that happening with Landry? In the Cowboy environment you always felt like a freak or a piece of meat or some objectified kind of exotic hybrid. And here's a coach interested in what you think about something other than football? This is a guy I can play for. This is a guy where our interests are aligned. He cares about people who aren't replaceable parts.

"There was a huge amount of respect. You could feel it. Madden wasn't going to bullshit us on any level. He'd stand there on the sideline, sort of helplessly, waving his arms, getting pink, but he gave us control, and it was great for the players."

Madden had to convince Davis that he was the right man for the job.

"I went into Al's office and told him, 'I know this team, I know these players. I know what they can do and I know how to get them to do it.'

"I told him, 'Age is a number. If you're made to be a head coach, you'll be successful whether you're thirty-two, forty-two, or fifty-two. I don't have to wait ten years. I know I can be a head coach now.'

"I had a plan. I had been thinking about this basically all my coaching life. Even as an assistant I'd thought as a head coach. Not second guessing, first guessing."

Former front-office executive John Herrera talked about the foot races that he and John had.

"As a linebacker coach, he was one of the boys. He was just a guy. We'd have foot races out in the driveway up at training camp. Between the cars parked outside the rooms and the boundary of the motel, there wasn't any room to run. He'd put his big, fat butt in front of me with the first step and beat me in a 40. We'd mark it off and he'd always win. He reminds me of it to this day.

"But I wasn't surprised when Al made him the head coach. He had a certain presence about him that stood out from the other assistants. It's hard to describe it in tangible terms, but he had it.

"Al told me that the players needed someone who would lead them but not demean them. And he knew both offensive and defensive football. He also had a feel for the passing game. He was on the staff. He was there. And I also liked the idea that he was younger than me."

Davis thought he would be a great coach.

"Anyone can see what a player is doing or not doing at the time; it was what you see in the future that matters. Can he coach? Can you develop him? I've seen it in a lot of young coaches. That doesn't mean they'll be successful with me. It's about the relationship. It's about keeping me informed and vice versa. It's like a marriage. Believing in each other. Anyone can get married. But can you make it work? At first my role was one of direction, and then it became one of assistance."

Tight end Bob Moore felt it was Madden's personality that drove the team.

"It was said that Al Davis was directing the team, calling the plays, doing all the stuff and John was just a hatchet man for him. That was absolutely not true! John was the one doing all the work. His attitude, disposition, and personality are what drove the team to greatness."

"It seemed to me that Al left John and his staff alone," said Kenny Stabler. "I think he let John make the decisions. Davis had a lot to do with the draft, but as far as who played? It was John."

According to Madden, Al may have been in charge of finding personnel, but it was John's team.

"That was never a question. Those things came up later. People had him calling plays and shit. But in those days players called the plays. I was never a headset coach anyway.

"I had a good situation. I always said that the fewer guys you have between you and the owner, the better. The best job would be

[George] Halas or Paul Brown, who coached and owned. The next best thing would be where you have an owner and you're the next guy. And that's what I had. It was a working partnership. He was a team player.

"Al was a friend. We used to have a box at the Coliseum during A's games in the off season, and we'd work during the day, and at night the coaches would leave and Al and I would go to the baseball game, watch three or four innings, talk, and go have dinner. We did a lot of talking at A's games. All football.

"I don't know anyone like him. He was total football."

Pat Toomay gives his perspective on the Davis/Madden relationship.

"However he negotiated the space with Al, whatever compromises Madden had to make, he made because it put him in the place he wanted to be. He was no dummy."

Linebacker Monte Johnson recalls his first day at training camp.

"At training camp, when we were all together for the first time, John would give his opening speech, and it was always the same: 'Our goal is to win the Super Bowl. Not make the playoffs. Win it all!'"

"John has a great mind," said punter Ray Guy, "but very few great minds make great head coaches. John's strength was that he had a way of making it simple. Whatever he was teaching us wasn't complex, something you couldn't understand. We wouldn't alter the game plan for this or that team. It would boil down to when the first ball is kicked; it's me against them. Line up and play."

"Teaching is repetition," said Madden. "Coaching is the same way. Some of the players couldn't understand why I'd repeat everything. Dave Casper and Ted Hendricks, for instance, got it the first time. But there were others whom you had to show film of the play, and then diagram it. And someone else who'd have to practice it and walk through it for two or three days."

Madden had three rules for his players. They were: be on time, pay attention, and play like hell when I tell you to.

"I always knew that the more rules you have, the easier they are to break," said, Madden. "And once you break one, you may as well break them all. It's easier to have fewer rules but be a stickler on those rules. Things that aren't important, that have nothing to do with winning or losing, don't have to be a rule."

According to offensive tackle John Vella, dress codes were nonexistent for the Raiders.

"I remember one time before a trip. Madden goes, 'Hey, guys, there's a few too many holes in the Levi's. Can we get the Levi's cleaned up a little bit? And you know, I don't know about the sandals. Maybe you should wear some shoes. Can you wear some shoes?' That was the end of the speech about dress codes."

Madden's philosophy regarding dress codes was different than that of other coaches in the NFL.

"I was coaching at a time when you had to wear white shirts and ties. Well, you don't have to wear white shirts and ties. Facial hair? That has nothing to do with winning or losing. Those things weren't important to me. I didn't give a damn. Some teams were making their decisions based on stuff like that. 'I got to get rid of that guy because he has a mustache.' I always thought that was dumb."

The only Raider rule was to win.

"Any rule or regulation regarding the Raiders had to do with nothing but winning, said Raiders running back Mark van Eeghen. "Otherwise it was not a regulation."

Kenny Stabler referred to the key word as play.

"On the field it was 'Go play,' off the field it was 'Go play.'"

Madden was also known for accepting the whole person; meaning accepting them for who they were and refusing to try and change them.

"The thing is you have a person, and he's made up of a total package. And you take all of that package. You don't just cherry-pick what you get. I remember one day I was walking off the field, and I was talking to our team doctor. I said, 'You know, we have doctors for everything now. Orthopedics, internal doctors, eye doctors, maybe we ought to get, like, a psychiatrist, a mind psychologist.'

"I'll never forget what he told me: 'You can do that, but you don't know what really makes a guy the person he is, and what trait it is that makes him a great player. You may remove that trait in bringing in psychology. And if you start messing with them, you may improve part of them, but the part that's improved might make them not play as well as they play.'

"I said, 'Oh, shit, forget I said that. There's no damned way I want to do it.'

"You have to accept the whole person and whatever they're going to do. If I give Marv Hubbard a card that says, 'If you ever get in a fight again, I'm gonna cut you,' what's that going to do? Nothing! I'm not gonna do anything."

Lineman Mike McCoy recalls his first pregame meeting as a Raider.

"During Madden's chalkboard talk, four or five players got up, walked out of the room, and caught a cab to the stadium. I was stunned! Madden didn't even mind. He knew they knew what they needed to know. And I don't think that's something you can teach or coach; I think it was just something he sensed. Basically, he was a laid-back coach, which was just right for this team. If he'd pushed and pushed and pushed, I don't think the Raiders would have won."

Like the players on his team, John Madden was also given nicknames.

"Our nickname for him was Fox, because he was so smart," said Stabler. "The other, more affectionate nickname we called him was Pinky.

"John received the name Pinky because his face would turn pink— sometimes even beet red when his temper would flare—or pretend to flare.

"I saw him come into dozens of meetings when he'd turn over a chair, raise hell, walk out, come back in, and wink. Like it was no big deal. That was his style."

Guard George Buehler tells how Madden's blow-ups were planned.

"I was sitting on the sidelines watching kickoffs when Madden walked up to me and said, 'I'll bet you that within five minutes, I'll blow my top.' I said, 'You plan that stuff?' He said, 'Oh, yeah. I don't do anything haphazardly or emotionally. I take a critical look and I see whether the team needs praising or being yelled at. I watch all the bad stuff and I ignore all the good, until I naturally blow up.'

"Less than five minutes later, sure enough, Madden was screaming, 'Goddammit! Get your asses . . .' And everybody straightens up. That's the way he coached."

Mark van Eeghen remembers one blow up in particular.

"It didn't matter if you were heralded or you were an unknown. He was a master of that. He knew everyone's hot spot. Knowing that everybody has to be treated equally, but maybe not all the time.

"During a game against the Broncos I missed a crucial block. During the film review session Madden kept clicking the play over and over and over. Fucking thirty times. Then he gets up, rips the reel off the projector, throws it in the trash can, and says, 'Get out on the field!'

"Once on the field Madden caught up with me and said, 'Mark, I got to let you know—that was one of the better games you had for me, and I thank you for your effort. I took advantage of you because I wanted to make a point to the team and I knew you wouldn't take it personally.'"

Madden reacted to his so-called premeditated—or not—outbursts.

"Whether it was premeditated or not, it would go away quickly. Sometimes you'd raise your voice, and then it would just go away, and I'd just say, 'I had to do that.' Sometime you felt you had to yell and scream. I tried not to do it to a player. I tried to do it collectively. There were some guys it didn't affect. They'd say, 'That's just Madden being Madden.'"

Nose tackle Dave Rowe recalls how Madden reacted to a fist fight between two players during practice.

"They're having this punch-up and he's going in between them and he slips. Everyone sees him fall, and the fight stops, and they all help him up. Then he says, 'We ain't having fighting.' I thought Madden would call practice. Instead he said, 'That was a damn sissy fight! I'll show you how to fight!' Madden started swinging his fists, comically, and that defused the whole situation. And we go back to practice."

Former Green Bay Packer defensive tackle Mike McCoy was traded to the Oakland Raiders in 1977. He compares Madden's practices to Bart Starr's practices.

"I thought to myself, *this is incredible. This is the way it should be.* He didn't want you to leave it on the field, so practices weren't what I was used to.

"I was used to hitting as hard as I could. One day I hit Pete Banaszak hard. He turned to me and said, 'Cool it down a little. This is offense day. Today the offense wins. Tomorrow the defense wins.' I turned around and Jack Tatum put his hand on my shoulder. 'Cool out, guy. Save it for the game.'"

Because of these laid-back workouts, the Raiders always had the fourth quarter because they were rested.

George Atkinson sums up Madden the man.

"You had to take your hat off to Madden as far as keeping everything from going haywire bonkers, you know? He kept us aware of what our mission was. In order to keep all of us organized and running smoothly, it took one hell of a guy."

TRAINING CAMP
AN EXPLOSIVE MIX OF TESTOSTERONE, ALCOHOL, AND INSANITY

THE EL RANCHO MOTEL:
THE PLACE WE CALLED HOME

Approximately 60 miles north of the Oakland Coliseum lay the quaint town of Santa Rosa, California. Here nestled in its quiet and serene Sonoma County foothills was the infamous El Rancho Tropicana Motel where for two decades the Raiders' veterans, rookies and coaching staff held training camp.

While for *six weeks* other NFL teams were enjoying the comforts and curfews of a college dorm, Oakland was held up for *eight weeks* at the seedy and rundown El Rancho. But to the Raiders, it was like a match made in Heaven.

The entire facility consisted of a hotel, two practice fields and a makeshift locker room that were built behind the motel. Each year the Jacuzzi would overflow with soapsuds, and firecrackers would be shot off at various times throughout the day. It was more like a summer camp for adult delinquent males than a training camp.

"My own, personal training camp memories and experiences are like nothing I had ever seen or heard— experiences I will never forget!

"I arrived almost two weeks late for my first training camp with the Oakland Raiders in Santa Rosa. Myself and three of my rookie teammates: Cliff Branch, John Vella, and Dave Dalby were selected to play in the *Chicago Tribune* College All-Star Game and we had spent the last few weeks at Northwestern University, just north of downtown Chicago, preparing to play the previous season Super Bowl champion Dallas Cowboys.

Here we were, a bunch of twenty-one and twenty-two-year-old kids right out of college with no professional experience and having never met each other—let alone played together—and we were supposed to compete in front of a national audience against the greatest football team in the world. The Cowboys were led that year by future Hall of Fame quarterback Roger Staubach. Another future Hall of Famer, the great Tom Landry, was their head coach, and both their offense and defense were filled with football legends like Bob Lilly, 'Bullet' Bob Hayes, Dan Reeves, Calvin Hill, and Chuck Howley to name a few. I remember in particular watching Bob Hayes in pre-game warm-ups because I wanted to see just how fast the Olympic gold medalist in the 100 yard dash could run and, after seeing him run, I thought to myself: who the hell is going to cover him?

Our squad was loaded with All-Americans from across the country; the best of the best from the college ranks and we were coached by outstanding Nebraska University coach Bob Devaney and his staff, who had just won the National Championship a few months earlier. Needless to say, we were no match for the Cowboys and they quickly proved why they were the best team in the NFL, as their offense scored at will against us and their defense shut us down completely with a shutout. I don't know who the genius was that concocted the idea of this event, but it was like the proverbial throwing the Christians to the lions—and the lions won easily that night at Soldier Field.

"Having flown from Chicago to Oakland the day after that game, we four Raiders rookies were picked up at the airport by a character nicknamed 'Charley Tuna,' who worked for Raider owner Al Davis. The drive from Oakland to Santa Rosa on interstate 80 was short, only about an hour or so, but when we finally arrived and the car stopped, the four of us looked at each other in amazement and wondered why our driver had stopped at a small motel complex called the El Rancho Tropicana? Surely this was not where the feared Raiders trained and honed their skills in preparation for the upcoming season . . . or was it?

"We quickly found out that we were in the right place and were led into a small wooden building behind the motel which served as a locker room. As I was led past rows of lockers and players getting ready for an afternoon practice, I was directed to where my locker was towards the end of the last row. Smoke filled the air of this section of the locker room, and it seemed that every player down that row was smoking a cigarette, cigar, or something they had rolled themselves. The language spewing from the players mouths was like nothing I had ever heard in the locker room at Villanova; the small catholic college I had graduated from only two months earlier—what a wake-up call!

"My locker was smack in the middle of the running backs, wide receivers, tight ends, and quarterbacks. I was suddenly thrust in the midst and surrounded by the likes of George Blanda, Darryl Lamonica, Ken Stabler, Fred Biletnikoff, Warren Wells, Marv Hubbard, Pete Banaszak, and Raymond Chester. Down the line were the lockers of the offensive linemen and I could see Art Shell, Jim '00' Otto, Gene Upshaw, and Bob Brown getting dressed for practice. They looked like they were getting ready for war. I had never seen players this big, wearing pieces of what seemed like homemade football equipment that resembled gladiators about to enter the Coliseum. I was intimidated and a little scared and I thought that I was in a prison cell and not an NFL locker room.

"Fortunately, Cliff Branch had been assigned the locker right next to me, so I was able to feel some relief as I looked at Cliff and could tell he was as nervous as I was. Now, let me remind you, this was the offensive side of the locker room. We were the cerebral players; we were the disciplined players, we were the organized players. I could only imagine what was going on across the way on the defensive half of the locker room where the lunatics were dressing for practice and were about to be let out of their cages!

For the next six weeks of my life, I learned what professional football is all about and about how the Oakland Raiders played football. These men who were now my teammates were amongst the best in the world at what they did and they did it with the attitude of the badasses that they really were!

Practices were hot, long and physically exhausting—even to a young twenty-two-year-old rookie like myself who thought he was in great shape. For two and a half hours in the morning and then another two and a half hours in the afternoon we hit the field at full tilt and never stopped until the last gasser was run and Coach Madden had finally blown his whistle.

"According to linebacker Phil Villapiano, I quickly became 'one of the guys.'

"Mike acclimated to the 'Raiders way' very quickly. He was right in there with the rest of us. He was a fucking wacko!"

Following the afternoon practices, we lifted weights, had individual position meetings with our coaches and then even had time before dinner to frequent some of the local drinking establishments to replenish the fluids we had sweated out with a few cold ones. After dinner were some more team meetings, breaking up into offense and defense and finally breaking up into position meetings again. Meetings ended around 9pm and normal people would have headed straight to bed to rest up for the next day's grueling schedule—but not the Raiders baby! The day just began for us when meetings were finally over.

From 9 p.m. until 11 p.m. we were on our own and we always made the most of our free time! For the next two hours the most of that time was spent escaping the rigors and discipline of the practice field. No matter how tired, soar, hurt or injured you were, nothing was going to keep you from hitting the streets of Santa Rosa and the Raiders hit them hard—as hard as Jack Tatum hit opposing receivers. The key was to hit quick and go to as many bars as we could in two hours because at 11 p.m., curfew was in effect and the fines were high if you missed bed check.

Just before eleven was considered to be the most treacherous time of the evening for the streets of Santa Rosa. At this time the cars, trucks, and motorcycles screeched and skidded into the El Rancho's parking lot. Like the beer and alcohol they had consumed, the players poured themselves out of their vehicles as they stumbled and stammered their way to their motel rooms. Most of the time, cars were left running as players sprinted to their assigned rooms to make bed check.

But the party was far from over after coaches had performed the nightly ritual. Five minutes after bed check players would once again pour themselves back into their vehicles and bikes and return for round two to their favorite haunts like the Bamboo Room, Melendy's, Al's Cactus Room, the Music Box, and other hot spots. Sometimes they would rendezvous with their favorite ladies of the night but most of the time the partying was simply a way of forming friendships and camaraderie with your teammates.

The El Rancho's motel-style rooms opened to the outside parking lots, making it easy for the renegades to escape undetected into the night.

"Anyone could play on Sunday. But if you could play with a hangover, you were a Raider," said former defensive end Ben Davidson.

"Those training camps were among the best times of my life," he added. "But you won't see them like that again. These players today . . . they're closer to their agents than they are to their teammates."

"There was no recession for Santa Rosa during Raiders training camp" said Pete Banaszak. "The owners of the establishments were overjoyed when the Raiders were in town. We were single-handily boosting their economy. The hookers rejoiced. We'd show up two days early. We loved training camp—we busted our asses and practiced hard but we also played just as hard off the field!"

"Only a team like the Raiders would stay at the El Rancho," said tackle Dave Rowe. "The other teams in the league stayed in dorms."

Kenny Stabler described it as big kids having fun.

"It was just kids having fun and life being good. We couldn't wait to get to training camp, to get away from our wives and girlfriends, play some football, have a few drinks at night, and do that for eight weeks.

"We also had a smoking room at the El Rancho. We changed a closet in one of the motel rooms into the marijuana room. But, of course, we didn't put any clothes in there."

The monotony of training camp was innovatively challenged by the players.

"The Oakland Raiders of my day trained in the long sucking heat of Santa Rosa, California, where the sweat poured like rain for eight weeks." The workouts were scheduled for ninety minutes in the morning and ninety minutes in the afternoon. But I'd like to have an Al Davis pinkie ring for every workout that lasted over two hours. We got so much conditioning in during practice we didn't have to do the extra running that other teams did.

All in all, I loved camp. First, because with the Raiders we went in knowing we were going to win every year; and second, because we also knew we were going to have fun. In fact, we expended almost as much energy devising and executing good times as we did getting ready for the season.

Quarterback Kenny Stabler described it this way: "The monotony of camp was so oppressive that without the diversions of whiskey and women, those of us who were wired for activity and no more than six hours of sleep a night might have gone berserk. I was fortunate to have four 'let's party hearty' roommates to pal with most of my years in Oakland. My roomies were halfback Pete Banaszak, wide receiver Freddy Biletnikoff, defensive end Tony Cline, and middle linebacker Dan Conners. We lived for the weekly football games and the football player nights in between. I liked to think of us as *The Santa Rosa Five.*

"The motel rooms of the El Rancho accommodated two players, but in order to 'socialize,' we shared one main room, with Pete and Dan in the adjoining one. Since there were only two beds in each room, Freddie chose to sleep in the closet. He had his mattress, pillow, and blankets set up there.

"At a used appliance store we bought three ancient refrigerators for $10 apiece and installed them in the suite. We kept the fridges full of beer, soft drinks, candy bars, and fruit . . . but mostly beer.

"Pete had a girl one year who baked us a pie every week. The pies were also stored in the fridge. The girl was strange. Given all the female 'players' who moved through our abode, it was inevitable that the girl would be replaced by new talent, and she was. Yet she kept bringing pies."

"Why don't you ease her out gently?" I asked Pete.

"I like pie," he said.

"She's a tad weird."

"Her pies ain't."

"The final week of camp, on her last pie delivery, the girl heaved it at Pete who ducked. Instead, it hit me in the chest and ran down my shirt."

"You're right, Snake." Pete said. "She's weird."

TEAM MEETING TRICKS, GADGETS, AND TOYS

After you've played a few years for John Madden and have the offense down, meetings end up being the most boring aspect of training camp.

"Biletnikoff taught me how to deal with that," said Stabler. "Freddy had already played eight years when I took over at quarterback and he had perfected a neat meeting trick.

"We always sat together in the back of the room. One night I leaned over and whispered something to him and got no response. I nudged him with an elbow and whispered. 'What the hell's wrong with you?' He had been staring straight ahead with the lifeless expression in his eyes that veterans get at meetings, but now he shook his head like a dog coming out of water and said, 'I was asleep.' *Goddamn*, I said to myself, *he's been sleeping with his eyes open!* Well, it took some practice to get that one down, copping Zs with your lids up and a semi-attentive look on your face. I guess that's when I decided that a determined man can do just about anything."

Many of the Raiders were into gadgets and toys. After all, being isolated at training camp for eight weeks could drive you crazy if you didn't have a few diversions.

"Center Dave Dalby brought the first moneymaking toys to camp. He hauled in two coin-operated pinball machines and set them up in his room. It cost twenty-five cents per game, and there was usually a line waiting to play that stretched out of Dave's room and all the way down the hall. You don't know the meaning of the word 'tilt' until you've seen a defensive lineman get mad at a pinball machine. But those two machines paid for all of Dalby's preseason bar bills.

"George Buehler, a six-two, 260-pound guard, inevitably brought the most interesting toys to camp; intricate models that he would assemble. Once he brought a remote controlled model airplane that cost about $7000. He spent every free moment in camp working on that plane. We'd watch him in his room, his thick, gnarled lineman's fingers fastening tiny parts. Finally, after weeks of labor, he took his plane out for its maiden flight.

"Naturally, we all went out on the field to see if his slick looking craft would actually fly and if George could control it. The plane was terrific and so was George. He had it doing loops, diving, climbing, banking, all kinds of maneuvers. A group of us stood there watching with admiration as George put his plane through its paces like a prized hunting dog. We let out cheers and he was rightly proud.

"Then, as he brought the plane down low for some lazy circles and figure eights, Dave Casper came walking by. Casper didn't know what was going on, which in itself was not that unusual; I never knew what was going on with Dave Casper either. He was a very intelligent individual able to hold two or three conversations at the same time. One on one, though, he was sometimes a tad hazy.

"The plane dove once right over Casper, a six-four, 245-pound tight end, and he sort of waved it away, like King Kong swatting at the bothersome planes that dove at him in the movie. When Buehler's plane made a second pass, Casper was ready. He grabbed a handful of lava rocks from the path and threw them at the plane, hitting the engine. The plane pitched straight down and crashed, pieces flying in every direction.

"Casper just kept walking, without a word to anyone.

"I went to George, who stood there dumbfounded. 'Maybe you're just too big to play with model airplanes,' I said.

"The year after his plane crashed, Buehler constructed a high-dollar, remote controlled tank. This machine was virtually indestructible. Just to make sure it stayed that way, though, George told Casper that if he so much as looked at the tank he was going to bite his face off.

"Inside the quadrangle of rooms at the motel was a sidewalk that skirted a courtyard of flowers, bushes, grass, and rocks. The courtyard was about fifty by fifty and George ran his tank all over it: over rocks, around flowers, through bushes. I saw that, remembered my firecrackers, and decided they would make a great combination—especially when Coach Madden was in his office.

"One afternoon between practice and dinner, Pete Banaszak and Ken Stabler requisitioned Buehler's tank. He left a note in Buehler's his mailbox: DON'T WORRY, THE SNAKE WILL RETURN.

"Next we went to our room, said Stabler which were directly across from the coaches' offices and timed running the tank over to them. We taped a handful of firecrackers to the tank and attached a long fuse that we calculated would be just the right length to set off the fireworks as the tank rolled into the offices. Our calculations proved to be accurate.

"Seconds after the bombs burst, a frantic Madden came running out of the office, jabbing index fingers into his ears and screaming, 'Who the hell did that? Where'd you go?' Meanwhile we turned the tank around, and while coach stood there hollering and turning pink and pulling at his hair as he tended to do whenever he got excited, we ran that little tank between his spread legs and brought it on home.

"After that we blew up the coaches' room maybe once a week. Good old John never got after us. At first I thought he just got used to the explosions. Then I noticed that whenever he entered his office he stuffed wads of cotton in his ears."

A COLLECTION OF MISFITS AND JOKESTERS

"Madden knew the kind of team he had." said offensive tackle John Vella. "He knew he was coaching a gang of distinctive individuals. Some called us characters. Others called us ruffians, mavericks, renegades, oddballs, intimidators . . . and there's no point in mentioning the curse words. But all the labels were fair enough. And I think that Madden decided that with the type of players we had that it was necessary to give us a certain amount of room to roam. We had more characters than any other team and John realized that we didn't care for a lot of restrictions—were happier without them—and as a result played better. John handled individuals very well, and I feel that was a prime reason why the Raiders had the best win-loss record in pro football while he was coaching the team." We all knew that we just needed to show up on Sundays at 1 o'clock, play our balls off and win and John would be a happy camper—so we did, and John was very happy.

"Al Davis liked to pick up so-called 'misfits' from other teams," recalls quarterback David Humm.

"He obviously figured that, while they may not have fit in elsewhere, they sure as hell could fit in with us. And those of us who were already Raiders welcomed anyone who could help the ballclub, and maybe even add another dimension to our festive occasions.

"In August 1975, Al grabbed veteran linebacker Ted Hendricks from Green Bay, where he had not meshed in the Packers defensive system. His nickname was 'Kick 'em in the Head Ted' because he had no qualms about applying his feet to opponents when the urge seized him. Hendricks had no qualms about anything.

"The day he reported at Santa Rosa he didn't turn out with the rest of us for practice, and we wondered where he was. Then we saw him coming over the hill that rose just beyond the field. He was riding a horse, in uniform. Except on his head was a spike-topped World War I German helmet that he'd painted silver and black, and on the sides were the Raiders symbol, patched-eyed pirate decals. Everyone cheered. Ted rode right up to John Madden and said, 'Okay, Coach, I'm ready to play some football.'"

In early 1976 during training camp, the Washington Redskins released six eight, two hundred and eighty pound defensive end John Matuszak. It didn't bother Al Davis that this was the third team to dump "The Tooz."

Ted Hendricks was standing next to Al Davis when John came out to the field.

"The day Matuszak arrived at practice; he suited up with us, but also delayed joining us on the field. Then he came running at full speed and let out a god-awful scream that made spectators cringe and the rest of us laugh like hell. Al Davis was not amused. He was standing next to me and Al, kind of thinking out loud said, 'I wonder if John's worth the gamble?'

I gave him a *you've got to be kidding* look and said, 'Al, what difference will one more make?'

When Pat Toomay joined the Raiders, he was ecstatic after playing the first seven seasons of his career with the Dallas Cowboys, the Buffalo Bills, and the Tampa Bay Buccaneers. "All my life I knew that somewhere in the league there must be a club like this!

"From what I learned in thirteen years, the Raiders were the only team that couldn't wait to get to training camp," Phil Villapiano said. "Santa Rosa was a little town and when we arrived, we were treated like gold.

Pete Banaszak compared the Raider workouts of the '70s to the NFL workouts of today.

"Madden worked the piss out of us in training camp. These guys today go out in their underwear, baseball caps, and sunglasses and don't put pads on. We practiced twice a day *in* pads."

When things got a little boring, Phil Villapiano came to the rescue.

"I thought I'd send a treat in for the boys. I got a girl from one of the clubs and gave her fifty bucks. She put on white sneakers and white socks and nothing else! She was to run around the practice field."

Banaszak remembered . . .

"They always kept the fence around us closed because they didn't want people watching. Then all of a sudden the gate opens just a crack. And here she comes, buck-naked. She was a pretty girl. She was a very appropriately-built young woman. And she starts running the entire length of the field. She then turns around and starts to run on the other field, and she gets winded—she can't run. She has to start walking; she's lost her breath. Madden doesn't know if he should be mad or laugh."

"Was she really pretty?" asked John Vella. "I don't know if I was looking at her face."

THE FAMOUS BAMBOO ROOM
AND OTHER PORTS OF CALL

Many of the Raiders frequented the 'spirit' facilities of Santa Rosa. One of those taverns was The Bamboo Room.

Pete Banaszak recalls a few fond memories of the old watering hole.

"One pitcher and you'd be shit faced. At five we would shower and by five-thirty we would in the Room slompin' 'em down. Then we would walk over to the El Rancho for dinner. One night Jim Otto was stumbling, bouncing off the wall. 'Rooster,' he said, 'it was too much, too soon.'

"We'd have those two a day practices," said linebacker Duane Benson, "and after those, in the heat, after a beer and a half you were so shit faced you couldn't make English a language. You'd suck them down, because it was a pretty cheap high. Pitchers of beer were the stable offering. Everyone was into volume. I don't remember anyone drinking out of a bottle."

John Matuszak remembered a particular night when a bar patron challenged him to a fight.

"One night I was sitting in the Bamboo Room with Dave Dalby and Ted Hendricks. Seated at a table, I suppose we looked like average sized guys. We were shooting the breeze when some guy I'd never seen before walked up to the table and interrupted our conversation. He was looking at me."

"What's your name, Fatso?" he asked.

"I didn't respond."

"I said," he repeated, "what's your name, Fatso?"

I unfolded myself from the table and stood straight up. The guy didn't look quite as cocky then."

"How would you like to eat this table," I asked the wise guy, "whole or in splinters?"

"Sometimes you have to speak to people in a language they understand."

It was at the Bamboo Room where Phil Villapiano got his nickname from Benson.

"I was trying to say 'Phil,' but due to the copious amounts of liquid refreshment, the syllable came out slightly askew. All I could say was 'Foo.'"

The Bamboo Room may have been one of the favorite watering holes of the Raiders, but it also served as an interview facility in finding a Queen.

"When Phil arrived to training camp, he had a fantastic inspiration," said linebacker Dan Connors. "He was going to find a Queen to reign over the Air Hockey Championships. There was just one requirement: she had to be ugly, ugly, ugly.

"Phil came up with the lady after many hours of interviews and elimination contests. He sure can pick 'em. The lady accepted the honor of being our Queen and we held a special coronation. Kick 'em in the head Hendricks, so named because of his favorite maneuver during a game, built a throne from old crates on the back of his pickup truck and drove Her Royal Majesty up and down the streets of Santa Rosa."

The Bamboo Room was also the venue for a wedding ceremony where, Phil Villapiano was the ring bearer.

"We called the Bamboo Room bartender 'the queen' (not to be confused with the Queen of the Air Hockey Tournament) because she served us pitchers and was nice to us," said Benson. "One night Queen announced that she was going to marry one of the patrons of the bar. So, the Raiders decided to host the wedding. Pat Toomay performed the ceremony in which he was paid one hundred dollars. Toomay was bestowed the name of 'Reverend Tombstone' from the Church of the Holy C-note.

"She came in a white dress. The guy she married was in a cowboy hat and boots. She thought it was legit. It wasn't, of course. We all chipped in and got them a week in Lake Tahoe, and a police escort on the way out of town."

BAR HOPPING WAS DOWN TO A SCIENCE

"We'd hit five bars in two hours," said Pete Banaszak. "The Bamboo Room, the Music Box, Melendy's, the Hilltopper, and the Hofbrau. The Music Box was a strip mall tavern. Melendy's featured a long bar with a jukebox and booths. We'd roll dice. Whoever lost the dice game bought the first round.

"Melendy's was out on the highway. It didn't have much local color. Local people didn't go there. You'd get the riffraff coming through. Exactly. We'd accuse Snake of studying his playbook by the light of the jukebox at the Music Box—although Stabler by his own admission seldom, if ever, studied a playbook."

Kenny Stabler loved it.

"We couldn't wait to get out of meetings and do the circuit. There was always a game plan to the madness. We had all the stops worked out; the same music stations on the radio. We ran in cliques like a pack of dogs, like a pack of wolves."

Stabler, at the time, like most of the Raider players, was not married. They drank hard and chased women even harder.

"It relieved the monotony of training camp and the pressure of games, said Stabler. "And, goddamn, it was fun.

"My roommates and I had a pact. We all took seats by the door at the 8 p.m. and met up the moment it broke up, which was around 9:30. We then sprinted to our rooms, where we'd comb our hair, slap on face juice, and dash to the biggest car we had, usually a Banaszak Buick. We only had ninety minutes to complete what we called 'The Circuit.' That consisted of hitting at least five bars before we had to be back for the 11 p.m. curfew.

"The Circuit started each night at Melendy's and ended at the Music Box. The Music Box had a large dance floor, the best live music in Santa Rosa, and also had the best looking women.

THE SIXTY MINUTE PLAYERS AND THE OT GIRLS

"Every year during training camp the women of Santa Rosa turned out in droves to greet the Raiders. Some of the women were beautiful, a great many were attractive, and the balance ranged from plain to ugly as a mud fence. We tried to be selective.

"We usually played Boss dice on the Circuit to see who would pay for the drinks. All the while, at each stop, we'd check out the women who appeared to be what we called 'players.' As we had to be in by the eleven o'clock curfew, all cars parked, dates would be set for 11:30. The experienced female players knew the routine, while others were quick to learn. They would drive to the El Rancho, pick you up, and haul you to their place or to another motel. Those players not familiar with the word 'shy' would join you in your room, uninhibited by the witnesses to the performances. There were a few tireless spirits who would attend to all five of us. They were known as the '60-minute Players' or the 'OT Girls.'

"When one of the roomies came in real late with a girl, those of us who appeared to be, but were not quite asleep, would peek at the action. Freddy liked to crawl on the floor and get right up close. I bought a kid's plastic periscope to peek around the doorframe into the inner room, but the damn thing didn't work unless all the lights in there were on.

"Many nights we'd go right back out after curfew, and many times I didn't return until just before breakfast. We left and returned the same way—through a back door and a hedgerow of bushes rimming the driveway. If I had a midnight date, she would pull in, turn off the headlights, and then slowly circle the driveway. Meanwhile, I'd creep through the bushes in a crouch and look up the driveway for her— and usually see about fifteen other veterans hunched down waiting for pickups.

"We had a teammate who kept professing how religious he was. He enjoyed reprimanding some of us for our womanizing. Then one night I went through the hedgerow and who was right beside me but that God spouting hypocrite. A woman stopped her car and he made for it as if she had the keys to the pearly gates. 'Caught, caught!' I half hollered. The next day he denied that it was him. For the next week, though, whenever I saw him I'd yell, 'Caught, caught!' and watch him turn red."

CURFEWS AND FINES

No matter the amount of late-night shenanigans the players embarked upon, Coach Madden was a stickler for curfew and the fines that went along with them.

"I never got caught with a woman in the El Rancho, though roughly half of our partying occurred right there," said Stabler. "But every year in camp a few guys would get nabbed by coaches. They knew the program. The coaches had been around longer than us and periodically would run a spot check after curfew, around 1 a.m. Invariably, it was a veteran who was found with a girl in his sack."

John Madden did this just to maintain some kind of control. He was not a guy to lay down rules and try to stop the fun completely— as most coaches did—because he knew that football players needed some relaxation. He drew a line, and it was a long one, beyond which you were not to tread. We just rubberized that line and stretched the hell out of it.

"Still, there had to be some policing, and at each camp six or eight players would be fined $200 for missing curfew, and four or five spot-check felons would have to cough up $500. The fines went into a fund for the end of the year team party.

"Coach Madden enjoyed standing up in the dining room and announcing the fines at breakfast, particularly when a player got busted with a woman in his room. 'I'd like to thank John Matuszak (or whoever),' John would say, 'for his contribution to the party fund. He was found to have given some poor, homeless young woman shelter last night. She had to be homeless to stay with him. And while we admire his big heart, we appreciate more his $500 party donation.'

"Then everyone would laugh and raise hell razzing the guy who had gotten caught.

"I did get tapped for not making curfew once. Our standard procedure was to drink in the last bar on the Circuit until 10:30. Then we'd jump in the car and race back to camp. But one night we blew a rear tire a couple of miles from the motel. 'Leave the car until tomorrow,' Freddy said. 'We can run for it.'

"Given my bad knees and all that booze in me, I wasn't about to run two miles. 'To hell with that,' I said. 'We'll speed-change the tire. Pete, you set the jack. Dan, you pop the hubcap. Tony, you get the spare. Freddy, you grab the lug wrench.'

'What are you gonna do, Snake?' Freddy asked.

'My duty. Go down with the ship if necessary.'

"Pete was so drunk he couldn't set the jack properly. I jumped in and it took me over ten minutes to get the flat off the blacktop. It's not real easy changing a tire in the dark—drunk. We didn't stomp into our rooms until 11:35. There was a note on the floor: THAT'S $200 X 5."

Pete Banaszak had his own way of letting it be known that he wasn't late for the 11:00 p.m. curfew.

"I'd come in there every night, and there was a long, long driveway to the back [of the hotel]. I'd peel off down that driveway, squealing the tires at about fifty miles an hour, at five till eleven. That was my way of letting the coaches know I was there. They'd hear the tires and say, 'OK, Banaszak's in, we don't have to check his room.'

"One night I was hurrying home to beat the curfew and I ended up scraping Stabler's Corvette. I go in the room and I see Snake sleeping. I bang him on the shoulder, 'Hey, I kind of hit your car coming in. It didn't look too bad. Rub it out with Turtle Wax. He got up real early and saw that I'd torn the fender off. Next morning he's banging on my door raising all kinds of hell.'

Shortly after the fender incident, Stabler's car was repossessed.

"A few mornings later I woke up and found that my wheels were missing. I accused Banaszak of hiding my Corvette. Banaszak said, 'No, I didn't fuck with your car. They'd repossessed it.' I got on the phone and said, 'You motherfuckers, you cocksuckers, you come up here and take my goddamn car? People are out there robbing people and you're repo-ing cars?' I ended up having to buy back my own car."

There was a lot of skill involved in sneaking out after bed check. The rooms at the El Rancho opened onto a courtyard, but they also had a door on the backside, right on the parking lot. Coach Bob Zeman would pull back the sliding glass door on the inside, say, 'Are you here?' then leave. The moment that happened, as soon as they would turn the corner, guys were bailing out the back door into their cars. It was like the Daytona 500 leaving the parking lot. Everyone knew it. But that was part of Madden's philosophy: 'I don't care what you do as long as you show up Sunday and play your heart out. And don't let anything happen that will have an impact on Sunday.'"

One night tight end Bob Moore got caught by Madden as he tried to escape the El Rancho.

"One night I snuck out and was headed for my car when I ran into Madden. I took off back to my room with Madden on my heels.

He was knocking and shouting, 'Let me in! Let me in!' We didn't let him in.

"We get up the next morning, thinking, 'Holy shit, this is gonna be really bad.' But we pass him at practice, he's going the other way, and he just says, 'How ya doin'?' I don't know if he had his boots full that night or what. But it did scare the hell out of us."

During training camp, everyone had their own way of sneaking out, but Fred Biletnikoff thought his way was smarter than most. His roommate, Pete Banaszak declined Fred's offer to go with him. It was the smart move.

"One night I didn't feel like going out," said Pete. "Fred wanted to go out after bed check. I was tired. I said, 'Fuck it, Fred. I'm staying in.' So Fred puts two tennis shoes under the covers, took the pillows and rolled them like legs, then he grabbed the lamp off the table and put it in there, and tucks his hat in there. It looked pretty real.

"I knew Coach would be doing bed checks that evening. I knew it was him because he never wore shoestrings in his sneakers and you could hear his feet dragging on the sidewalk outside the window. Well, he came to our room and turned the light switch on. Freddy's bed lit up and Madden walked out. The next morning at practice, Madden calls the team together. He says to Fred, 'By the way, Biletnikoff, I came in last night and your head lit up. It's gonna cost you big time.'"

THE WALL OF SHAME

What would Raiders training camp be without a Wall of Shame? Biletnikoff explains.

"We partied so much in our rooms that they became very popular with various female players. At times we had to take reservations. We also began finding, the morning after, various bras and panties that women had left behind. That gave us the idea to start a collection of women's undergarments. Kind of our trophies. We tacked the garments up on the walls and watched the items multiply. Women readily contributed, with monogrammed panties being the choice donation of the elite.

"Undergarment collecting became an annual rite of training camp. Someone called us the 'Frederick's of Santa Rosa.' In subsequent years, we tended to judge our preseason success not by how many passes were completed or receptions caught, not by how many tackles were made or how much yardage was gained. The bottom line was: how much lingerie did we collect?"

Sometimes the guys didn't feel like going out, so the entertainment was brought to them.

"There were some nights when we were all tired or maybe needed a night off the sauce and we'd decide not to go out on the Circuit" explained Stabler. "We'd all just sit around the rooms, read, talk, have a couple of beers. It felt damn good—for about an hour.

"Then one of us would feel the need to get some entertainment going. A ball boy would walk past our door and we'd tell him to find the two rookies we named and send them to us.

'Tell them it's their ass and yours if they don't get here pronto.'

"Usually we'd just send the rookies out for pizza or hamburgers. But the really fun times were when their assigned mission, a bit more difficult but one of the more important ones in their young lives, was to bring us back women."

'This is a major test of your abilities,' I'd tell them. 'Raiders have to be resourceful, determined, and quick-witted at all times. This is one of those times. Raiders are also expected to know how to sweet talk women. So regard this as just part of your training. Failure won't be looked on kindly.'

'I'm sure,' Pete would say, 'You don't want to be standing on your chair at every meal singing your rotten school songs.'

'Go get 'em,' Tony would say.

'And remember,' Freddy would always add, 'no coyotes.'

"One night, though, we suffered a terrible disappointment. The two girls were so cute, I about felt my eyeballs sweat. Both girls were wearing white short-shorts that did little to disguise what was under them. They were also braless and walked into our doorway like players of the first rank. But when the redhead opened her mouth, it was like we were two TDs down to the Steelers with thirty seconds left to play.

'Are you guys serious?' she said with sarcasm you could chew on. 'We just wanted to check out you jerks who had the balls to send kids to score dates for you.' Her eyes scanned the room. 'Did you really think we would be a couple more of your playthings?' If looks could melt, we would have all gone up in smoke.

"She hooked a finger under the lower edge of her panties, tugged it down on the side of her thigh, and let it snap back. Her girlfriend turned, bent, and mooned us through her shorts, saying, 'Enjoy yourselves.' Then they were gone."

"*Win some, lose some*," I thought. "But within ten minutes we were out on the prowl again. No way could we stay in after that simmering short-shorts show."

Married veterans had to be even more resourceful than their unmarried teammates. Stabler recalls an incident that occurred on the football field when a married vet was kicked in the balls . . . and thankful for it.

"For example, what do you do when you are about to go home to your wife from camp bearing crabs? This story concerns a former teammate who is still married to that wife, so he will remain anonymous."

"Crabs, back then, were treated with an ointment called Pyrinate A-200. It was so popular with the 'Santa Rosa Five' that we pasted a Pyrinate label on our bathroom mirror over a sign that read: COMBAT YOUR ENEMY. But back then it took a week to kill off crabs, and my teammate would have to join his wife in two days after the final preseason game. He would be expected to take care of his homework . . . and what could he do?

"What he did was get lucky. In the game against the Rams, with his wife looking on from the stands, he was kicked in the nuts on a kickoff. It was the only time in his life he was thankful for a kick in the nuts, but he saw that as a solution to his problem.

"After the injury, he was carried off the field into the locker room. At game's end he had very swollen testicles, and to emphasize this he stuck two athletic socks into his Jockey shorts. He then put on slacks and a sport coat and gingerly walked out to meet his wife.

'Sorry I can't go home with you, babe,' he said, pointing at his bulging crotch. 'I'm hurting and everyone who got hurt today has to go back to camp for treatment.'"

THE ARRIVAL OF BOB BROWN

In 1971, Rams offensive tackle Bob Brown was traded to Raiders. Brown talks about his way of dealing with fines.

"I didn't have to sneak out. I'd leave at ten at night and just leave a blank check signed on my bed, and if they came in and fined me, they could just fill out the check."

Linebacker Duane Benson had this to say on his reaction to meeting Brown.

"He shows up in '71, the first day, in a Cadillac, wearing a basketball shirt, with this huge upper body. And he's got a driver. Shit, the rest of us were driving junkers, and he shows up with a driver and a suitcase full of pistols. It was like I told Jim Otto, 'I don't think the son of a bitch needs a pistol. He's got arms as big as your legs.' Brown immediately fit right in."

Pete Banaszak recalls an incident between Brown and the goalpost.

"Bob went on to the field before practice had begun. I saw him get into a three-point stance in front of the goalpost, then run into it. I swear, those goalposts were four by fours. He snapped it right in half! My eyes fell out of my head. You got to remember that every weird guy who ever played football those days came through the Raiders."

Being an offensive tackle, Bob Brown was not a big fan of the headslap. Raiders' cornerback Willie Brown tells the story that Brown told to him.

"Bob was traded by the Eagles to the Rams," said Willie Brown. "There he met Deacon Jones. Deacon was famous for his 'headslap.' Bob was definitely not a fan of it. He finally asked Deacon to stop using the tactic on him during practice. As usual, Jones ignored his request. At the following practice, Deacon slapped the side of Bob's helmet and tore up his hand. Boomer had replaced a small screw [that held the helmet pad in place] with a longer screw that stuck out of the helmet."

Phil Villapiano learned a lesson on dealing with Boomer when he was asked to help him with his pass blocking.

"One day Boomer asked me to stay and help him with his pass blocking. He tells me, 'I'm going to get back off the ball and you're going to try and get to the quarterback.' I fucking come up field, hard, come in, make a move and the fucking guy blasts me in the stomach, nearly fucking kills me. I go, 'Bob, what the fuck?' I mean we didn't even have helmets on!"

As much as Brown was known for his hard hitting, he was also known for his style . . . and for Villapiano to say that Bob Brown was an extravagant dresser would be an understatement.

"I called him 'El Boomo.' We'd go to Golden Gate and Bay Meadows and play the horses. You should have seen his outfits. You'd get on the airplane with him, he'd have these tight spandex pants, 300 pounds with a silk guinea T-shirt showing off these large muscles, gold chain, a fucking hat, fucking boots. You'd go, 'What the fuck is this?'"

In the seventies it didn't take much for players to stand out, and Bob was no different. As stated earlier, Brown carried a suitcase to training camp that was filled with only firearms. One night he decided to use one of them.

"We were all sleeping when all of a sudden we heard gunfire," said Villapiano. "We're all ducking and running down the hallway like the Black Plague's here. It turned out that Boomer had shot out his television."

Another time, Brown riddled Willie Brown's mattress with bullets. "Gene Upshaw and I were roommates and down the hall from Boomer's room. Boomer used to come into our room and raid the refrigerator. Gene and I would be watching TV and I'd be telling Bob to do this, do that: 'Bob, cut the light out." Then I'd say, 'Get me some cheese.' Then I'd call him back and say, 'Bob get me a soda.' Then, 'Bob, turn off the TV.' So the next time I call him he comes back and shoots three bullets into my mattress. Not near me; he wasn't trying to hit me, or anything like that, but that didn't stop me from backpedaling in that bed so fast that I almost climbed the wall. Hell, I was scared to death. He says, 'That'll teach you to make me your servant.'"

When it was time for pay raises, Bob had a way of getting his point across. "The story had it that Boomer was negotiating his contract with Al Davis, and that Al didn't want to give him a raise, so he pulled out a gun and sat it on the desk," said center Jim Otto. I don't know if he got the raise or not."

Whether on or off the field, Bob Brown brought his own style and personality to the Raiders.

"Bob Brown brought his technique and style to the team and that's what he taught our guys," said Madden. "They were tough anyway, but from Bob they learned that even in relatively passive situations they could be aggressive. You feed off Boomer Brown's aggression on your offensive line, and pretty soon everyone's playing that way."

THE INFAMOUS AIR HOCKEY TOURNAMENTS

Raider training camp was famous for its air hockey tournaments. Phil was my roommate and, together, we declared ourselves co-commissioners of all tournaments, games, and activities during training camp.

"It all began during the 1973 offseason when the Raiders and Rams played a charity basketball game. The halftime entertainment included a tricycle race. Phil beat the Rams linebacker Isiah Robertson, and his prize was an air hockey table. That summer at training camp, Phil brought the air hockey table to Santa Rosa and it stayed in our room all summer during training camp. During the day and night when we were not practicing football, Raider players routinely entered our room to hone up on their air hockey skills. Of course, come tournament time, skill had nothing to do with whether you won or lost, it was how well you cheated that advanced you to the championship. The table later found a home at Melendy's, where it remained for several years.

"As co-commissioners of the tournament, Villapiano and I had responsibilities of that prestigious position which required us to come up with rules and regulations for all such events. So, for our annual air hockey tournament, which was a round robin format, like the NCAA basketball tournament, we came up with thirty odd rules for the tournament, with the last and most important rule reading: *Cheating is Highly Encouraged.*

"Rule number 30 was taken to heart by all members of the team entered in playing in the tournament, and it also meant that rules 1 through 29 meant absolutely nothing!"

Now veterans Pete Banaszak and Fred Biletnikoff derived a method of cheating that can only be described as genius!

As the tournament progressed, we knew they were cheating, but we couldn't figure out how they were doing it. They had already won six games in a row and were now in the finals against John "Happy Fella" Vella and Dave "Double D" Dalby, and still no team had scored a goal against them. Vella and Dalby themselves had come up with an ingenious way of cheating as they wore extra long trench coats weighed down with extra heavy sleeves enabling them to block many a shot on goal with those sleeves. But even their ingenuity was no match for Biletnikoff and Banaszak in what was dubbed as the most creative cheating in Oakland Raider tournament history.

"After another resounding 7–0 victory for Biletnikoff and Banaszak as they ripped through the dumbfounded Vella and Dalby on their way to the championship. However, before they walked away with their trophies and a couple of more beers in their hands, all participants needed to know just how they cheated so well. They were not walking out of that bar without an explanation as the door was blocked by 6'9" defensive end John Matuszak. Their explanation was exhilarating as they told how they corroborated with equipment manager Dick Romanski in designing an apparatus constructed of clear plastic, which somehow strapped undetected to their left hand. As they played with their right hand on the stick and hit the puck around the board, they slipped their left hand under the table and into the mouth of the goal. Thus, with the speed of the puck flying around the table, no one—including the co-commissioners—ever realized that the shot of an opponent would occasionally enter the goal and then quickly and simply ricochet back onto the playing surface—truly ingenious! The rowdy and inebriated crowd of Raiders exploded in applause as the champions were lifted in the air and paraded around the bar for their creativity and effort for cheating at the highest level.

"Just Win, Baby" was a phrase coined by Raiders owner Al Davis, and that night Biletnikoff and Banaszak had followed Al's advice to perfection in doing anything and everything to just win.

"The number one rule for the air hockey tournament was 'Cheating is encouraged,'" said Monte Johnson. "And, of course, it was only cheating if you get caught."

Villapiano used to say, "If you're not cheating, you're not really trying."

"What the air-hockey tournament revealed was how we played football. The original rules were lost over time, but here's an example of what they said:

- Cheating is encouraged
- Motherfuckages and verbal abuse of opponents is encouraged
- No physical abuse to table, players, or judge (penalty: one unmolested free shot; guilty party must cruise with the Tooz)

- Long sleeve shirts are illegal. Tooz will remove all sleeves personally
- All hose bags must be registered with Rooster
- Drunkenness is mandatory—urine must be clear
- Rookies cannot win
- Phil Villapiano Most Disgusting Player Award will be presented to the most outrageous display of baffoonism or illicit behavior
- Ray Guy's Poor Sportsmanship Award to the biggest shit sport.

Of course the air hockey tournament would be nothing without an appearance by San Francisco's topless stripper, Carol Doda. She was invited by Fred Biletnikoff.

"Carol Doda, the famous topless dancer of the '60s and '70s was our *honorary queen*. I invited her to the air hockey tournament. She put her tits on the table and blocked shots with them. She was a big hit!"

Rookie night and the annual parade were two of the biggest events in Santa Rosa.

"It was a huge event," said Banaszak. "It was like a ticker-tape parade. The guys who won the various tournaments would ride through town on the back of our pick-up trucks. Dan Connors used to drive his El Camino with a bra tied to the trailer hitch. We usually had to kick in some money to clean the place up afterwards. We'd always end up throwing food at each other.

"Rookie Night was held at a local strip club. The veterans loved it and the strippers were more than willing to welcome the newcomers to the league."

The exploits at the El Rancho bonded the players and, at the end of training camp, the Raiders were ready to take on the season.

OAKLAND NIGHT LIFE
ONE FOR ALL AND ALL FOR ONE

THE EDGEWATER WEST MOTEL was where Al Davis hosted his post-game parties. As Villapiano said, "It was one seedy place. A real dive.

"We had a great time there," continued Phil. "It was all you could eat and drink for free. But you have to remember that the NFL was just getting started and these teams didn't have a lot of money to spend. The Raiders were the only team that threw a full-fledged party for all the players, their family and their friends. And if you didn't go, someone would be down your fucking throat. We all went, we all had a good time . . . and of course, shit happened.

"The one great thing about the Edgewater parties was you'd get to know everyone, and that had a lot to do with the team's camaraderie."

John Madden liked family oriented events. The team and their families were family to the Raiders.

"Everything was always family with the team. I used to let my players and coaches bring their kids to Saturday practices for home games. I had my two kids, too. Then when we all went in to take off the pads and shower, the kids would play a game on the field—on the game field, the day before a game. Those were great practices. They were fun. You could still do that back then, you could still have fun."

Center Steve Sylvester remembers the Tuesday afternoon golf tournaments.

"We had a two-man scramble match every Tuesday. Dave Dalby and Gene Upshaw were always partners, they both cheated, and everyone fell in line after that. Madden used to stand in front of the chalkboard that featured our twosomes and look at the matchups. He always had a towel over his shoulder and a bottle of Maalox in his hand."

Tuesday night was considered to be Camaraderie Night, and it was *mandatory* that all players attend. Villapiano explains.

"Everyone had to be there; we didn't accept excuses. We'd tell the new guys, 'Tell your wife anything, but you gotta be there.' No wives. No friends. No girlfriends.

"Our first stop was Big Al's Cactus Room. It was in the middle of nowhere. During the day the downtown area would be full of life, but by nightfall there would be nothing; nobody . . . except for the Raiders. The Cactus Room would be packed with Raiders and with fans.

"Al was the sweetest man of all the bartenders. He's also my daughter's godfather.

"Al Punzak was our Hungarian guy. It was the perfect hangout. Big, long bar and down at the end he had this bell. As soon as you'd step in, he'd ring the bell, and call out, 'Villapiano in the house! Ken Stabler in the house!'

"He'd make these delicious beef ribs for us and every player who walked in had a drink named after them. Mike Siani's was called a 'Mohair Special.' It had something to do with Bailey's Irish Cream. We paid nothing for anything. Of course, part of why he did it was because it brought hundreds of people into his restaurant every week."

The second stop was Jack London Square.

"After the Cactus Room, we'd head to the Grotto to eat, then to Clancy's, and later to Uppy's," said Pete Banaszak. "Christ, we were drunker than skunks. But we had a way of policing each other. If a guy was too drunk, we'd always find a way to get him home."

Ken Stabler remembers one particular night at Uppy's on the Square. It was owned by Gene Upshaw and his brother, Marvin.

"One night I heard a voice call out, 'Hello, Snake.' When I turned around I saw that it was Huey Newton of the Black Panthers standing there."

The Black Panthers would frequent the Raiders' practices.

"It was just our style," said Willie Brown. "Bobby Seale would come to practice sometimes. The Panthers loved the Raiders. They were part of us. All the different organizations and groups that were disengaged, we took them and brought them in and accepted them. The Angels? That's part of us. The Panthers? That's part of us. We didn't think of it then as what it means today."

Stabler became friends with Hell's Angels then president Sonny Barger.

"I was always a huge fight fan ever since I was a kid and I'd watch the Friday night fights with my dad. Freddy and I used to go to this gym in downtown Oakland. Freddy would live in there and watch the fighters work out.

"One day Freddy asked me to meet him at the bar near the gym. There was a guy at the bar with a sleeveless jean jacket that said 'Hells Angels' on the back of it. Everybody knew who we were. So he introduced himself, wanted to know if we wanted to shoot a game of pool with Sonny Barger. And we did."

Defensive tackle Art Thoms remembers drinking with the Angels.

"I remember one story when Stabler was out drinking with the Angels till a.m. It was the night before a game. Kenny went to the game. The Angels went home, watched him on TV, then passed out"

Villapiano used to work out with the Angels.

"I used to life weights with Sonny in a gym in Hayward, on East 14th Street. Sonny and his bodyguard were serious lifters. Matuszak and I would meet them there a lot during the offseason. If you met them at a bar, you'd have beer together. They'd be on the sideline during the game—you'd see Sonny a lot."

Offensive guard George Buehler remembers one night when Villapiano had not returned to the hotel. It was long after curfew and Phil was nowhere to be found.

"All of a sudden, around the corner here comes Phil, a bloody mess. His shirt was torn and he was stumbling badly. The guys got him over to the room."

Phil said it all began while drinking in the Bamboo Room. He had had a bad day.

"I was pissed off because I was changed to inside linebacker. On top of that I had pulled a muscle in practice and knew I wouldn't be practicing the next day. I hung out at the bar and had a few more beers. When I came out of the bar there were a couple of guys leaning on my car.

"I told them, 'Get the fuck off my car.' The next thing I remember is I got a hammer to the side of my head. If I didn't know Sonny, I'd probably be dead. As soon as I mentioned his name, those guys stopped. It wasn't as bad as it looked. Head wounds just tend to bleed a lot.

"Jack Tatum wanted revenge, as well as a few others, but I told them that we didn't want to go there. Someone is going to get hurt and it's going to ruin our season.

"Guys were still yelling to go out and get those assholes, but Madden came into the room and said, 'No one's leaving!'

"A week or so later, I made up with the Angels. I had to invite them to practice. When Madden saw them he began yelling, 'What the fuck?' I explained to him what happened, practice went on as usual, and we were friends with the Angels once again."

* * *

The Raiders had a Junior Board and a Senior Board that was in charge of various Raider functions. The Junior Board was made up of the younger and newer guys, and the Senior Board was made up of the veterans. Since they all were together so much throughout the week, they decided to purchase a limo to drive them from one bar to another. In addition to driving the players around town during the week, the limo was used to pick up friends and family members who would fly into Oakland for the weekend when we played at home—and we always had family and friends come to see us play.

"We always had a lot of Board functions," said Art Thoms, "so we had to have the Board Limo. We all kicked in like $500 apiece. Couldn't have cost more than $2,500 tops. It was a black, run-down piece of crap. Hell, it must have been at least ten years old.

"After a 49ers game, we went down to a bar on Union Street in San Francisco. We parked right in front of the bar and we put all our girls on our shoulders and walked into the place.

The bouncers weren't real happy. They tried to keep us out, but we weren't leaving. The 49ers weren't very good at that time and the Raiders dominated both sides of the bay. That night Phil Villapiano got up on one of the tables. He was singing along with the dueling piano's, and he fell off the table crashing to the ground and dislocating his right elbow—I think he pulled a groin too but he never missed a beat and never missed a day of practice.

"Another time we used the limo to go to a Boz Scaggs concert. He was a Raiders fan. Used to say I was his favorite player said Art Thoms. So we pulled the limo up to the very front of the place, and there was this line of people waiting to get in. There was this little area, this red zone. I backed in and I hit the curb and the tire blew. It was like a shotgun going off. Everyone turned and looked and we just walked in. I left the limo there. It's a miracle I didn't get sued."

Pete Banaszak always thought that Thoms' behavior was strange.

"We referred to Art as 'King Arthur.' He was kind of fucking strange. He would travel with a Snoopy lunch pail under his arm. I have no idea what he kept in it.

"Otis Sistrunk and Art were 'Salt and Pepper.' Everyone had a gimmick. You had to have a gimmick. Otis was black and bald and Art was white with long hair, so Art would wear a black hat and Otis would wear a white hat. Otis brought the cigars and the two of them would smoke the cigars on the way to the stadium."

RIVALS, ENEMIES, AND FOES

THE RAIDERS AND THEIR rivalries represented everything that was great about the 1970s. Back then, the Raiders were the most hated team in the NFL. The Kansas City Chiefs, the Denver Broncos, and the Pittsburgh Steelers were among their major rivalries of the era.

Oakland dominated each of their rivals during that decade. The team records were as follows: Raiders vs. Chiefs: 12–6–2; Raiders vs. Broncos: 14–6–1.

But the dominant rivalry was that of the Raiders and the Steelers. When the NFL and AFL merged in 1970, the Raiders and the Steelers played eleven times, including five playoff games against each other. At the end of the '70s, the Raiders led the regular season series 4 to 2, and won 2 of 5 in postseason play.

In the '70s, the Steelers and the Raiders met in three straight AFC Championship games, with the winner taking the Super Bowl each time.

The San Diego Chargers were always a rival of the Raiders, but during the '70s, there was little rivalry as Oakland dominated by winning fourteen out of twenty-one games, with one tie. This is why the Chargers are not listed in this section. The rivalry came back to a short-lived life on September 10, 1978, after a 21–20 Oakland victory in a game noted simply as "The Holy Roller," which will be retold later on in this book.

KANSAS CITY CHIEFS

The Red versus the Black.

The fierce rivalry began during the early days of the AFL, and from the beginning no member of the opposing organization could escape the fury.

It wasn't just the rivalry that was fierce, but also a fierce hatred for the Chiefs' mascot.

"They had a horse that Madden hated," said Pete Banaszak. "Every time the Chiefs would score, the horse would be running up and down the field and the Chief would be waving the spear. I remember me and Biletnikoff coming on the field and throwing ice cubes at the horse."

But according to Kansas City running back Mike Garrett, the cheap shots were not just reserved for the horse.

"If you're behind, it's kind of natural to give an elbow here or throw some dirt there or trip the player to make the other guy look stupid."

A lot of players didn't like each other if you get right down to it. One of those players was defensive end Ben Davidson.

"When Buck Buchanan corkscrewed George Blanda upside down and threw him down on his head, that rubbed us the wrong way. It was now payback time."

Defensive back George Atkinson remembers the personal rivalry between the Chiefs defensive back Jim Marsalis and Fred Biletnikoff.

"Biletnikoff had this running thing with cornerback Jim Marsalis. Once when he caught the ball for a touchdown, he spiked it in front of Marsalis and pointed his finger at him. I don't know what he told him, but evidently it wasn't very pretty. When it came to Kansas City you could say hello to a guy and a fight would break out."

It wasn't just the players who had issues. Pete Banaszak was forthright about the fact that he didn't have a lot of respect for the Chiefs' legendary coach Hank Stram.

"It all started with their coach Hank Stram. He was always so neat and proper. You could always hear that squeaky voice yelling, 'Hey, you're holding #63!' You would want to go over there and spit on him, too."

But there was one classic fight between the Raiders and the Chiefs (in 1970) that executive assistant Al LoCasale will never forget. It involved Lenny Dawson and Ben Davidson.

"It was late in the game. The Raiders had used all their time-outs and things were looking very bleak. The Chiefs had a three-point lead and Dawson called a bootleg. What should have been a game-clinching first down by Dawson was instead wiped away by actions typical of two archenemies."

What Ben Davidson did next would now be considered an "illegal" move.

"Lenny very much needed to be touched down, but I figured being a conscientious defensive end, I should touch him down—which is illegal now—with my helmet in his back. Immediately after that Otis Taylor came at me and the referees penalized the Chiefs. We got the ball back as a result of that.

"We drove to near midfield and with three or four seconds left in the game Blanda kicks a 48-yard field goal and we tied the game, 17–17."

Their contests were punctuated by more than just malice. During the '60s, the Chiefs and the Raiders were the *class* of the AFL.

Chiefs running back Ed Podolak talks about his early years of the Raiders rivalry.

"For the first five years that I was with the Chiefs, every time we played them, it was either for the lead in the division or the conference championship."

Such was the case in 1969, when Oakland beat Kansas City twice during the regular season.

"So we had to go out there to play them for the right to go to Super Bowl IV," said quarterback Lenny Dawson.

He continued: "They were so confident that they were going to win that the players had their bags packed for New Orleans and had stored them at the stadium because they were going to go right to the airport."

"We were up going into the third quarter and we had Lenny Dawson with a third and about fifteen," said George Atkinson.

"Unless a miracle could be performed, Coach Stram knew his team was in deep trouble.

"We're in the end zone. We hid Otis Taylor between the right guard and right tackle, went on a quick count, and Otis went deep down the sideline and made a one-handed catch. It gave us a first down and enabled us to win the game."

But was Taylor in bounds? Atkinson doesn't agree.

"He catches the ball with one foot out of bounds. This was a real bad call. They went in and scored and beat us."

Dawson added salt to the wound—and enjoyed every minute of it.

"It makes it so satisfying because as we are going to our bus to catch a plane—go back to KC to get ready to go to New Orleans— here come the Raider players with suitcases in hand. They had to walk by us to get to their cars. And I'll never forget that. It was the most enjoyable thing that I can recall."

The defining legacy of this rivalry is not only the championships, but the intense battles that were endured in order to reach those victorious feats.

"Those moments and those games were special," said Banaszak. "Now I'll sit and watch a Raiders–Chiefs game on TV and I start reliving all those certain situations. It's almost like I'm looking across at Bobby Bell screaming out something and all of a sudden I got sweat coming out from under my arms down to my waist . . . it's like reliving all those moments that you cherished."

DENVER BRONCOS

The Raiders and Broncos rivalry is as bitter today as it was during its heyday in the '70s, when an established Oakland team clashed with the up-and-coming Broncos.

Running back Floyd Little felt that beating the Raiders was imperative.

"We had to beat the Raiders. Guys that were injured would get ready to play the Raiders because we needed everybody we had to play."

Broncos coach Red Miller (1977–1980) had only one thing to say about the Oakland renegades.

"I hate the Raiders. I hate them. The Oakland Raiders, I hate them!"

Hell, back in those days, who didn't hate the Raiders?

Broncos linebacker Tom Jackson had no trouble hating the silver and black.

"They were easy to hate. They dressed in black which made them look bigger than life. They had some guys who were real characters on that ballclub, and I think that physically I had never run into a ballclub like that when we began to play."

"The only way a rivalry ever heats up is when both teams are good," said Coach Madden. "When Denver was down, it wasn't a good rivalry."

Denver didn't stay down long, sparked by the emergence of their hard-hitting defense. But hard hits were old hat for the Raiders.

"When [defensive back] Jack Tatum would hit a receiver, it was unbelievable," said George Atkinson. "The contact, the sound that I heard was incredible. But Tatum wasn't happy with just the hit."

"I said, 'Man, great hit. What's wrong?'

"Jack said, 'He didn't drop the ball.'"

For Denver, Jack Tatum became public enemy number one. And the Broncos player he, Upshaw, and Stabler despised most was Tom Jackson.

"There was no guy on the field that had a bigger and louder mouth than Tom Jackson," said Gene Upshaw.

"Tom Jackson was a tremendous athlete that talked all the time," said Stabler. "He was always jawin' and always trash talkin'."

Jackson remembers his first words coming out of the locker room.

"I intend to kick your ass today!"

Jackson's remarks were backed up when, in Week 5 of the 1977 season, the Broncos finally blew away the Raiders, 30–27, in Oakland.

Denver was ahead in the second quarter and had a chance to go for a field goal, but special teams coach Marv Braden had something different in mind. He ran the idea by Coach John Ralston.

"Marv Braden comes up to me, and I mean he was serious, man. 'Coach, it's time for that play—the play where we fake the field goal and throw to Jim. I know it will work.' I said to him, 'It better work!'

"We fake the field goal and Jim Turner runs down the left side line with nobody in miles of him. He scores a touchdown."

Tom Jackson recalls Turner's remarks to John Madden as he ran by him.

"Turner ran by the bench and said to Madden, 'It's all over, fat man! That's it, it's done!'"

While there was much hatred on the field, fuel was added to the fire by the fanatical fans of Denver.

"That Orange Crush group was tough," said Stabler.

"They'd stomp their feet while you were trying to talk. They would throw stuff at you," said Madden.

"They would pelt you with everything they had," said Upshaw.

Jack Tatum remembers getting hit with snowballs.

"We got bombarded with about twenty or thirty snowballs. We turned around, and all the people are booing and cussing at us."

The defining moment of this matchup came in 1977. It would be the ultimate test for the Denver franchise, and was best said by Terry Frei of the *Denver Post*:

> In the AFC Championship game, with Denver holding a 7–3 lead in the third quarter, Oakland's Clarence Davis fumbled at the Raider 17, and Broncos defensive end Brison Manor recovered. Moments later, Craig Morton hit Riley Odoms for 13 yards to put the ball on the 2. On first down from there, Denver rookie running back Rob Lytle went off the left side, was hit by Jack Tatum, lost the ball, and Oakland's Mike McCoy recovered and took off the other way with the ball.
>
> But hold up . . .
>
> Linesman Ed Marion ruled that Lytle's forward motion was stopped and the whistle had blown before he fumbled. Replays, though, seemed to show he fumbled the second he was hit, before

he was knocked back. Denver was awarded the ball and a penalty on the Raiders was added on top of that for arguing the blown call. Denver scored on the next play and the Raider bitterness reached a boiling point along with their shot at the Super Bowl.

The following day, Ted Hendricks saw the photos of the fumble in the *Oakland Tribune.*

"The *Tribune* clearly showed the fumble out of his hands while he was trying to jump across the goal line. We got screwed."

John Matuszak, who did not have what one would call a great game, had this to say about the NFL refs.

"There wasn't much you could say when you were burned by the refs. If you got too abusive, you would end up hurting only yourself. Yes, NFL refs do hold grudges. I've seen refs make calls for one reason only: because they were angry at something you said. As for the anti-Raider calls, I don't think every ref got a memo reading, 'Screw the Raiders.' I think it was more of an unwritten rule, and it wasn't all the refs, there were definitely exceptions."

But for Denver, the emotion from that game transcended time.

PITTSBURGH STEELERS

Of all the Raiders rivalries, this one was an accident. The Pittsburgh Steelers, an NFL franchise since 1933, were sent to the newly formed AFC after the NFL–AFL merger. Long a dormant presence, never having won a single league championship as part of the NFL, the Steelers came to life after the merger and built their first dynasty in the Super Bowl era.

"We were two tough, blue-collar cities against each other," said Gene Upshaw. "You know when you play against the Steelers, you had better have your chin strap on tight."

Pittsburgh linebacker Jack Lambert loved playing the Raiders.

"The most fun I've ever had in my life was playing against the Oakland Raiders. To me that was what football was all about."

"My arms and the back of my neck would be covered in goose bumps 'cause they would boo us so bad," said Villapiano. "It was fueled by the hatred for each other, fueled by the want of going to the Super Bowl, and it just exploded."

The most famous of all Steelers–Raiders games was the 1972 play-off game in Pittsburgh, where the "Immaculate Reception" was born. But the match between these two competitors actually began the night before the big game.

Early Friday night, both tight end Bob Moore and linebacker Greg Slough had planned an early dinner, an early movie, and reporting back to the hotel for an early turn-in. Well, things didn't quite work out that way.

Upon arriving at the hotel, Moore and Slough noticed a large group of fans blocking the entry to the hotel entrance. As they worked their way up to the front of the mob, they were greeted by a row of police that were stationed there to keep the belligerent fans at bay.

Moore describes what happened next.

"We go up to the front, and there are these cops. We tell them we're with the Raiders and we want to go up to our rooms. This policeman kind of hits me and says, 'I don't care who the fuck you are. You're not getting to the front of this line.'

"I didn't think a cop with a nightstick was going to beat up an Oakland Raider in town for a playoff game, so I make a comment I regretted pretty quickly.

"I said, 'Look, motherfucker, I'm going to my room.'

"And then, *boom*! This guy comes down on the top of my head with a nightstick, which is like a baseball bat. Solid wood. The next thing I know, I'm on the ground and I got a guy on my chest trying to beat the shit out of me and another guy holding my legs. I'm trying to cover up, and I get my hands pulled away, and *bang!* I get it again! You get hit by one of these things while you're conscious, and you think you're going to die.

"'Motherfucker!' I shouted to the cops. Then they drag me away to a paddy wagon. I get in the back. The first guy comes in. I went after him. Just attacked him. Hit him with everything I had. He goes out and they slam the door. A couple of minutes later, the driver comes back and says, 'We're going to take you down and book you.'

"I said, 'Book me for what?'

"Then he sees I'm drenched in blood. He says, 'No, we're going to rush you to the hospital.' Turns out it wasn't bad. Seven stitches, cuts on both sides of my head. I was swollen like a son of a gun. I'm on the operating table and the young surgeon says, 'You're real lucky.' I said, 'You have to explain this to me. I don't feel very lucky.'

"So he said, 'Generally, guys who get this kind of treatment don't come here. We pick them up at the morgue after they dump them in the river.' I said, 'Thanks, that's comforting.'

"The next morning in the locker room I can't get a helmet on. Our defensive lineman Kelvin Korver had a big head and wore a size eight helmet. They took his helmet, took all the insides out of it, and made these Styrofoam donuts strapped to the inside.

"I don't remember a thing about the game. I wandered like a mummy off the field, knowing we lost. But I had to figure out what the hell happened."

The Immaculate Reception: December 23, 1972

It's been over forty years since Franco Harris was involved in what's been called the miracle of all miracles . . . and the play has been a mystery ever since.

This is the story of a play that's lived a life of its own.

"The Immaculate Reception is a myth, a miracle, a cottage industry, a conspiracy, a crime, and a detective story." But before it became all these things, it was just a football play: the last desperate hope of a team and a town that has always been destined to lose.

"I'm lying on the ground and I heard this roar—huge roar—definitely our roar," said quarterback Terry Bradshaw. "I'm going, 'You son of a gun, you pulled this sucker off.' Then I got up and asked 'What happened?'"

People have been asking that question ever since.

Franco Harris crossed the goal line at approximately 3:29 p.m. EST. For fifteen full minutes, referee Fred Swearingen and his five-man crew deliberated over the play.

"There was no indication as to whether or not there was a score because nobody saw what took place," said Steelers running back Rocky Bleier. "So Fred Swearingen pulled all the other officials together and asked, 'What happened?'"

Villapiano thought it was a touchdown.

"When I turned to our sideline, I saw Madden going crazy. And I felt like saying, 'Coach, he caught the ball.' I had no clue about this double hit rule.

"I was covering Franco. When they snapped the ball, Franco set up to block. Now, in the NFL, when someone sets up to block, you run in and grab them, and it's pretty much over. I ran in and grabbed him, shoved him, and when Bradshaw rolled out to the other side, Franco just started jogging down the field. I'm like, 'What the fuck is he doin'?' I'm just jogging right next to him. Then when I saw Terry throw the ball, I'm gone. I just shot over downfield to help. Then the ball bounced right over my head.

"As I was sprinting towards it, it was going right over my head. See, I'm figuring Franco's running down the field, 'cause he's a rookie and he knows the coaches are looking at him. He's just trying to be a good boy. I always tell Franco when I see him: 'I was right on your inside. All I had to do was be as lazy as you and that ball would have come to me.' If I jog with him, it's over. Instead, I sprinted away from him. He kept running, and look what happened."

Jack Tatum was certain of what happened.

"I hit Frenchy Fuqua in the back, and the ball *had to* have hit him for the ball to have come back to Franco. Back then, the 'two-touch' rule mandated that two offensive players couldn't touch the ball consecutively."

Willie Brown saw Tatum hit Fuqua.

"I was on the right side. I saw Jack hit Fuqua in the back. The ball bounced off Fuqua, and I knew it was over right there. I knew the ball was dead. He hit the guy from the back. When you hit a guy from the back, it means you're knocking him forward. So how could Jack have touched the ball? I mean, come on, the laws of physics and the laws of common sense say there's no way Tatum could have hit it if he knocked Fuqua into the ball.

"He hit Fuqua, and Fuqua hit the ball. And I thought the game was over.

"When I saw the referees get together I knew something was going on. So the next thing I know, since I'm the captain, and so is Upshaw, we're running up to them and saying, 'The game's over.' They say, 'We don't know yet.' They kept saying 'We don't know yet.' I'm saying, 'Bullshit. It's over.'

"Then I hear one of the referees say, 'Do we have security on the field? If you do, I'm going to make this call in favor of the Raiders.' So someone says, 'Well, we'll get you out of here as fast as we can.'

"If they'd ruled in our favor, they would never have gotten out of there alive. That was the reason they changed the call."

Pittsburgh defensive end L. C. Greenwood was headed back to the locker room while the refs deliberated.

"I was actually headed for the locker room then I heard the crowd cheering. I was actually running to the locker room to get off the field before people got carried away, as I expected them to anyway. They would have been upset if we had lost. Pittsburgh fans are pretty energetic fans. They don't like losing."

Raiders safety George Atkinson was on the other side of the field.

"I unsnapped my helmet. I'm headed to the locker room. It never hit me that it counted. When Jack hit Fuqua and the ball ricocheted, I thought it hit the ground from my angle. I also registered the two offensive players rule. So I thought, *Even if Franco has it, it's dead.* The officials knew it was dead, too, but they couldn't reverse that call, man. In Pittsburgh?"

The then director of officiating, Art McNally, defined Rule 7, Section 5, Article 2, Item 1.

"The first player to touch the pass, he, only, continues to be eligible for A—in this case, for the Pittsburgh Steelers."

Atkinson continues. "You could not have a double touch. If Fuqua touched the ball, as soon as the second player on his team touched the ball—incomplete pass. That's the end of it."

Madden knew that the officials didn't know what had happened.

"In the history of football, when a guy crosses a goal line, it's either a touchdown or it's not. They didn't call a touchdown because they didn't know if it was a touchdown.

"I ran out on the field. They said, 'Get away. We don't know what happened.' I said, 'I *know* you don't know what happened.' So I went off the field, and then they talked and talked and talked, forever.

"So now the referee leaves that huddle and goes into the Steelers sidelines. He gets on the phone and makes a call to somebody, hangs up, then walks out onto the middle of the field and signals touchdown. This is five or ten minutes later.

"I mean, that's not the way you call a touchdown! My thing, to this day, is if they knew it was a touchdown, why didn't they call it a touchdown? In the history of football, a touchdown is a *touchdown*! You don't have to go talk about it.

"And he calls it a touchdown. Well, what didn't you see before that, and what did you see after that? That was my argument. If you knew it was a touchdown, call it a touchdown.

"They said that they didn't look at replays. They didn't do anything.

"That's a hell of a damn game that has to go down to someone up in the press box.

"I still don't know who he made the call to because he won't admit it. No one knows. Of all the investigations and investigative reporters, no one knows who that guy talked to and what was said on that telephone call. That question has never been answered to this day."

The play had lasted for just seventeen seconds. Tens of thousands had witnessed it, but nobody saw it, and people are still talking about it today—over forty years later.

"I don't know if I got knocked down or what," said Bradshaw. "But I looked up and Franco was taking that Italian army right down the field."

The mythologizing of the Immaculate Reception began shortly after the final gun in the Pittsburgh locker room.

Steelers linebacker Andy Russell corrected Fuqua's answer to the media.

"The press was wild. Some of them were smart enough to come over and talk to Frenchy. They said, 'Well Frenchy, could you explain what happened exactly?' Frenchy said, 'Well, the ball bounced off my chest.'

"I knew that that was not the right answer. Frenchy didn't know the rule. He didn't know what happened because he got hit in the head. I grabbed him and said, 'Frenchy, what you meant to say was . . .'"

Frenchy Fuqua stopped by the Raiders locker room and whispered in Raymond Chester's ear.

"After the game, Frenchy came into the locker room, leaned over to me, and said in my ear, 'You know the ball hit me.' I said, 'Yeah I know the ball hit you.' He said, 'Yeah, it did hit me, but that's the way it goes.' And that's a true statement."

Seven days later the plot thickened when a new angle of the play emerged on the nationally syndicated NFL Game of the Week.

The iconic image captured by Ernie Ernst's camera in the north end zone, when spliced together with the camera of Jay Gerber who had been positioned at midfield, created the enduring image of the play—an image that would be replayed millions of times.

Stephen Dubner, co-author of *Freakonomics,* sees this piece of film as the "Zapruder film" of sports.

"The Immaculate Reception and the film of it became the Zapruder film of sports. The Zapruder film was the film of the Kennedy assassination shot in Dealey Plaza in Dallas, Texas. Conspiracy theories being what they are and the assassination of a president being what it is, that film has been analyzed and dissected and argued about more than any other short piece of film in history.

"Similarly, the film of the IR has been pored over the same as the Zapruder film. Frame by frame, image by image, idea by idea to look for incontrovertible proof that the play was not legitimate."

Franco Harris's touchdown was shrouded in mystery and had an image that would become iconic. But to become a play for the ages, it would need a name.

Steeler fan Michael Ord coined the term *Immaculate Reception* in a Pittsburgh bar.

"At the bar, I climbed up on the table and said, 'I would like to suggest that from this day on, we refer to this day as *The Feast of the Immaculate Reception.* That night my girlfriend called Myron Cope, a local sportscaster, and he pronounced Franco's catch as *Immaculate* that night on the eleven o'clock news."

None of Pittsburgh's newspapers referred to the play as the Immaculate Reception until September of 1973, and reporters outside of Pittsburgh didn't know what to call it.

Art Rooney was against the name because he felt it was sacrilegious.

Joe Gordon, former Steelers PR director, said "It was a stroke of genius. Once it was dubbed the IR, it took on a life of its own. You saw it everywhere."

NFL president Steve Sabol called the Immaculate Reception "the most important play in NFL history."

"'*The Catch*' was a great play," said Steelers halfback Rocky Bleier, "but it doesn't have the pizzazz, it's not marketable. The Immaculate Reception is so apropos."

"That play, if you were a Steelers fan, you believe it; if you're a Raiders fan, you'll never accept it," said Fuqua. "So it's almost like a bible and a faith to others."

Like Al Davis says, "Winning Is Everything."

Unfortunately, in our culture, there is only one thing that matters: who wins. The winner writes the history books, the winner gets the Super Bowl trophy, the winner is the genius. You have to win. It's one of the great moments in NFL history, but it's not a great moment in Oakland Raiders history.

The Immaculate Reception changed the Raiders forever. And the silver and black erected a myth of their own.

George Atkinson has a different name for the Immaculate Reception.

"We don't call it the Immaculate Reception. We call it the Immaculate Deception. The public was deceived, the officials were deceived, and we were deceived."

Raiders tight end Raymond Chester describes the anger and frustration of that loss.

"If you could have packaged all the anger and frustration, it would have probably been nuclear. It probably would have been equivalent to a nuclear bomb."

More than forty years later, emotions are still painful, especially for John Madden.

"That play bothered me then, it bothers me today, and will bother me till the day I die."

Every person who experienced the play was scarred by it. The Raiders were able to use it as a motivation which led to the next ten years in which no team won more games. And that all started in the seconds after the Immaculate Reception.

George Atkinson believes that there was some kind of conspiracy theory.

"There was a vendetta against the Raiders. Here's what the truth and the facts of the matter are. There were *three* infractions that were never called that leads to a conspiracy theory."

The Fuqua Theory

According to Rocky Bleier, "The story that needs to be unraveled, if it ever can be, is the story from Frenchy Fuqua. Did it touch him or didn't it touch him? Only he knows."

When Fuqua was asked if he touched the ball, his response was, "Maybe, maybe not."

George Atkinson saw Fuqua knocked into the ball.

"Jack Tatum hit him from behind into the ball."

"I saw it with my own eyes," said Villapiano. "I saw Jack Tatum hit Fuqua right in the back. I saw the whiplash. It definitely, definitely hit Fuqua."

But Andy Russell disagrees.

"That has been proven to be wrong. The film clearly shows that it was off of Tatum's body, not Frenchy's."

"Did Jack Tatum hit the ball?" asked Willie Brown. "It clearly shows that the ball hit Frenchy's shoulder pads and bounced off of that."

"Look at the tape!" said Bradshaw.

He continued: "If you look at the tape, Frenchy's hands are stretched out to catch the ball. There's no way it hit his hands and then bounced back twenty feet."

The Trap Play Theory

Author Stephen Dubner talks about what we didn't see.

"Let's be honest. We never see the bottom tip or half of the ball and whether or not it touches the turf. That seems to be the most legitimate conspiracy theory objection. I asked Franco about it, and Franco doesn't give a straight answer.

"When asked if the ball hit the ground before he plucked it out of the air, Franco's answer is: 'I can't say. From the time that Bradshaw threw the ball, it was like I lost all sense of consciousness and before I knew it I was up and running. Before that everything else is just a blur.'"

"Franco is a good ballplayer, don't get me wrong," said Willie Brown. "I'm not knocking him, but he knew what had happened. He knew he caught the ball off the turf."

"I saw it from across the field," said George Atkinson. "The tip of the ball touched the ground and he trapped it."

"More than likely because Franco doesn't speak, he probably trapped it on the ground," said Bradshaw. "No one will ever say, Frenchy won't say and Franco won't say and I understand that it is one of the greatest plays in the history of the sport, as long as we all sit here and say, 'Did they touch it, did they trap it?' then it keeps it going."

The Riot Theory

"Once Franco got in the end zone, he then started getting piled on," said Stephen Dubner. "The people started jumping from the stands.

It was a total mob scene. I think, if I recall, you never actually see a touchdown sign. Humankind does not have the ability to reverse that kind of thing."

"It was absolute mayhem," said Raymond Chester. "And given the fear that was in the hearts of the officials, I don't think they were going to change their decision."

"I know for a fact that those officials knew that that play was not a legal play," stated Atkinson. "I did hear one of the officials say, 'How much security do we have?' They talked a little longer then one of the officials went out on the field and signaled touchdown."

Villapiano remembers it being out of control.

"There was no control. It was crazy what was going on. I think if he had reversed that call, that man might have died—and all the other officials, too."

The Clip Theory

"Look at Gerber frame 325," said Villapiano. "That will tell you all you need to know. Look at McMakin's head. You can't see his head 'cause it's in my back. I was clipped and we totally got screwed. The officials had no clue what was going on and were afraid to throw flags. If it wasn't for that trip, I would have made that play and there would be no Immaculate Reception."

Steelers tight end John McMakin refutes Villapiano's statement.

"It's always been clear in my memory that it was a clean block with the head and shoulders in front. That's why I call it the Immaculate Obstruction. That's a pretty good name for the block."

"That was no Immaculate Obstruction!" said Villapiano. "That was an Immaculate Clip!"

"I do think it's puzzling that he feels that it was a clip from behind," said McMakin. "But if you look at Gerber frame 325, you can tell that my head and shoulders are plainly visible in front of Phil."

Mysteriously, both the network film and the coaching staff film have vanished. The network broadcast of the game was also believed to be lost. Then, right before the 1997 AFC Championship game, the tape mysteriously resurfaced.

Everyone loves a mystery, and that's why the IR will always remain unsolved. There's no way to prove it one way or the other.

"I personally thought we got taken," said Al Davis. "We should have had that football game but we didn't get it. Fuqua knows he hit it and it should have been our game."

After the Immaculate Reception, the Steelers wilted in the heat of battle against the Raiders. They lost two of their next three games to Oakland—including the 1973 AFC divisional playoff game. The team was desperate for guidance—especially Bradshaw.

As the two teams moved toward a rematch in the 1974 AFC Championship game, another Raiders player would utter the words that pushed the Steelers too far.

Steelers defensive tackle Joe Greene responds to Madden's claim.

"The Raiders had just played and beaten the Dolphins. Madden said that the best two teams in the NFL had played today and that was the real Super Bowl."

Just prior to the 1974 AFC Championship game, Chuck Noll heard what Madden had said and replied with, "Well I want to tell you that one of the two best teams in the NFL (the Steelers) is in this room."

The Steelers used 21 fourth-quarter points to beat Oakland after they had led 10–3. Pittsburgh's 24–13 win humbled the confident Raiders in front of their home crowd. Oakland would have to wait a year to get even.

In the 1975 AFC Championship game, the plot thickened around a curious pattern of ice.

"The night before that game there was a mysterious tear in the tarp," said Upshaw. "And we go back the next day and the field is frozen. The only part not frozen was between the two hash marks."

Al Davis describes the effect the ice had on his team.

"Our game was to throw the deep ball. If there was one play that Mel Blount dreaded, it was the long ball to Cliff Branch. So with that ice, we had to move those receivers in and that narrowed the field for us. I'll never forget what Pete Rozelle said to me, 'Well it's the same for both sides.' I said, 'Damn it, Pete, you don't even know what you're talking about. It's not the same for both sides!'"

The Steelers won 16–10 as the ice along the sidelines neutralized Cliff Branch. But safety George Atkinson and the Raiders found their own way to neutralize Pittsburgh leading receiver Lynn Swann.

"We never go out on the field with the intentions of trying to hurt anyone, but we do go out on the field with the intentions of getting the job done. If he don't want to get hit, his best bet is not to show up on Sunday, 'cause I guarantee he will get hit."

"Swann is going to be thinking about it," said Jack Tatum. "He knows that we are back there. And he knows that if he comes in my area or George's area to catch a ball, he's gonna get hit and hit hard. He's a professional athlete too, and he has a job to do. If he can't do it he's going to have to be replaced by someone who can. He knows this and in the past he has done a lot of mouthin' off, but personally I think he is more interested in being an announcer than he is a football player."

Pittsburgh wide receiver Lynn Swann says that the Raiders' key was to try and use intimidation.

"The Raiders' secondary as a group attempted to intimidate people by playing on the fringe of what was legal and beyond the fringe. And I'll tell you that as a fact. What you had to do as a receiver is not let that bother you."

On opening day, September 12, 1976, on a running play, George Atkinson struck the rivalry's most vicious blow.

"Whenever you end up with the Steelers and the Raiders, you're going to have a tough football game, everyone's gonna be angry when it's all said and done, and eventually someone is going to get sued about it."

After that game, Chuck Noll called Atkinson a "criminal." Atkinson said he was slandered, and filed a two-million-dollar lawsuit against Noll. Atkinson's claim was thrown out of court.

Villapiano sees it from a different perspective.

"It was such a joke. You got those maniacs over there and they say we're too rough for them? Give me a break!"

The feud was taken back to the field during the 1976 AFC Championship between the two teams. But first we need to tell the story of how they got there.

In the first three games of the 1976 season, the Raiders beat the Steelers, Chiefs, and Oilers. But the loss to New England in Week 4 left a bad taste in their mouth, and the team decided to hold a players-only meeting. During that meeting the players said, "If you want to win the Super Bowl, we are not losing any more games."

And they didn't. The Raiders went on to beat San Diego, Denver twice, Green Bay, Chicago, and Kansas City. In Week 11 we beat the Eagles to clinch the division.

As usual, there were pregame parties in all of the cities, but the one that stands out most in my mind was the pregame party the night before we played Denver. Kenny Stabler and Fred Biletnikoff were the hosts.

"Sometimes the pregame partying would make you feel loose the next day and you'd come up with a real good game," said Stabler. "I know a lot of players who would agree with that. Bobby Layne of the Detroit Lions always did. They used to say that if Bobby didn't go out and get plowed the night before he played, he wasn't going to have a big game. I loved his style."

"In Denver, Freddy and I called a couple of girls we knew after dinner and asked them to come over and bring four bottles of wine. Freddy was between marriages at the time, so what the hell? We already had a nice glow from our dinner wine and wanted to keep it alive. No problem. We got so ripped that by 4 a.m. we were all sitting around nude, making shadow puppets on the walls using the light cast by the bare bulbs from the table lamps. We laughed like there was no tomorrow.

"We finally went to bed around five. When I got up at eight-thirty for the pregame meal, I opened the blinds and it was snowing like hell.

"'Look at this shit, Freddy,' I said. 'And we gotta play today!'

"We went down to breakfast and got a bunch of cold drinks to put out the fire, had coffee, then went out and had a big day. I threw four touchdown passes—two to Freddy and two to Cliff. They received game balls. I thought a third should have gone to Bobby Layne."

Week 12 was special for the Raiders as the Tampa Bay Buccaneers came to Oakland. Former Raider Bob Moore had been taken by the Bucs in the expansion draft and we all looked forward to seeing him once again. Art Thoms, along with Villapiano and Dave Dalby, met Moore with a limo.

"This was before terrorists, so we talked to some people at the airport and they agreed to let us drive onto the runway," said Thoms. "Well, not the actual runway, but the apron. So the Tampa charter plane pulls up. They bring out those stairs they used to have to get off a plane, and right then we pull the limo up.

"Moore came out, walked down the stairs, and walked across the red carpet. We all hugged him, he got in, and we pulled away. The Bucs coach, John McKay, I think, wasn't real happy about that."

According to Moore, Coach John McKay was definitely not happy with the gesture.

"McKay had no idea what the hell was going on. In fact at first, I had no idea what the hell was going on. Or how they got to the tarmac. The doors open up and Phil and Dalby and Sistrunk all pour out to welcome me.

"I still had my condo in Alameda so we all went there to have a party. A couple of my Tampa teammates were with me. So girls are going in and out, and the television station shows up at about nine. It gets on the eleven o'clock news.

"When I get back to the hotel the following day, John McKay was really pissed off. He said he was watching the eleven o'clock news, and there I am drinking with the guys we're playing the next day. At the same time, actually, I think Steve Spurrier, our quarterback, went over to the other side of the bay and had the same kind of party with his former San Francisco 49ers teammates."

"We had a team that was not in very good shape that day—or for that matter on any Sunday."

Oakland beat Tampa Bay 49–16, and the Bengals the following week. The defeat of the Bengals meant much more to John Madden than just a win.

"That was really big to me. Of all the games we played, I have as much pride in what we did to Cincinnati as any game I coached, because we had everything clinched. People were saying we were going to lose because we didn't want to play Pittsburgh. And whoever said that said the right thing to get me pissed off."

George Atkinson says it all.

"That was us telling Pittsburgh, 'No, we're going through these motherfuckers. We're going to do you a favor first, and then we're going to fuck you up next.' The thing that was so beautiful about that Monday night game against the Bengals was the way we were calling Pittsburgh out: 'Come on, guys, you're not going to stop us this year.'"

The AFC divisional playoff game pitted Oakland against the New England Patriots. According to tackle Dave Rowe, "The team that won that game would win the Super Bowl."

The Steelers beat the Colts 40–14 for a rematch with the Raiders.

The 1976 AFC Championship game was once again between the Steelers and the Raiders.

"The two Super Bowls that they went to were through Oakland," said Villapiano. "They had beaten us up both times. We just couldn't take it anymore. It was like we were going to leave it out there. If we don't win that day, forget the season and here comes the Steelers all cocky, and we wanted them."

The Steelers had to play the title game without Franco Harris and Rocky Bleier, and the Raiders took full advantage of the circumstances.

"I wanted to play Pittsburgh all along," said George Atkinson. "Baltimore made the Steelers look better than they were. The Colts were intimidated. That won't happen to us. We have a team that can't be intimidated."

Steelers defensive tackle Joe Greene guaranteed revenge on Atkinson.

"I guarantee that if Atkinson starts pulling that stuff, I'll come off the bench to get him if I have to."

"The Friday before the game, we go in after practice, and then Madden calls us all back out," said Villapiano. "The word came out that the Steelers might use a formation we hadn't practiced; two tight ends and a fullback. Two tight ends are pretty effective. We were laughing, because we figured they were trying to surprise us. We didn't realize Rocky [Bleier] and Franco [Harris] weren't playing until game day."

"I vividly remember the introductions to that game," recalls George Buehler. "The Steelers had been introduced before us, and they were all over there on their sidelines jumping up and down like high school kids. I thought that was kind of amusing. I was thinking, 'That kind of thing can disappear pretty quickly in a game.' We were calm. Besides, they had snuffed our hopes too many times. This was something we wanted to close the book on."

The Raiders were the first to strike with an Errol Mann field goal in the first quarter. From that point on, Pittsburgh tried to pull ahead, but their efforts were all in vain.

"Late in the game I ran a sprint out to the left, chased by Joe Greene and L. C. Greenwood, and I was right on that line of scrimmage when I threw the ball to Casper," said Stabler. "Joe and L. C. screamed at the officials, 'He was over the line! He crossed the goddamn line of scrimmage!'"

The referee spotted the ball and cried, 'First down!'

"'Close, wasn't it?' I said to Joe and winked.

"'Close, shit!' he said. 'The goddamn ref needs a seein' eye dog!'"

The best the Steelers defense could do was to keep the score down to Oakland 24, Pittsburgh 7. After that first score, the Raiders never looked back. Oakland was off to the Super Bowl.

Pittsburgh's linebacker Jack Lambert was devastated after the game.

"The biggest heartbreak that I ever had on a football field. After the game I said, 'Give me a six pack [and] a half hour rest and let's go back out there and play them again. I think we can beat them.'"

George Atkinson had a few words for the critics of the Raiders.

"Critics said we couldn't make it to the Super Bowl and that we were a dirty team. I say to them, 'Eat your words.'"

Of course, Chuck Noll made excuses for his team.

"We played without fifty percent of our offense. I'm sorry we didn't have more weapons."

Madden's response to Nol:

"That was our time. They weren't going to stop us that day. They could have had Franco and Bleier and the whole thing, and it wouldn't have made any goddamned difference. That was our day. That was our year!"

"Come on, the game was a blowout," said Dave Rowe. "We beat them in every aspect of the game. You're talking about two players. That game was not won or lost on offense or defense. That game was the Oakland Raiders going through the Pittsburgh Steelers. You're talking about scoring 24 points against an incredible defense. And it wasn't like we scored by intercepting a pass or recovering a fumble and getting the ball on the 10 or something. We put some drives together. We drove the football on a great defense. We scored 24 points on them pretty easily."

After the 1976 championship game, the feud subsided, and as time passed, the players on both sides mellowed with age.

"Pretty much their guys got older and we got older and it ended," said Villapiano. "I go to Pittsburgh now and I love to show my ring to these people because all those Steelers fans in all those office buildings and I go in there and show them this ring, and I show them the side of the ring that shows the score Al Davis had written on the side of the ring: Raiders 24 Steelers 7."

With the Pittsburgh game and win now behind us, the Raiders were on their way to Pasadena to play the Vikings in Super Bowl IX and maybe do a little partying.

SUPER BOWL XI

One of the stories that stands out in my mind is the great time that Kenny Stabler, Freddy Biletnikoff, and Pete Banaszak had the week prior to the Super Bowl. Here's how Kenny told it to me.

"Pete, Freddy and I had adjoining rooms at the Marriott Hotel in Newport Beach, where we stayed the week before playing the Super Bowl against the Minnesota Vikings. We prepared for the game as we would any other game: Monday we were off, workouts Tuesday through Saturday. Thanks to John Madden, we didn't have a curfew until Thursday night and we took full advantage of it.

"Freddie and I were friends with actor James Caan. We called Jimmy to get into some action the first night. Jimmy was on location, but his bother Ronnie picked us up in a Rolls and took us to the Playboy Mansion. It was full of beautiful women who gave us a tour of the place. We had so much fun that we didn't leave until about four a.m.

"The next night I went to the condo of a girl I had met at the Playboy Mansion. I stayed with her till morning. On Wednesday, Freddy, Pete, and I just barhopped in Newport Beach. That ended the partying, except for a little scotch sipping in my room to relax. I never got to sleep before two."

On January 9, 1977, the Raiders met the Minnesota Vikings at Pasadena's Rose Bowl for Super Bowl XI.

"When you have to go through the Steelers, you feel pretty good about playing Minnesota," said Stabler. "We felt good about the matchup. We felt a little bit stronger."

Vikings quarterback Fran Tarkenton felt the same about Minnesota.

"We are going to go there and we are going to win."

Madden's offensive strategy: Never be predictable!

"You never want to be predictable because offenses and defenses are based on predictability. They were the type of team that was fundamentally disciplined and organized. Just by doing something a little different, it was better than doing the things they focused in on.

"From coaching Pro Bowl teams and observing the Super Bowls, I always figured that the team with the fewest complaints always won the game. The team that was complaining about extra tickets, extra people, the practice facility, usually lost. So the first week I said, 'We're going to get everything out of the way.' I got all the players' tickets right off the bat and told them to get rid of them before we flew down to Los Angeles.

"I made sure that everyone would have an extra room at the hotel. Other teams complain, 'You take wives down, how about if you don't have a wife? A girlfriend? A mother?' Those things could become issues. So I made sure everyone had an extra room for whomever they wanted. Then I made sure everyone had an extra seat on the airplane. I wanted all the extra-curriculars out of the way.

"We did some football work that first week but we watched a lot of film so we could get acquainted with what they looked like. If you practice the game plan the first week, if you have something done early, you just have to go over it again, and the next thing, I figured boredom would set in. And my team wasn't a team that handled boredom well."

Raiders linebacker Monte Johnson was the one that found the Vikings' Achilles heel.

"During my prep for the Super Bowl I noticed their offense had a tendency on the goal line with how they lined the backs up, how they determined which side of the center they'd run the ball. At one point we were practicing short yardage defense and I went to [assistant coaches Bob] Zeman and [Don] Shinnick and said, 'Guys, trust me and allow me to call the defense on the line of scrimmage in short yardage.'

"They said, 'Why would we ever do that?'

"I said, 'Let me tell you what I've seen.'

"They watched a number of reels. They went to Madden and said, 'This is what we want to do.' John said, 'Sure.'"

The week leading up to the Super Bowl was business as usual for Madden.

"Our week leading up to the Super Bowl was normal. Our football was normal. Our meetings were normal. Other than the press conferences, everything was a normal work week. No distractions. The only thing that's a distraction if it's something that isn't planned. I had everything planned."

"We were fine-tuned," said Atkinson. "That practice was like no other. We were crisp, we were sharp. No mistakes. No balls hit the ground. Receivers didn't drop a ball that week, come to think of it."

"The day before a game we'd always just have a thirty-four-minute practice," said Banaszak. "Just light stuff. So after about twenty minutes, Madden calls us in. He said, 'Let's stop right now. Go on in. If we play like we just practiced, it won't be a game. We play like this, we're going to kill them.'"

John Madden called up Al Davis the night before the game.

"I said to him, 'We're going to get these guys. This might not even be close.' Al said, 'Don't talk like that!' Like I'm gonna jinx it.

"I wasn't that type of guy, normally. Even if I had those feelings, I wouldn't normally say it. It was just that I had a feeling, after the way we practiced that second week. The way Stabler was so sharp in that last offensive practice. I just knew that I liked the matchup. I liked the way we were prepared. I liked the game plan. I felt as confident as I've ever felt."

Villapiano remembers Madden's words just before kickoff.

"He looks around the room and all he says is, 'Guys, this will be the single biggest event of your lives—as long as you win. Act like it and play like it. You don't remember losing. It has to be a win to be the greatest day of your life. Make a memory.'"

The Raiders did make a memory. They beat the Vikings 32–14 and, after scoring 16 points in the second quarter, never looked back.

After the win, the locker room was ecstatic.

"John's face was lit up like a Christmas tree, like a jack-o-lantern, like a big Howdy Doody, happy as hell," said Banaszak. "He was hugging everyone. We were all hugging each other. Even Al was hugging us. It was the first time I ever saw Al hug anyone."

"It was euphoric," said Atkinson. "Pure euphoria! It was joy, pure joy. There was a feeling and an energy that if you could capture and put it in a bottle and share it, it would be worth its weight in gold. You'd be a millionaire. I mean, it was a matter of closure, and I looked around at these faces of joy, these faces of happiness that understood we had finally done it."

"The look on everyone's faces, all these guys, all your friends, all your family," recalled Banaszak with a smile. "We were so happy for one another. At that moment it was just the consummate team feeling, not an individual thing.

"We just wanted to sit and savor the feeling. I think I must have sat in my uniform for half an hour before I ripped my tape off. I was numb."

"You just sit there and try and figure it all out," said Stabler. "You let it all sink in. It was about appreciating what you did."

"I'll never forget the smile on Al's face when Pete Rozelle handed him the trophy," said Villapiano. "It was the most beautiful smile I'd ever seen. He took that trophy in his hands and he just shook it."

Madden reassured his guys, "They can't take it away from you!

"I wasn't one to say, 'All the hard work you put in,' and all that bullshit. It was just, 'Goddamnit, we did it! We're the world champions! We did it, and it's forever. They can never take it away from you.' I get shivers when I think about it to this day."

After being thrown in the shower, Madden greeted the media and had this to say to say at the press conference.

"We've lived with the fact that we haven't been able to win the big one for a long time. And we felt it was time to disprove that."

That night the team stayed at the Newport Beach Marriott. It was the best party I've ever been to in my life! The team was drinking all night. I remember Matuszak throwing a football with a buddy of mine. Someone from the hotel came over and said, "You can't do that." The next thing I saw was the hotel guy running away.

The next day we were supposed to fly back to Oakland. I think out of the entire team, thirteen guys made the plane. The rest of us couldn't get up.

OAKLAND RAIDERS HIGHLIGHTS
1970-1974

1970 SEASON (8-4-2)

In 1969, a young John Madden became head coach of the Oakland Raiders and faced the awesome challenge of maintaining the Raiders' winning ways. He met the challenge in '69 with pro football's best record: 12–1–1 and the AFL Western Division Championship.

The Oakland Raiders emerged from the '60s with the finest three consecutive years in the history of professional football. No team was more respected, none more feared than the team who proudly wore the silver and black.

But 1970 began a new era, a new challenge. The question now was: Could the Raiders continue to rank with the great organizations of professional sports? Were the Raiders ready to meet the challenges of the '70s?

Week 1 @ Cincinnati

The Raiders' challenge began in Cincinnati at the Bengals new Riverfront Stadium. Not even the wizardry of Fred Biletnikoff's two touchdowns or the 63-yard punt return by Alvin Wyatt could tame the Bengals as Oakland lost their first opening game since 1964 by a score of 31–21. But in the heat of defeat, a star was born—a rugged, determined rookie from Morgan State—a tight end named Raymond Chester.

Week 2 vs. San Diego

In San Diego, the Raiders appeared ready to rip off a victory. George Atkinson led the defense with two interceptions and a powerful offense that included two touchdowns by Pete Banaszak, one by Fred Biletnikoff and two field goals from George Blanda that totaled 27 points, but the Chargers rang up 27 points of their own to end the game in a tie . . . two games without a victory.

Week 3 @ Miami

In Miami it was fire and rain. The Raiders started with fire as Charlie Smith scorched the soggy synthetic turf for a 60-yard touchdown that was washed out by a penalty. Two field goals by George Blanda and a solo touchdown by Warren Wells were not enough. The Raiders' hopes were swamped as the Dolphins stepped to a 20–13 win. Three games and still no taste of victory.

Week 4 vs. Denver

The Raiders finally came home to meet the undefeated division-leading Broncos, and John Madden rallied his forces for a mission of destruction. The offensive line of Shell, Upshaw, Otto, Jim Harvey, and Bob Svihus gave the runners room to roll and they moved like a relentless silver and black tide that ultimately crashed on a goal-line beach. Then it was Daryle Lamonica unleashing the Raiders' famed precision passing. Lamonica's arm whipped and the ball whistled. There was no derailing the Raiders this day as they roared by Denver, 35–23. Victory had returned and loyal Raiders fans sighed with relief. But it was a bittersweet victory, as All-Pro cornerback Willie Brown was out with a shoulder injury on an interception.

Week 5 vs. Washington

Washington arrived for a Monday night national TV game, and the Jurgensen air strike was shot down by Kent McCloughan and Nemiah Wilson. Tom Keating and Duane Benson dismembered the ground strike. Then came Hewritt Dixon, whose single purpose was to put a flash of silver and black into the end zone. Behind the blocking of Jim Otto and Harry Shiu, Dixon was more than the Redskins could handle as he ran for 164 yards. He demolished the Skins defense and set it up for the bomb that convinced the TV audience that the silver and black were back in the fight to be number one—back with a vengeance. Final score: Oakland 34, Washington 20.

Week 6 vs. Pittsburgh

Pittsburgh and rookie quarterback Terry Bradshaw arrived in Oakland. Gus Otto shut down the corner and Kent McCloughan shut down the end zone. Lamonica streaked one to Raymond Chester and then forty-three-year-old George Blanda came off the bench and hurled thunderbolts to Chester. One was called back, one was good, and one was superb. A veteran and a rookie had wreaked havoc, begun a phenomenon, and Oakland was battling toward first place in the West. Final score: Oakland 31, Pittsburgh 14.

Week 7 @ Kansas City

The World Champion Chiefs were pitted against the Raiders and the Oakland offense earned the lead with two touchdown passes from Lamonica to Chester. The Raiders defense led by Dan Conners and Carleton Oates struck with a fury, but the talented Chiefs came back to lead 17–14 late in the last quarter. Then all that remained was part fantasy, part outrage, and totally incredible. Raiders radio announcer Bill King described it this way.

> Here's the bootleg now by Dawson running to the right himself. He's got a first down. He's down to the 35 and he's brought down at the 28-yard line. Here's a flag and here's Ben Davidson being jumped on by one of the Chiefs. Two more Chiefs come in. There's a big pileup. Davidson and Taylor are going at it. There are at least eight Chiefs, and here come all the Raiders. Holy Toledo, it's a free for all! It's all along this near sideline here. Stram is out and getting Lenny Dawson out of there. He doesn't want Dawson to get killed!

After the brawl was over, the defense still had to stop the Chiefs. With eight seconds left in the game, George Blanda was handed the incredibly difficult job of kicking a 48-yard field goal. Lamonica spotted the ball at the 48. The ball was snapped and the kick was good. George Blanda landed a 48-yard field goal to tie Kansas City, 17–17.

Week 8 vs. Cleveland

The Raiders were back home against the Cleveland Browns for the first time ever, and led in the game early with a George Blanda field goal and a Charlie Smith touchdown. But the Browns, a perennial NFL power, came roaring back. With time running out, Cleveland led 20–13 until a near disaster struck—Lamonica was injured. It was now up to George Blanda. On the next play, Blanda threw to Wells for the score. With seven seconds to go, the game was tied at 20. Once again it would be George Blanda who would come in for the game-winning 52-yard field goal. Stabler held for Blanda and it went through the uprights. Final score: Raiders 23, Cleveland 20.

Week 9 @ Denver

In Denver, Oakland followed the script perfectly by taking a quick lead with a 36-yard pass from Lamonica to Warren Wells. But the Broncos rallied to lead 19–17 so late in the game that Denver fans were already celebrating victory. But no one should celebrate victory over the Raiders until they hear the fat lady sing. The phenomenon is pride and poise. It's Blanda zeroed on Wells. The phenomenon is class and courage. And it's Blanda hitting Biletnikoff for a score. The phenomenon is discipline and desire, and it's Jimmy Warren shutting off Denver's last hope with his second interception of the day. The phenomenon is an Oakland Raiders victory under any pressure. Final score: Oakland 24, Denver 19.

Week 10 vs. San Diego

The Raiders came home without a defeat in their last six games. But the Chargers went ahead in the third quarter. Oakland answered with catches by Biletnikoff that set up two Charlie Smith touchdowns and the game was tied at 17 in the fourth quarter after the teams traded field goals. Then it was Tony Kline spinning the Charger attack to the ground. It was Dave Grayson pulling butterflies out of the air. It was Bill Laskey giving the Raiders one final chance for Daryle to drive them to victory. It was unbelievable! It was Oakland 'hanging from the cliff' again. Then Daryle dropped back to pass from the 45, but decided to run the ball himself. He ran it all the way to the 34 and a first down. Oakland ran the clock down to seven seconds and then brought out George Blanda. From the 16-yard line and with four seconds left in the game, Blanda kicked it straight through the uprights giving Oakland the lead and the win. Final score: Oakland 20, San Diego 17.

Week 11 @ Detroit

The Raiders played Detroit on Thanksgiving Day, four days after the Chargers game. Charley Sanders scored twice for Detroit as Oakland lost a 14-point lead and the game as the playoff-bound Lions bellowed out in victory for a 28–14 win.

Week 12 @ New York Jets

There was more trouble to come for Oakland in New York against the Jets. Despite Blanda to Wells, the Jets led 13–7. Time was fleeting when a now-healthy Willie Brown intercepted the ball, and Oakland had only eight seconds and one chance to win; but if anyone thought that Oakland could do it, the Jets should have. For it was in the historic *Heidi* game of 1968 that these Jets were certain winners until the Raiders exploded. In less than twenty seconds, Oakland scored twice and sealed the Jets' fate . . . a fate that, in the '60s, had doomed many opponents. For the Raiders were a team with last-second victories stashed somewhere beneath their battle-scarred silver and black helmets. It wasn't miracles and it wasn't luck. It was instead a team poised, a team responding to the challenge—ready to make and take any break. Any team is allowed one miracle—maybe two—but the Raiders defied all odds to become the winningest team in the American Football League since 1963. Now this tradition, born in the

'60s, would be most severely tested as the Raiders confronted another impossible must-win situation. With the ball on the 33 and eight seconds to go, Lamonica threw deep to Wells in the end zone for a touchdown. With the score tied 13–13, it was once again Blanda who came off the bench to kick the extra point and win the game for the Raiders. Final score: Oakland 14, New York 13.

Week 13 vs. Kansas City

This was the big one, the game to decide who would reign supreme in pro football's toughest division: Kansas City at Oakland. No last-second heroics today. The Raiders made no mistakes. And when Marv Hubbard came in, he screamed at the Chiefs, "I'm coming at you!" And he went at them. And when Lamonica and Madden talked they spoke of going right over them. And Lamonica went to Biletnikoff— right over them. No miracles today, just mind and muscle—silver and black—and number one in the West for a record-breaking four straight Western Division Championships. Final score: Oakland 20, Kansas City 6.

The regular season closed in Week 14 with an anti-climatic loss to the 49ers at the Coliseum, 38–7. But the challenge continued. For now the Raiders, with the amazing George Blanda as their most inspirational player, would host Miami in the playoffs.

AFC Divisional Playoff vs. Miami

The AFC Playoff looked like it would be played in Dolphin weather. Before kickoff, the sun and the eighteenth straight sellout crowd filled the Coliseum. But the field hadn't dried and the going was tough for both teams. The Dolphins scored first and seven points might have been enough to win in this mud. But a determined defense dug in and while the destroyers put Griese to sleep, Lamonica picked the Raiders up and passed them goalward. The score was now 7 to 7, but a tie meant nothing and the defense knew it. Griese was kept down in the mud but the Raiders still needed more points. The 82-yarder to

Rod Sherman, a clutch performer all season, meant victory to Oakland with the final score, Raiders 21, Dolphins 14. So it would be silver and black in Baltimore in the AFC Championship.

AFC Conference Championship @ Baltimore

But in the AFL championship game in Baltimore, Lamonica would miss by inches, and then would miss from the game after being leveled by a bulldozer named Bubba Smith. Blanda replaced him, and the Raiders fought back. Oakland scored two touchdowns—one by Biletnikoff and the other by Wells. But in the end it was John Unitas, *NFL Player of the Decade*, who hit for the big play. And just like that, it was over. Final score: Baltimore 27, Oakland 17. The Colts went on to Miami, while the Raiders returned to Oakland.

So what kind of a season was it? After eleven years of struggles and dedication, a day of defeat curtailed the destiny of the Oakland Raiders, but nothing could blot out another year of glory. What kind of a season was it? A season that saw the silver and black maintain their lofty position as one of the finest organizations in the history of professional sports. It was a season that merits a salute to the coaches, back up men, and special team warriors like George Buehler and Pete Banaszak, Eischeid and Stabler, Thoms, Todd, Koy, Highsmith, Budness, Irons, Buie, Weathers, and MacKinnon.

In 1970, the Oakland Raiders thrilled our country as no other team in professional football history has ever done. They won victory upon dramatic victory and always with poise. Poise above all. What kind of a season was it? Here's what Bill King had to say:

"If a television scriptwriter tried to write the kind of finishes that the Oakland Raiders have produced this year, they would send him to the Looney bin before he ever got passed the first proof reader!"

In 1963, Al Davis made the total *Commitment to Excellence* for the Raiders' organization. But the only real test of any great organization is how long its success can endure. The Oakland Raiders had met this test. People said it couldn't be done. They said that it couldn't continue. But this was the challenge, and the Oakland Raiders stood ready to meet the challenge of the '70s.

1971 SEASON (8-4-2)

In 1971, for the first time in five years, the Oakland Raiders did not play in the Conference Championship game.

Disaster stalked the Raiders from the get-go. Running back Hewritt Dixon was gone for the year with an injury as was receiver Warren Wells. Running back Charlie Smith was out for six games. What would have happened if the Dallas Cowboys had lost Duane Thomas, Calvin Hill, and Bob Hayes? Or if Miami had lost Csonka, Kiick, and Warfield? They would have dropped from contention as the Raiders did. Yet in 1971, despite losing players responsible for 3,000 yards and 18 touchdowns, the silver and black remained feared championship contenders because of a dedicated organization and sterling field leadership from gifted head coach John Madden; talented veteran assistants Oliver Spencer, Tom Dahms, Ray Malavasi, and Bob Zeman; skillful trainer George Anderson; and capable equipment director Dick Romanski.

There is no substitute for victory now, so the true greatness of the Raiders must remain in their future and their glorious past. But if battling insurmountable odds is still a virtue, then in 1971 the silver and black may well have had their finest hour.

Week 1 @ New England

The season opener was held in New England's new Schaefer Stadium against the Patriots' new quarterback, Jim Plunkett. The Raiders unveiled three rookie starters of their own. Safety Jack Tatum was one and recovered two fumbles. Despite several personnel losses, Raiders running behind Gene Upshaw showed promise with another newcomer, Clarence Davis, gliding for 39 yards.

Pete Banaszak had the lone Oakland score as he slashed into the end zone. But inches spelled the Raiders' doom and, in the end, Plunkett passed his Patriots to a 20-6 upset victory.

It was the last time the Oakland Raiders would lose for nine weeks.

Week 2 @ San Diego

In San Diego, Oakland faced the second of four demanding consecutive road games. The Raiders' defense dominated as All-Pro Willie Brown challenged John Hadl's air attack. Rookie ends Horace Jones and Harold Rice blasted in on Hadl and forced the Chargers into desperate gambles made even more desperate when the determined silver and black dug in and refused to yield. Then the Raiders' famed precision passing flashed into action. Lamonica to Biletnikoff accounted for two scores. Clarence Davis, behind blocking by Shell, Upshaw, Buehler, Otto, and Bob Brown, raced into another.

Middle linebacker Dan Conners picked off two interceptions. Lamonica and Stabler finished the Chargers with a lopsided 34–0 triumph, which was Oakland's first shutout ever over San Diego.

Week 3 @ Cleveland

Oakland was in Cleveland next in a Monday night national TV game. Lamonica's throwing hand was giving him trouble. Early in the contest the offensive missed by inches, but the undefeated Browns weren't missing and led 14–0. Then the Raiders' rookie wreckers went to work. Linebacker Villiapiano shut down the corner and Horace Jones shut down passes while Jack Tatum made a great interception and return. Daryle arched a bomb to tight end Raymond Chester and utilized the diverse design of the Raiders attack, then threw a screen to Marv Hubbard who powered for 31 yards.

The relentless Raiders rolled for 24 fourth-quarter points. Clarence Davis put Oakland ahead 24–20, and Banaszak finished Cleveland off as the nation learned that though the Raiders had lost key players (including vet Tom Keating with a broken leg in this game), they had lost none of their class or courage. Final score: Raiders 34, Cleveland 20.

Week 4 @ Denver

In Denver, a punishing Oakland defense set the tone. Phil Villapi-ano was everywhere at once, making the inches count. And suddenly inches meant points as Jimmy Warren intercepted and streaked 55 yards for a touchdown.

Stabler to Chester gave an indication as to why the Raiders would finish second in scoring in the entire NFL in 1971. Stabler then pro-vided the insurance himself, and the Raiders had won their third in a row. At last they were ready to come home. Final score: Oakland 27, Denver 16.

Week 5 vs. Philadelphia

Finally, five weeks into the season, the silver and black returned to the Oakland Coliseum—and the stadium responded to their monumen-tal rise to a football power. They had come home to meet the surging Philadelphia Eagles, who quickly took a 10–0 halftime lead. But even though shorthanded, the Raiders would not shortchange the total sellout colloquium crowd.

A wide-open Fred Biletnikoff fooled everyone as he scored six, and Raiders runners led by powerful Marv Hubbard were end zone bound regardless of obstacles. Lamonica hit Eldridge Dickey for a 27-yard score, followed by the Eagles fumbling the kickoff which Atkinson returned for a touchdown. It was Oakland's second touchdown in fifteen seconds. It destroyed the Eagles and gave the silver and black their fourth win in a row. Final score: Oakland 34, Philadelphia 10.

Week 6 vs. Cincinnati

For the Bengals, the inches went against them as Raiders' Chester just managed to score. Marv Hubbard continued to shred opponents' defenses and Hubbard showed his versatility by taking a perfect George Blanda pass in for six points. However, Paul Brown's Bengals were always tough for Oakland, and Cincinnati led 27–24 with time running out.

But Art Thoms smothered the Bengals offense. Then Clarence Davis put the Raiders in close. Marv Hubbard rushed in and gave Oakland another great come-from-behind victory. Final score: Oakland 31, Cincinnati 27.

Week 7 vs. Kansas City

Archrival Kansas City came next and, as always in the tough AFC Western Division, it was an all-out war. Ben Davidson dropped in on Lenny Dawson often, as did Tony Cline and Dan Conners to sabotage the Chiefs' attack. But football remains a game of inches, as rookie linebacker Terry Mendenhall found out when, with the Raiders trailing, his fumble recovery was allowed but his touchdown run wasn't.

With the Chiefs ahead 20–10, the Raiders' defense shut down the Chiefs passing game. Then the Raiders' air attack burst to life. Twenty-two-year pro veteran George Blanda connected with Raymond Chester and then hit Fred Biletnikoff to make it 20–17.

George Blanda's last-minute field goal not only earned a 20–20 comeback tie to keep the Raiders' six-game unbeaten streak alive, but also made Blanda pro football's all-time leading scorer.

Week 8 @ New Orleans

Meanwhile, in New Orleans, the Oakland secondary played the game of inches just right. While the defense made the inches count, the offense grabbed up enough yards to take a 14–0 lead. But the Saints benefited from a puzzling roughing call and went on to score. The Raiders countered and the lead looked safe, but misfortune struck a season-ending injury to linebacker Gus Otto, followed by a game-ending fumble recovery, which was disallowed. And finally there was the untimely penalty that gave the Saints a second chance and a 21–21 tie.

Week 9 vs. Houston

The Oilers came to Oakland and paid dearly for the Raiders' frustration at two consecutive ties. Nemiah Wilson's interception paved the way as Lamonica, behind protection from veteran Ron Mix, lifted a 63-yard strike to Drew Buie. Two more interceptions proved the Raiders would settle for no tie this day. Buie's second score ballooned the Oakland lead to 21–0. Silver and black might and muscle ruled this day. Once again Jimmy Warren slashed in, stole the ball, and weaved to pay dirt. It was the Raiders' eighth game without a defeat. Final score: Oakland 41, Houston 21.

Week 10 vs. San Diego

When the Chargers arrived in Oakland, they set out to avenge the earlier shutout and leaped to a substantial 24–10 lead. But unlike many teams, the Raiders are traditionally most dangerous when behind. And soon they stuck back for yardage that blew away the Chargers' lead. Rod Sherman's great catch made it 34–24 Oakland, but the Chargers rallied, making the score 34–31.

With time fleeting, they were driving again when an intense rush set up Dan Conners's clutch interception. Then Coach John Madden instructed punter Jerry DePoyster to take a safety when running out the clock, preserving a nine-game undefeated string that experts had labeled impossible for injury-wracked Oakland. Final score: Oakland 34, San Diego 33.

Week 11 vs. Baltimore

The defending world champion Baltimore Colts came next, and the bat-tle-worn Raiders had problems—problems that turned opportunities into mistakes by inches. Even Blanda's two touchdown passes to Biletnikoff could not stop the Colts, who rolled on and put an end to the hard-earned Oakland unbeaten streak. Final score: Baltimore 37, Oakland 14.

Week 12 @ Atlanta

In Atlanta the following week the weather was rainy, the field muddy, and the ball slippery. Slippery enough to contribute to a pair of crucial fumbles which were the key to a Falcon win and Oakland's second straight loss. The two field goals by Blanda and the Lamonica-to-Biletnikoff touchdown were too little too late. Final score: Atlanta 14, Oakland 13.

Week 13 @ Kansas City

And so it came down to the big one. The Raiders and the Chiefs battling for the title in pro football's toughest division. It had been that way for years, and was always a hitting, bruising, punishing conflict. Kansas City took an early lead on a Dawson-to-Otis Taylor touchdown and a Stenerud field goal. The Raiders struck back when Nemiah Wilson intercepted. Then Marv Hubbard blasted in for the score and almost drove the ball underground. It's that kind of rivalry.

As time was running out in the first half, the Chiefs made a big first down. And with just one second left their lead jumped to 13–7. Inches, seconds, and penalties proved decisive. An obvious interference led to Hubbard's second TD, and the silver and black battled back to a 14–13 fourth-quarter lead. Safety George Atkinson's interception halted a KC rally. Then George Blanda's field goal was blocked. As the Chiefs struggled to survive, Nemiah Wilson dove for the game-clinching interception, but it was not to be. The officials called it a trap. Given another chance, Dawson hit Taylor in heavy traffic. A no-harm interference was called on an overthrown desperation pass, and then Stenerud kicked and denied Oakland their fifth consecutive division championship. The season had come down to one game, one play, one inch, one penalty, one second, and heartbreak for the Raiders. Final score: Kansas City 16, Oakland 14.

Week 14 vs. Denver

In a game that was played for pride alone, the Raiders struck first with a 67-yard pass from Lamonica to Raymond Chester. Charlie Smith rushed for a one-yard score while Pete Banaszak rushed for a two-yard score. The Raiders finished out the season by beating the Broncos, 21 to 13.

But in 1971, the valued Raiders had challenged overwhelming odds and blasted them head on.

As the season closed, twelve-year All-Pro center Jim Otto was voted the Gorman Award by his teammates as Oakland's most inspirational player; and against Denver, every Raider deserved awards. They had lost the title but never their pride. Against Denver, Pete Banaszak got his eighth rushing score—a Raider season record. Lamonica playing with a hand that would require off-season surgery found Raymond Chester for another score. A now-healthy Charlie Smith made big plays. His return added a missing dimension to Oakland's potent offense. The defense with Tatum, Duane Benson, and the rest stood tall on a goal-line stand that gave meaning to the motto "Pride and Poise." The Denver victory gave Oakland an 8–4–2 record—better than teams winning division championships and playing for conference titles.

In Oakland, 1971 was a year when newcomers Moore, Slough, Seiler, Maxwell, and Gipson had fought and won beside vets Jim Harvey, Gerald Irons, and other unsung heroes. One league championship and four consecutive division championships are Raiders history.

The total commitment to excellence made by Al Davis in 1963 continues, and the greatness of the Raiders is in their future. But when this grueling 1971 season is examined against all the great glory years, the silver and black may well have had their finest hour.

1972 SEASON (10–3–1)

In 1969, under young head coach John Madden, the Raiders molded explosive, precision offense with quick strike defense. Their 12–1–1 record led all of pro football and what was emerging in Oakland was an unrivaled level of excellence.

In 1970, it was a fourth consecutive championship and a season of last-second victories that rocked the sports world and showcased Oakland Raiders pride and poise. Winning against all odds had become a Raiders tradition and it seemed that this *wave of glory* might roll on forever.

But in 1971, the wave broke and, despite an amiable 8–4–2 record, the Raiders lost the championship to Kansas City by inches and seconds. Consecutive championships had finally ended, but never the total commitment that made them possible. From narrow defeat rose a solemn promise: that in 1972 the Oakland Raiders would once again return to glory.

Week 1 @ Pittsburgh

The cross-country opener in Pittsburgh was played without the injured Ben Davidson. Kenny Stabler started at quarterback, but the Raiders ran into bad breaks and the rugged Steelers forged a big lead.

Ageless George Blanda celebrated his forty-fifth birthday by arching a bomb to tight end Raymond Chester. But the scoring gap was not narrowed until Daryle Lamonica connected with rookie wide receiver Mike Siani on a 24-yard pass, making the score 27–14. Lamonica hit Siani again in the fourth quarter on a 70-yard pass, but it was too little too late.

Despite nearly 400 yards total offense and Lamonica's 8 for 10, Oakland's furious finish fell short, 34–28.

Week 2 @ Green Bay

In Green Bay, the Raiders challenged their second eventual division champion in a row. Behind crushing blocking by George Buehler, Bob Brown, Jim Otto, Art Shell, and Gene Upshaw, Marv Hubbard bulldozed for 125 yards in search of victory and a 1,000-yard rushing goal. The Packers led early, but Coach John Madden's young defense was maturing under fire and allowed Green Bay to succeed on only one third down situation.

Jack Tatum's recovery and record 104-yard return exemplified the alert Raiders defense, which held the Packers scoreless for the last forty-three minutes of an inspired 20–14 victory, in which Oakland completely dominated play.

Week 3 vs. San Diego

Finally the Raiders returned home and, in their first game in the NFL's toughest division, met the stubborn San Diego Chargers.

Behind beautiful protection from All-Pro pair Gene Upshaw and Art Shell, Lamonica hit running back Don Highsmith to drive Oakland goalward. But the Raiders trailed the fired-up Chargers 17–14 in the fourth quarter until an off-the-dirt 40-yard field goal tied the score and gave Oakland a 1–1–1 record.

Week 4 @ Houston

Then in the Houston Astrodome for a Monday night national TV game, the Raiders exploded. Sure-handed Fred Biletnikoff caught six passes as the mighty silver and black offense rolled up 34 points.

While Stabler hit Bob Moore for one score, the defense led by Art Thoms shut out the Oilers. Gus Otto and Phil Villapiano were instrumental in holding Houston to just 89 yards of total offense. Nemiah Wilson had one of five Raiders interceptions while Houston completed only four passes.

A 34–0 triumph was a total team effort that gave notice to the nation that the silver and black were once again bound for glory.

Week 5 vs. Buffalo

The Buffalo Bills visited Oakland and the man to get was O. J. Simpson, who gave the Bills a 16–7 fourth-quarter lead by rushing for 144 yards and paying for every yard he got.

But in that fourth quarter, the Raiders came on relentlessly. Clarence Davis slashed in for one score then rode behind, pulling guard Gene Upshaw to add to the Raiders' 21-point last-period explosion, as the silver and black won going away, 28–16.

Week 6 vs. Denver

With a 3–1–1 record, an offense, defense, and special teams steaming along, it looked like the Raiders' return to glory was inevitable, but the AFC West is pro football's toughest division and danger faced the Oakland glory caravan.

The tough, talented Denver Broncos had just come to town. Broncos quarterback Charlie Johnson had one of his best days ever, ringing up a 24–3 Denver lead, but the comeback-conscious Raiders fought back.

Charlie Smith set up one score and top draftee Mike Siani got another on great effort, but time ran out on the Raiders, who lost 30–23.

Week 7 vs. Los Angeles

The Los Angeles Rams walked into a cyclone as the Oakland Raiders faced a must-win situation in their championship drive.

Six and a half minutes into the game, the Raiders grabbed a 21–0 lead over the Rams. And the cyclone roared on as newcomer Otis Sistrunk, Gerald Irons, and Horace Jones closed down the Ram offense. The cyclone then continued as Marv Hubbard added to the eventual club record of 2,376 yards rushing and an NFL high of 297 first downs.

Lamonica hit Pete Banaszak to put the Raiders in a position for another score. Later, Lamonica hit Raymond Chester in the end zone. Interceptions by Willie Brown (who had three), Nemiah Wilson, Jack Tatum, and Phil Villapiano (who ran for a touchdown) gave the Raiders a 45–17 win. But there were greater challenges still to be met.

Week 8 @ Kansas City

In Kansas City's fantastic new Arrowhead Stadium, the Raiders found themselves unloved before a record crowd of over 82,000.

Oakland was missing the big play by inches and the Chiefs raced to a 20–0 lead. The Raiders battled back with touchdowns by Marv Hubbard and Raymond Chester, but lost 27–14 and dropped to second in the division with a 4–3–1 record. Now any return to glory depended on two must-win games before facing the Chiefs again.

Week 9 @ Cincinnati

In Cincinnati, the Raiders were superb, blocking passes and field goals and destroying the Bengals' offense. Blanda kicked two field goals and Clarence Davis scored on a one-yard run. Behind disciplined, almost flawless blocking, Charlie Smith rushed for an eight-yard TD and raced for 146 total yards. Oakland had their first must-win, 20–14.

Week 10 @ Denver

In Denver, pressure mounted but the Raiders were ready. Oakland's defensive mind and muscle were magnificent as first-year find Otis Sistrunk was everywhere. The secondary with Jimmy Warren closed down the Denver scoring lanes and Coach John Madden's meticulously designed offense was devastating, rolling up 25 first downs and punting not even once.

Fred Biletnikoff continued his march to another AFC receiving title with two touchdowns. Marv Hubbard and Charlie Smith added scores of their own, and George Blanda kicked three field goals as the proud, poised Raiders met the test with must-win number two, 37–20.

Week 11 vs. Kansas City

Now it was time for a showdown with the Kansas City Chiefs.

There was always special tension in the air before a Raiders–Chiefs encounter because for the past six years, these meetings had decided the championship. This time, Oakland held a 1.5 game lead over Kansas City. A Raiders win now and the return to glory was but one step away.

From the very outset, it was silver and black dominance. The powerful Raiders grabbed an early lead, blasting for sixteen rushing first downs—the most in their proud history.

Just three weeks earlier they had been humiliated in Kansas City. But the Raiders never lost sight of their championship goal. They grew tougher, more determined. The Chiefs learned this first hand.

Charlie Smith scored from 2 yards out to open the scoring, and Blanda added a 27-yard field goal for a 10–0 lead. It was 10–3 when Lamonica hit Biletnikoff, making it 16–3. The Raider lead ballooned at 26–3 and stayed there, protected by George Atkinson and the entire silver and black defense.

With Oakland victorious, 26–3, it was all over, and more than 54,000 loyal Raiders fans knew their team needed but one more win to gain the division championship—their fifth in six years.

Week 12 @ San Diego

A large group of Raider boosters followed their team to San Diego, anxious to see the division title clinched.

The defense was shocked, earning breaks for the offense. The famed Raider precision passing built leads at 7–0 and 14–10. But the Chargers rallied late in the last quarter and led 19–14, threatening to score again, but quarterback John Hadl threw deep into the end zone. The ball was deflected and landed in the hands of Dan Conners.

The Charger threat continued, but it was as if the Raiders fans willed a miss kick and all that followed. Trailing by five points and with time draining away, the silver and black marshaled the attack team. Lamonica began a relentless move on the Chargers goal. He rifled one to Mike Siani, who was injured on the play and was replaced by Cliff Branch. Lamonica hit Branch on the 20 and took the ball to the nine. With first and goal to go, Lamonica gave the ball to Smith, who took the ball in for the touchdown. Final score: Raiders 21, San Diego 19.

The pledge had been kept. The Oakland Raiders had returned to glory, for they were the 1972 champions of the rugged AFC Western Division.

Week 13 vs. New York Jets

The Raiders and Jets played before the largest TV audience in Monday night pro football history. Joe Namath was spectacular and threw an early TD pass to give New York the lead. But the now battle-wise Raiders played sound team defense and, thirty-nine passes later, the Jets had been prevented from scoring even one more touchdown.

As the record Oakland Coliseum crowd of 54,843 cheered, the Raiders made it five in a row, beating the Jets 24–16.

Week 14 vs. Chicago

Marv Hubbard, who finished with a record 1,100 yards rushing, was presented with the annual Gorman Award before the start of the game.

Charlie Smith scored twice and Pete Banaszak once. Then Clarence Davis and the offensive line went on to beat the Bears 28 to 21 before a thirty-eighth consecutive sellout crowd, and Oakland entered the playoffs with a 10–3–1 record.

AFC Divisional Playoffs @ Pittsburgh

The playoff game in Pittsburgh was one of pro football's defensive struggles. Led by Otis Sistrunk and Tony Kline, Oakland held the Steelers to just two field goals, but with 1:57 left in the game, the Raiders trailed 6–0. Then Kenny Stabler began a brilliant drive that marched the courageous Raiders downfield in what appeared to be another heroic finish.

Next Stabler went back to pass, then decided to run the ball into the end zone, making the score 7–6. Unfortunately, Raider heroics were short lived, for the Steelers in an impossible fourth down situation came up with a play that has been called miraculous, freakish, illegal, and certainly controversial.

Pittsburgh quarterback Terry Bradshaw dropped back to pass, but the Raiders flushed him out of the pocket to the right. He saw running back John (Frenchy) Fuqua over the middle at the Raiders' 35, and with defenders closing, Bradshaw fired a pass toward Fuqua.

Fuqua, Raiders safety Jack Tatum, and the ball converged simultaneously, and out popped the ball. The Raiders began to celebrate, not realizing that rookie running back Franco Harris, trailing the play at the Raiders' 42, had picked the ball out of the air at his shoe tops and taken off down the left sideline. Some Raiders gave chase, but they could not stop Harris from running to the end zone.

Touchdown? Nobody knew, including the officials. The Raiders argued that Fuqua had batted the ball to Harris (the rules of the time did not permit consecutive touches by offensive players). If Tatum had batted the ball, the play would have been a touchdown.

Referee Fred Swearingen, after consulting with NFL supervisor of officials Art McNally, came back on the field and ruled the play a touchdown. Pittsburgh kicked the extra point to take a 13–7 lead with five seconds left, a score that was finalized moments later.

As suddenly as the Raiders had forged ahead, their 1972 season was ended. But a moment of defeat cannot erase years of glory. The years 1963 through 1972 were when the Oakland Raiders proved that the true test of any great organization is its ability to maintain a level of excellence.

The Oakland Raiders, the famed and feared silver and black, now proudly stood as pro football's winningest team over the past ten challenging seasons. Every Oakland Raider sacrificed to fulfill the destiny of this organization whose greatness was in its future, and all now proudly shared in their gallant return to glory.

1973 SEASON (9–4–1)

Defending champions of pro football's toughest division, the Oakland Raiders faced a tough 1973 schedule, including the undefeated World Champions plus every AFC playoff team. Of the first seven games, only one would be at home.

Sunday night, November 18, found the silver and black, pro football's winningest team the past ten years, third in the AFC West.

Experts buried Oakland's chances for their sixth division championship in seven years, but the Raiders knew what remained to be done on the battered Coliseum turf. Forged in the fires of adversity, fueled by an unyielding total commitment to excellence, the character of the Raiders rose to heights of greatness in a thundering drive to the playoffs.

Thus was written another heroic chapter in the proud history of an organization that ranks atop the sports world. Thus was written conquest and character—the story of the 1973 Oakland Raiders.

Week 1 @ Minnesota

The challenge began in Minnesota against the eventual NFC champions. Daryle Lamonica started at quarterback and hit Mike Siani with six passes as Oakland gained 353 yards against the vaunted *purple gang.*

Top draft choice Ray Guy marked his pro debut with a 50-yard punting average, while George Atkinson's electrifying punt return, which gave the Raiders a 13–10 lead at the half. But in the end, veteran Fran Tarkenton and Rookie of the Year Chuck Foreman spearheaded the Vikings' 24–16 win over the silver and black.

Week 2 vs. Miami

The next Sunday found Coach John Madden and the Raiders at California Memorial Stadium against the World Champion Miami Dolphins.

The order of battle was set early as Dan Conners blocked out Larry Csonka power. Then Bubba Smith and the young Raiders defensive unit turned out the light of flashy runner Mercury Morris.

Oakland played errorless football and over 74,000 appreciate fans, the largest crowd to ever see a pro game in Northern California, knew Miami's eighteen-game win streak was in danger.

Charlie Smith and Marv Hubbard rampaged goalward. Four times this duo drove within field goal range. Four times Coach John Madden called upon veteran George Blanda. George was a perfect 4–4 and, coupled with superb defense and determined special teams, he helped the mighty Raiders to a 12–7 streak-breaking conquest of the World Champions.

Week 3 @ Kansas City

In unfriendly Kansas City, Oakland faced the first of five straight grueling road games. Clarence Davis darted on a 76-yard kickoff return, but the Raiders registered only three points. The powerful Chiefs managed only three field goals themselves as punter Ray Guy boomed the football into the land of no return.

The Oakland defense held the hard ground savagely. But with only two minutes left to play, a deflected pass intercepted by Willie Lanier and returned for a touchdown sealed the Raiders' fate. The 16–3 loss to the Chiefs left Oakland with one win in three games. With four straight road games still ahead, the Raiders' character would be severely tested.

Week 4 @ St. Louis

In St. Louis, the silver and black faced soaring temperatures and an explosive Cardinals offense. Ignoring the heat, the fired-up Raiders defenders, led by Otis Sistrunk, Tony Kline, Art Thoms, and Phil Villapiano, limited the high-scoring Cards to only ten points (who averaged 20 per game that season). Behind flawless protection from Jim Otto, George Buehler, Gene Upshaw, Art Shell, Bob Brown, and John Vella, Kenny Stabler completed 19 of 31 as the surging Oakland offense gained nearly 450 yards.

Marv Hubbard helped achieve a club record of eighteen rushing first downs. Defense had been paramount in the first three games, but offensive came forth as Hubbard blasted in for the 17–10 clincher.

Week 5 @ San Diego

The traveling Raiders were on the road again, and this time it was San Diego that challenged Oakland's closed end zone policy. The silver and black took advantage of every Charger miscue. Pete Banaszak recovered one fumble and Bob Moore's score, along with touchdowns from Cliff Branch and Marv Hubbard and two Blanda field goals, gave Oakland the victory with a final score of 27–17.

Week 6 @ Denver

Next, in a Monday night road game at Denver, the Raiders faced another team crusading to overtake them. Twenty-four-year veteran George Blanda became the first player to ever kick 300 field goals, but even more important kicks were yet to come.

Twice the Raiders rallied from behind. An 80-yard bomb from Kenny Stabler to Mike Siani brought Oakland back once, and the Raiders defense fought valiantly to protect the lead. Despite clutch plays such as Jack Tatum's interception, the rugged Broncos forged a 17–13 lead. Cliff Branch then put Oakland ahead, 20–17. With Stabler injured, Lamonica came in and hit Branch to set up a go-ahead field goal. But Denver came back to tie the game at 23, and Oakland's 3–2–1 record left the AFC Western Division title up for grabs.

Week 7 @ Baltimore

Now the Raiders were cross-country in Baltimore for a fifth straight road game. Ken Stabler hit Mike Siani, Fred Biletnikoff, and Bob Moore with six passes each, while completing 25 of 29 to set an all-time NFL completion percentage record. This record performance again brought to national attention the precision passing that has for so long been a feared weapon in the Raiders arsenal. When the Colts tried to immolate the Raiders' success, they ran into trouble from alert Alonzo "Skip" Thomas. With the riddled Colts secondary playing deep, Clarence Davis rolled behind Gene Upshaw for two scores and a 34–21 Oakland victory. Five straight away games, and yet this young Raiders squad had allowed but one game to result in defeat.

Week 8 vs. New York Giants

Finally the silver and black were finally home to the Oakland Coliseum. Their opponent in this eighth week of the season was the New York Giants. With a fortieth consecutive Coliseum sellout crowd in attendance, the fatigue of travel and battle was temporarily forgotten as Coach John Madden skillfully unfolded a devastating game plan. Against New York, Oakland's superiority was evident from the opening whistle. Yard by yard, man by man, point by point, Oakland vanquished the Giants in a surge of raw power.

The defense, with linebacker Gerald Irons leading the way, zeroed in on the Giants. Down after down, the Raiders displayed the intensity of a proud team in search of its ninth consecutive winning season.

On the offense side, Kenny Stabler threw a touchdown to both Bob Moore and Charlie Smith, while Clarence Davis, and Marv

Hubbard (twice) rushed for scores. Daryle Lamonica came in during the fourth quarter and whistled one to wide receiver Steve Sweeney. It finished the Giants 42–0 and raised Oakland's record to 5–2–1.

Week 9 vs. Pittsburgh

Against the playoff-bound Pittsburgh Steelers, the Raiders were plagued by turnovers and penalties, and Ken Stabler suffered a knee injury. Behind Lamonica, Oakland ran and passed for nearly 400 yards against the prestigious Steelers defense. Despite this display of strength, the Raiders scored only nine points—a field goal by Blanda and a touchdown by Biletnikoff. As things went awry, Oakland suffered its third loss of the 1973 season. But while the 17–9 defeat was damaging, the bruising defensive struggle with Cleveland the following week was even more costly.

Week 10 vs. Cleveland

Both defenses played tough, tightfisted football. For the silver and black, the 7–3 loss seemed deadly because that night when the scores were in, the Raiders stood third in the AFC West and many thought they were finished.

Week 11 vs. San Diego

With San Diego in Oakland, it was a must-win situation for the Raiders. The Chargers employed trick formations, but Coach Madden's competent staff had the silver and black poised and ready.

Horace Jones and Kelvin Korver pressured the Chargers' offense into big mistakes. The Raiders' conference-leading defense forced a miscue that safety man George Atkinson turned into a score, and the Chargers were never close.

The defiant Raiders dug in and overpowered San Diego 31–3 with TDs from Smith, Biletnikoff, and Moore. The victory was crucial. Oakland's comeback tradition blended with its strong pride that would not allow this team to give an inch despite the imposing obstacles that barred their charge to the division title.

With this victory, the Raiders were now tied for second, but faced yet another must-win in Houston.

Week 12 @ Houston

Against the Oilers, Marv Hubbard raced for 121 yards to contribute to a new Raiders season rushing record of 2,510 yards. But the Raiders were in a rugged battle inside the Astrodome.

The Oakland defense bent, but a touchdown saving effort by Willie Brown epitomized the Raiders' determination. Two plays later, the Houston scoring threat was smashed when linebacker Phil Villapiano picked up a forced fumble. Fred Biletnikoff's clutch catch finished the Oilers, 17–6.

Week 13 vs. Kansas City

The Raiders were atop the AFC West, but on the horizon was the team that hated them most: the Kansas City Chiefs.

Nemiah Wilson came up with a timely interception that helped limit the Chiefs to only seven points. Then the Raiders offense zeroed in with their big guns, and the explosion shook the football world. This was the offense that would finish number one in the AFC, and KNBR's Bill King describes the relentless role of the onrushing silver and black way:

"Stabler gives the ball to Hubbard. He breaks a tackle at the 25, the 20, the 15, the 5, TOUCHDOWN, RAIDERS! Hubbard with a 31-yard touchdown gives the Raiders the lead of 13–0. Marv Hubbard did another crunch job."

And after the crunch came the crumble as the Oakland defense got it back and the Chiefs were ground to dust, 37–7. Now only two teams remained, and the last regular season game was the only one that mattered.

Week 14 vs. Denver

The Raiders had battled back and now faced the final challenge to their championship plans: the Denver Broncos. They forged an early lead and then added to it, as Stabler handed off to Davis for a score.

Throughout the year, the aggressive Raiders defense allowed only 175 points—58 less than any previous season. This intense pressure forced the Broncos to falter. Only the strong survive in the final quarter of a title game, and on this December day, once again it was the silver and black who conquered. A big play by the offense of Stabler to Siani for the score, and then another by the defense when the Broncos were intercepted by Thomas, rendered the final verdict, 21–17.

The Raiders, for the sixth time in seven years, had won the Western Division of the American Football Conference.

AFC Divisional Playoffs vs. Pittsburgh

Just six days after defeating Denver, the Steelers and Raiders met at an AFC playoff game marked by Oakland's methodical mayhem at the Coliseum.

With a first and ten to go at the Pittsburg 39, Villapiano intercepted the ball at the 40-yard line of the Raiders. Later, Bradshaw was looking for Barry Pearson and overthrew him. Waiting in the midst was George Atkinson for the second interception of the day. Once again, Bradshaw set up and fired down field, and the ball was intercepted by Willie Brown, who raced 54 yards to the end zone for the score.

With design and desire, the awesome Raiders juggernaut ripped out huge chunks of Steelers turf. Time and time again they drove to the end zone door and battered it down. In the end, it was Raiders pride that dominated the day with a resounding 33–14 victory—a triumph saluted with a standing ovation by the ecstatic Oakland fans.

AFC Conference Championship @ Miami

Fifteen weeks after the league opener, the Raiders journeyed cross-country to meet the Miami Dolphins for the AFC Championship.

On the initial series, the Raiders mounted a strong drive that was killed by a heartbreaking penalty. Miami came right back and powered in for the score. The Dolphins had won twenty-three straight in the Orange Bowl, and Raiders efforts went for naught.

A George Blanda field goal and a Mike Siani touchdown were the only points that Oakland could muster that day. Final score: Miami 27, Oakland 10. The Raiders' season had ended.

The silver and black had fought their way into the championship game with a thundering drive down the stretch that earned new respect and admiration. And the single loss could not erase another glorious season to which every Raider contributed. The excellence of head coach John Madden continued, as did the contribution of able assistants.

The pledge first made in 1963 by Al Davis was a simple one: "Unrivaled Excellence." As pro football's winningest team for the past eleven years, the Raiders' monumental rise to glory stems from a dynamic organization whose motto is "Pride and Poise," and whose lifeblood is and always will be "Conquest and Character."

1974 SEASON (12–2–0)

December 29, 1974: the AFC Championship game between the Oakland Raiders and the Pittsburgh Steelers.

The Raiders led 10–3 with only one quarter left before another glorious chapter could be added to the most memorable sports history of our time. A Super Bowl return marred the Oakland Raiders' unrivaled record of accomplishments, but fate would write a new ending—a rarely called tripping penalty wiped out a Raiders scoring opportunity.

The football itself bounced away, defying Oakland's attempt at capture.

Super Bowl laurels faded in a mist of heartbreak and tears. What remained was a brilliant 12–2 season—best in the game. What remained was a magnificent playoff triumph over the defending World Champion Miami Dolphins in one of the greatest games ever

played. What remained was a total domination of professional football since 1963 in terms of consistent victory. No organization even
approaches the Raiders' unbelievable 115 wins against only 42 losses
(and 11 ties) during these twelve years. What remained was ten consecutive winning seasons—seven championships in eight years.

These monumental achievements are history, yet the true greatness
of the Raiders remains in its future; a proud future fueled and fired by
their relentless, unceasing commitment to excellence.

Week 1 @ Buffalo

In Buffalo, the Raiders opened on the road for the fifth consecutive
year. Before a Monday night television audience and 80,000 unlov-
ing fans, George Blanda kicked two field goals and Clarence Davis
rushed 15 yards for a touchdown to put Oakland ahead, 13–7. Art
Thoms scored on a fumble return late in the fourth quarter to put
the Raiders ahead, 20–14, but a final Buffalo rally sealed a 21–20
Oakland defeat made more damaging by the loss of dependable Tony
Cline for two months.

Week 2 vs. Kansas City

Cross-country travel left Raiders head coach John Madden and his
assistants just five days to prepare for Kansas City. But five days were
all that Oakland needed.

Mike Siani was on the receiving end of one Ken Stabler strike. Then the
diverse Oakland attack sprung Pete Banaszak for 20 and a touchdown.

The silver and black defense was overwhelming. Monte Johnson
stormed for one of four Raiders sacks. He also grabbed one of five
Raiders interceptions that limited the Chiefs to only 86 yards passing.

Rookie tight end Dave Casper's second score of the day made the
final score, 27–7.

Week 3 @ Pittsburgh

In Pittsburgh, the Raider defense was overpowering, making quarterback Joe Gilliam's day a disaster. Big Bubba Smith dropped him

for a 20-yard setback on one play. The defense rendered them score-less for the first time in 132 games. Ken Stabler was neither sacked nor intercepted and his bullet to Cliff Branch finished Pittsburgh, 17–0.

Week 4 @ Cleveland

In Cleveland, Jim Otto, George Buehler, John Vella, Art Shell, and Gene Upshaw gave near-perfect protection to a surging attack sparked by Clarence Davis's extra-effort score. Twice the mighty Raiders fell behind by 10 points before rallying, while ringing up 445 yards and a record 90 offensive plays.

The defense clicked on interceptions by Jack Tatum and three in the last quarter by George Atkinson. Defensive captain Willie Brown picked off another as the Raiders rolled for 40 points en route to becoming 1974's top scoring team. Final score: Raiders 40, Cleveland 24.

Week 5 @ San Diego

In San Diego, Coach Madden's team was on the road for the fourth time in five weeks, and the defense was angry.

On offense, Snake struck twice—once to Cliff Branch and once to Bob Moore—giving the Raiders a 14–10 win and upping their record to 4–1.

Week 6 vs. Cincinnati

The tough Cincinnati Bengals jumped ahead to a quick 14–3 lead. Ageless George Blanda, the oldest player in NFL history, kicked two field goals to keep the Raiders' attack moving. His second put Oakland ahead, 23–21, but the Bengals bounced back and led 27–23 with 1:36 to go.

Daring comebacks are a Raider trademark, but the silver and black needed more than just a field goal. With calm and poise, Ken Stabler marched them goalward. Although playing without time-outs or huddles, the Raiders remained disciplined, cold, and relentless. Finally the game hinged on a few seconds and a few plays.

Stabler threw to Siani and he made it to the five with thirteen seconds left. Stabler next handed off to Charlie Smith and he rushed for the winning score.

The Raiders with their 30–27 win now carried a five-game winning streak as they traveled to meet their cross-bay rivals.

Week 7 @ San Francisco

The silver and black had triumphed in San Francisco during preseason play. The return visit would end the same way, as Marv Hubbard powered for 117 yards and one touchdown.

Next, Stabler passed to Cliff Branch for 64 yards and another Raiders score. It was exhibition season revisited. The domination continued, as under unyielding pressure the Niners lost the ball and George Atkinson's recovery set up a Stabler-to-Dave Casper score.

Then Ray Guy, pro football's leading punter, boomed a punt, and the 49ers return man dropped the ball. Harold Hart recovered and ran it back 60 yards for the score to end the San Francisco earthquake of 1974. Final score: Oakland 35, San Francisco 24.

Week 8 @ Denver

In Denver, the Raiders were undaunted by a Rocky Mountain winter. Even in the snow, John Madden's forces were ready. Twice Ken Stabler found Fred Biletnikoff for scores. These helped Biletnikoff to become the first player in Raiders history to score 60 touchdowns. Cliff Branch also hit pay dirt twice to continue his route to the playoffs and a league-leading 13 TD catches. It was seven in a row for the silver and black. Final score: Oakland 28, Denver 17.

Week 9 vs. Detroit

Back in Oakland for the season's ninth week, the Raiders faced the Detroit Lions, who saw their own four-game winning streak demolished. Linebacker Dan Conners came up with two interceptions to help Oakland finish second in that NFL department. Then came time to remind pro football that the bomb was back in Oakland, as

Stabler threw long to Cliff Branch for a score, while the Raider runners blasted out 284 yards.

Final score: Oakland 35, Detroit 13—eight in a row.

Week 10 vs. San Diego

The San Diego Chargers came to Oakland with lightning bolts on their helmets, but the real lightning wore #21 for the silver and black, as Cliff Branch scored on a 60-yard bomb from Kenny Stabler.

The defense pounded the Chargers, while Oakland's Gerald Irons and Skip Thomas destroyed Charger hopes.

Final score: Oakland 17, San Diego 10—their ninth in a row.

Week 11 vs. Denver

When the Broncos came to Oakland, they were meeting the first team in the entire NFL to earn a playoff spot. Seven times in eight years the Raiders had won the Western Division Championship. But despite Ken Stabler's two TDs to Biletnikoff and a field goal by George Blanda, it wasn't enough for the win. The Raider winning streak ended with the final score of 20–17.

Week 12 vs. New England

Unfortuantely for the New England Patriots, they would have to pay for that loss to Denver. It was an enormous love-in for Oakland fans, as Stabler hit Branch (twice), Biletnikoff, and Moore in the end zone for scores.

Twin terrors Horace Jones and Otis Sistrunk pounded Plunkett and company all day. Pressure paid off when Skip Thomas scored on an interception. Then rookies Larry Lawrence and Harold Hart ran an option and finalized the Oakland victory, 41–26.

Week 13 @ Kansas City

In a cold, windy Kansas City, the Raiders played the Chiefs for the first time in a decade without a championship at stake.

Throughout the bitter day, the Oakland defense made big plays as Horace Jones recovered a fumble and ran 45 yards. With Brown and Tatum still out, Jimmy Warren stepped in and made a crucial interception.

Then, in an intense finish, veteran quarterback Daryle Lamonica hit Cliff Branch for a narrow 7–6 Raiders win.

Week 14 vs. Dallas

Before the final league game against Dallas, Kenny Stabler was presented the 1974 Gorman Award as the player who best exemplified the pride and spirit of the Oakland Raiders.

Then a national TV audience saw a Raiders team bound for glory as Fred Biletnikoff led the way while achieving his eighth consecutive season of 40 or more receptions.

Ken Stabler then found Charlie Smith on a pattern that would loom large in the upcoming playoff classic. Suddenly the Cowboys were struggling for survival when Phil Villapiano recovered a fumble.

On the next play, Blanda found Branch for a score. It was the first pass that Blanda had thrown since 1972. This pass helped close the league season with a 27–23 Oakland victory, and George Blanda was named NFL Man of the Year.

AFC Divisional Playoffs vs. Miami

From the opening kickoff, the Raider–Dolphin playoff game exploded with excitement as Dolphin Nat Moore raced 89 yards to score. The sellout Coliseum crowd despaired, but the pride and poise that made these Raiders so feared and respected never wavered.

Next, Charlie Smith caught a Stabler pass in the end zone for a score.

After missing the end zone by inches the first time, Biletnikoff caught a deflected pass in the end zone for a second Raiders score. Following in Biletnikoff's footsteps, Branch caught a bomb from Stabler on the 30 and ran it in for a touchdown, sending the crowd into a frenzy.

Miami trailed 21–19, but they had not become two-time world champions by giving up. They roared back and powered into the end zone to lead again, 26–21. With only 2:01 left and with pro football's most disciplined defense to overcome, the Oakland Raider hopes hung by a thread.

But Stabler took the reins and led the charge. He went to Biletnikoff for 18 and then again for 20 more. With forty seconds left, Stabler hit Frank Pitts for a crucial five yards. Now it was do or die.

Stabler then faded back, was hit, and lobbed the ball to Davis for the score. With twenty-one seconds left, Griese was intercepted by Villapiano. Raiders 28, Miami 26.

AFC Conference Championship vs. Pittsburgh

The Raiders would once again play their formidable foes: the Pittsburgh Steelers. But with two Blanda field goals and a touchdown by Cliff Branch, it would not be enough and, once again, the Raiders would go down in flames. Final score: Steelers 24, Raiders 13.

SECOND HALF: 1975–1980

A COLORFUL CAST OF MISFITS
PLAYERS, NICKNAMES, SUPERSTITIONS, AND THE TWO COKE CUPS

THE OAKLAND RAIDERS, by far, are the most colorful, unusual, and bizarre team in the NFL. Despite their outlaw appearance, this menagerie of misfits and rebels is damn entertaining!

From their inception in 1960 to their Super Bowl wins this renegade team has displayed a number of colorful characters and personalities unmatched by any other NFL team.

FRED BILETNIKOFF

Fred Biletnikoff's football hero was a 5' 9", 178-pound wide receiver for the Philadelphia Eagles by the name of Tommy McDonald. He was the inspiration for Biletnikoff wanting to be a wide receiver. Freddy himself was a 6' 1", 190-pound wide receiver drafted out of Florida State by the Raiders in the second round of the 1965 AFL draft.

Freddy knew from the very start that he had to be not only a physical ball player, but also a mentally fit player. Biletnikoff was inducted into the Pro Football Hall of Fame in 1988. His presenter was his former boss, Al Davis.

Freddy may have not been the biggest guy on the team or the fastest, but Stabler knew that he had the heart to play . . . and play well.

"Freddy represented everything the team was. He wasn't the biggest, and hell, I could outrun him, but he had a tremendous heart. He would always find a way to come up with the ball—those rawboned hands always snatching a ball out of the air when you needed it most.

"As a wide receiver I had the opportunity to play my entire career with Freddy. He was incredible. I've seen players today drop more passes in one game than I ever saw Fred Biletnikoff drop in his entire career!"

During quarterback David Humm's rookie year, he had the opportunity to work out with Biletnikoff.

"My rookie year I measured 6' 1" and weighed in at 180 pounds. I decide I'm going to stay behind and work out as late as the latest guys, and the last one to leave was always Fred. I would work out with Freddy and his bag of balls, jump rope, hit the speed bag, do all the stuff in cycles.

"I'd say to Freddy, 'You done?' He'd say, 'No, no, no!' I mean we would be out in the dark working out by the light of the back door."

"I just loved going out there and staying after practice," said Biletnikoff. "It was fun to be able to think about your routes, your footwork. I mean, the ball's not always going to be perfect. I liked being able to think about how high it might be, how low, covering my ass and catching all of those balls, too. You got to practice like you're going to play."

Freddy made his opinion clear regarding the NFL's uniform "dress code."

"You can't go out on the field unless you feel good. The more comfortable you make yourself, the better you feel. So to make the uniform roomier, I would cut underneath the jersey—underneath my arms, and you'd feel like you didn't have a jersey on.

"Then I would slit the back of my pants, because they were real tight pants. It looked ragged, but it was comfortable. And right where the jersey comes around the front, I would slice that down so it wasn't so tight around my neck."

Pat Toomay remembered Al Davis' response to Freddy's unique uniform.

"One time we won a game in Cleveland late in the year. There are three buses for the players afterwards. I always got on the last one, and this time there was just Fred, Snake, and I in the back. Snake had a pint of whiskey in his bag. They had a drink. We were about ready to go. Then [Al] Davis gets on, the last guy. He sits behind the driver. Next he turned around and looked towards the back of the bus, stands up, and holds up a letter from the league, points to it, and says to Fred, 'You cost me another $2,500 with the way you mess with your uniform.'"

"Biletnikoff says, 'Fuck you, Al! You told me, 'Whatever it takes.' Davis looked at him, and he laughed, and sat back down and just shook his head."

Fred turned and said to me, 'I guess I told him.'"

Back in the day, Freddy used a then 'legal substance' that was rightfully named Stickum. Stabler recalled what equipment manager Dick Romanski would have to go through.

"Dick Romanski would get the stuff for Biletnikoff. It looked like a huge glob of goo. From afar, it looked like it might be a four-inch bloody gash seeping through his socks. After he catches that first pass you have to go right to the official and get a new ball because that one was all sticky. He was that way the whole game. Madden swears he once caught a pass that stuck to his forearm."

"You needed paint turpentine to get the stuff off," said Pete Banaszak. "Fred would have it everywhere—his uniform, his head, his nose, and his mouth."

"It took me a day to wash off Biletnikoff's helmet," said Romanski. "But Freddy didn't really need the help in catching a ball. He just used it to remind himself to hold on to the ball. Not that he needed to. Best pass catcher I ever saw!"

According to Freddy, it was more psychological than anything else.

"It was more psychological than physical. I never used it in practice or training camp. Only games. The biggest thing was you were able to hold on to the ball when you were fighting with the defensive back, and you have to have any opportunity you can to get a grip on it. But yeah, you're going to pull some balls out of your ass with it. Sometimes it helped a great deal."

"Whenever he fell, he'd try and protect himself and turn to where he didn't get his hands in the dirt and the grass," said tackle John Vella. "I'd be across from him in the huddle, and there were times when his fingers would be stuck together, and he had a bunch of grass stuck to them. Stabler would be calling the play, and Freddy would be saying, 'JV, help me out.' I'm reaching over to separate his fingers because they're all stuck together.

"I remember being in the locker room at halftime and Fred couldn't hold the cigarette. He'd have Romanski actually hold the cigarette for him so he could smoke it!"

Monte Johnson describes Freddy's "dinosaur-like" noises as part of his pre-game ritual.

"Madden made the comment one time, 'Depending on how many times Freddy threw up, you knew what kind of game he'd have.'" I think it was superstition, but whatever it was, Freddy would disappear into the bathroom, calling *dinosaurs*. That's what we called it, because he would make these odd, groveling, groaning noises. Like a dinosaur might make."

This was Freddy's response to Johnson.

"I was just real nervous and intense. It was the waiting, waiting for hours. Every game to me wasn't just a game. It was a big game. Every game meant something to our team, and to me. The thought that you were never prepared enough when you went on the field—putting that on yourself is going to make anyone sick—until everything starts. And then you're fine. Then everything falls into place."

Stabler's locker was next to Biletnikoff's.

"Freddy was always a mess before games—nervous, hyper. He'd smoke a pack of cigarettes in the locker room and drink four or five Cokes. And he had a whole elaborate program for getting dressed to play. It would sometimes draw a crowd.

"First he would take a pair of scissors and snip off every little thread hanging from his pants. The threads could be so minute that most naked eyes couldn't detect them, but Freddy twisted and turned those pants in the light till he got them all. His pants had to come just over his knees, and he would cut them in back for more freedom. He wore his black socks just over his calves so the flesh was bare to the knee.

"Then he would go through the ceremony of what shoes to wear. Receivers tend to be real picky about their shoes, depending on the field conditions and the weather. Even on perfect days, Freddy was picky. He might put on a pair of Riddells, then go to a pair of Spot-Bilts, then pull on a pair of Converse. One day I saw him put on one Riddell and on Spot Bilt. I guess one cut better to the left and the other to the right.

"He was so superstitious he'd put a dime in one shoe and two nickels in the other. He literally turned on a dime. And he always taped a crucifix under his shoulder pads that looked like they were made out of a couple of Kotex.

"Once he finally decided on his shoes, Freddy would tie them about twenty-five times to get them just right. Whatever that was. Pete and I would drive him crazy. Sometimes we'd hide a shoe or lace up a pair and skip an eyelet near the bottom.

"Freddy would tape over his shoes up to the ankle, which was called 'spatting.' He would tape his arms from just below the elbow to the wrist, then take a can of Stickum and spray the tape. Finally he would pull on his helmet and adjust the chinstrap.

"Then Pete would walk over, wink at me, and say, 'Goddamn, Freddy, your uniform looks like shit today!'

"So Freddy would take the whole son of a bitching thing off and start all over."

'Hey, Freddy, be a little more careful,' I'd say."

Biletnikoff was also very superstitious. He'd wear the same pair of socks every game and chew the same number of pieces of gum. Before every game Fred would tie and untie his shoelaces about fifty times.

Then he would lie on his back on the locker room floor, tossing a football to himself over and over and over. When it came to Stickum, Fred used twice as much as Lester Hayes ever did. Fred had a routine: he would come back to the huddle and go right to John Vella. John would literally pry Fred's fingers apart or tear off the grass that was stuck to the palms of his hands.

Dick Romanski had to carry Biletnikoff's gum with him throughout the entire game.

"Every time he came out of the game, he had to have new gum. He was superstitious like that. Sometimes he would want Spearmint, sometimes Juicy Fruit. It was always three sticks. At times I'd mix 'em all up and he wouldn't know the difference."

GEORGE BLANDA

George Blanda was a 6' 2", 215-pound quarterback out of Kentucky. He was drafted by the Chicago Bears in the 12th round of the 1949 NFL draft. He played ten years with the Bears, a year with the Colts, seven years with Houston, and nine with the Raiders. Blanda was cut by the Raiders prior to the next to last preseason game against the 49ers in 1976.

Blanda's replacement was a twenty-three-year-old kicker out of Boston College by the name of Fred Steinfort. By 1977, after only a half year with Oakland, Steinfort was on his way to the Atlanta Falcons.

In 1981, Blanda was inducted into the Pro Football Hall of Fame. His presenter was none other than Al Davis who, at that time, was the managing general partner for the Raiders.

What makes this even sadder is the fact that once you retire from the NFL, they are basically through with you. You are just a commodity. Once you are used up, they get rid of you. George deserved better than that.

For Blanda, it was humiliating.

"It was embarrassing. It's like waiting to be beheaded. I was like a cancer out on that field. The players treated me like I had leprosy. I wish I had known what the situation was before I got here. I never would have come. I have no animosity toward Al Davis or John Madden. I just don't care. Have you ever gotten to the point where you don't care? I don't care."

Blanda said his final goodbyes after one last practice.

"It's was really sad," said Biletnikoff. "They owe you something. There should have been some way of having him leave that would give you a good feeling. There should have been something to bring a tear to your eye . . . it's like the guy going to the electric chair."

"I thought for sure that there would be a big press conference and he would go out with glory," said Stabler. "George deserved it. As cold and hard as he was, I enjoyed being around him. He would tell you what he thought. If you liked him, fine. If you didn't like him, the hell with you."

BOB BROWN: *BOOMER*

The only way to describe Bob Brown is that he was one tough, mean son of a bitch! An offensive tackle out of Nebraska, Bob stood 6' 4" and weighed 280 pounds. He was absolutely massive! Brown was drafted by the Philadelphia Eagles in the first round—second over-all—of the 1964 NFL draft. He spent five years with the Eagles before being traded in 1969 to the Los Angeles Rams. After two years with the Rams, Bob was traded to the Raiders in 1971, where he completed his final three years in the NFL. After becoming a four-time finalist for the Pro Football Hall of Fame, Brown was finally inducted into the prestigious fraternity in 2004. Bob's son, Robert Brown Jr. was his father's presenter. Brown's nickname was "Boomer."

Bob Brown left his mark not only on the Raiders organization, but many other NFL teams. Kenny Stabler found Brown to be a most intriguing character.

"Bob had a massive upper body and little bitty calves. Brown could run (and keep up) with some of the backs. But most of all, he was mean. He wrapped his forearms from wrist to elbow over lengths of hard molded plastic. It was like he carried two clubs. He just hated defensive linemen and was devoted to making them pay for troubling him, particularly those who used the head slap. Bob punched back and would always go for a blow to the solar plexus."

Stabler continued.

"He was the only offensive lineman I ever heard say things like: "I try to punish defensive ends. My game is based on an attack formula. I use a Two Hand Rip Up to attack soft spots like the spleen, the liver, and the solar plexus. I think the universal quotient for the particular occupation is pain, and I attempt to apply pain constantly!"

Bob Brown was different and he was proud of it. He did things his way, and if anybody didn't like it, well, he did not send sympathy cards."

He was always weight lifting. We had a lot of guys who regularly pumped iron, but Bob was the only one who ever pumped in the dining hall. He carried a dumbbell to lunch and did curls with one hand while he ate. An ambidextrous eater, he would then switch his fork and dumbbell into the other hand and continue. Dumbbells looked like cufflinks in Bob's hands.

Bob was one of the most powerful men Pete Banaszak had ever seen.

"On his first day of training camp after coming over from the Rams in 1971, guys were just jacking around on the practice field. Bob Brown lined up in his stance in front of one of our wooden goalposts. Then he fired out and laid a forearm smash on the upright. The post shattered and toppled over dragging the crossbar to the ground.

'Can you believe that big fucker?' I said to Stabler. 'Breaking a damn goalpost with his forearm?'

"'He's in the room next to ours,' Pete said. 'I hope he doesn't slam the wall.'

"I think everyone was about half scared of Bob Brown, including his roommate Gene Upshaw," said Banaszak.

"One night I head six or seven gunshots go off in rapid fire right outside my room. Freddy came in and I asked him what was going on.

"'Bob Brown brought some pieces from his handgun collection to camp,' Freddy said. 'He's out back firing into the air to check the gun's action or something.'

"'Or something?' I said. 'Did you tell him that might not be the best idea?'

"'Would you tell him that?' Freddy asked.

"'No.

"So Bob continued to fire his gun—without complaints.

"Bob played the weak side of the line. This made him uneasy. He took his complaint to Kenny Stabler.

"The Raiders got the reputation in 1973 of being a left-handed team," said Stabler. "The media kept reporting that we ran mostly to the left side because I was left handed. We did run left more, even without the tight end set over there, but it had nothing to do with me. We had Shell and Upshaw over there and they buried people.

"Bob Brown didn't like to be thought of as a player on the *weaker side* of the line, and he kept complaining in practice that we didn't run off right tackle enough. The next thing I knew, we went to the line of scrimmage in a game and Bob registered his complaint so that all could hear.

"'Can I please get a few fucking plays run to my side?' he said in that booming voice of his.

"I looked over at that small mountain glaring at me and I nodded. The next play went right over the top of him, and everyone on the opposing line knew it would. All Bob did was drive his defensive end about four yards off the line while tying up the linebacker at the same time.

"Bob Brown kept himself in great shape, loved to play, and he was that rare offensive lineman who played football mad . . . all the time

GEORGE BUEHLER: *THE FOG, THE MAD SCIENTIST*

Guard George Buehler stood 6' 2" and weighed 260 pounds. He was drafted by the Raiders out of Stanford in the second round of the 1969 draft.

George was considered to be the strongest man on the team. He was a stellar athlete, but had a habit of losing interest in the game. Sometimes the other linemen would have to slap him around in the huddle to bring him back. Left guard Gene Upshaw said this about George: "He did have a tendency to drift a bit. Yelling at him didn't always work. He seemed to have his mind on a hundred different things other than the game. It took a good slap to get him concentrating again."

Fullback Pete Banaszak tells about a particular game when the Raiders' were behind and driving for a last minute go-ahead touchdown.

"Everyone was deadly serious as they listened to Kenny Stabler call the play. Then, all of a sudden, Buehler started talking to me and asked, "Where'd you get those shoes? I've been thinking about changing mine and maybe I'll try a pair like yours. I like that fancy design.'

"We called George 'The Mad Scientist' because he loved electronic gadgets. He made a little remote controlled tank that he used to send out to pick up his mail every morning."

George also liked remote controlled airplanes. Unfortunately for George, he didn't know how to use the controls. He brought a plane to training camp one day. We were all in full gear ready to scrimmage and George started flying his airplane around the field. The coaches told him to put the toy away but something was wrong with the controls. The plane started diving at us almost as though there was a crazed pilot flying it. Buehler was punching the control box with his fist and cussing while everyone else was running around ducking and dodging. Finally, the plane crashed into the goal post.

Someone screamed, "Buehler, what the hell happened?"

He answered, "I lost contact!"

CLARENCE DAVIS: *C. D.*

Clarence Davis was a 5' 10", 195-pound running back out of USC. He was the fourth round pick of the Oakland Raiders in the 1971 NFL draft.

One time we were playing in Pittsburgh and Clarence Davis came up to my room with a big smile on his face. He said, 'Tate, I just gave an interview for you.'

'Meaning what?' I asked.

"Clarence started explaining with a smirk on his face. 'You remember the time we went out to dinner in Oakland and you left me? Remember, Tate? Remember that time when you left with that big dude's lady friend?'

"I remembered what C. D. was talking about. One time, when he and I went out to dinner, I noticed this nice looking lady sitting across from us staring and smiling at me. Well, she got up to powder her nose and I just happened to get up to make a phone call. Anyway, I talked with her in the lobby and we both decided to leave together. She left her boy friend and I left C. D.

'Damn, C. D., I hope you didn't get upset about me sticking you with the check for dinner.' I replied.

"'Oh, no, Tate, I wasn't angry about the check I got stuck with. The lady's friend had a knife and she wanted to stick me with it. I was lucky to get away with my life so I decided to do you a favor. That's why I gave an interview for you.'

"C. D. was overly excited. I knew that he must have really stuck it to me, so I asked, 'Okay, tell me about it.'

"'Well, Tate, I was down in the lobby just minding my own business when this man comes up to me and starts asking questions. It was strange, though, because he kept calling me Mr. Tatum.'

"I knew what had happened. A lot of times reporters and even fans mistook Clarence and me. Really, though, I can't see the resemblance. I'm much better looking.

"The man who came up to C. D. was a reporter and he wanted to interview me. He asked C. D., 'Tell me, Jack, what receiver of the Steelers do you fear the most?'

"C. D. answered, 'Steelers receivers! Ain't none of them worth a damn.'

"Obviously, the reporter was startled at my arrogant display of verbal abusiveness or, I should say, at C. D.'s. The man asked a second question: 'Tell me, Jack, what do you think of the Steelers' running backs?'

"'Chicken, all of them, chicken!' C. D. replied.

"The reporter was really taken in and he started firing more questions at C. D.

"'Do you have any respect for anyone on the Steelers' club?' asked the reporter.

"'Mister, if I told you the Steelers were gutless suckers, that would be a compliment. Ain't none of the Steelers worth a damn, and tomorrow me, Mr. Jack Tatum, will personally beat them all over the stadium. You can quote me on that!' Clarence told the man.

"The man did quote him and the Steelers read the story. Let me tell you, I had a hell of a time explaining everything to the few friends I did have on the Steelers club."

DAVE CASPER: *GHOST*

In 1976, tight end Bob Moore was sent from the Raiders to the Tampa Bay Buccaneers in the expansion draft. Dave Casper took over his position.

Casper was one of the bigger tight ends of his day. A product of Notre Dame, "Ghost" stood 6' 4" and weighed in at 240 pounds. In 2002, Casper was inducted into the Pro Football Hall of Fame. His presenter was his former coach, John Madden.

Dave Casper, like the rest of the team, was a little "different." According to offensive guard and former Notre Dame teammate Steve Sylvester, Dave was sometimes a bit . . . weird.

"Sometimes he was one of the guys. He played golf on Tuesdays and he was involved in all the tournaments. But sometimes, after games, when we would go hang out, he would go down to the estuary by himself and get his fishing rod and fish. Hey, on that team everybody beat their own drum.

"Madden loved Casper. He loved his weirdness. 'He's off the wall!' John would say.

"Casper would draw up these crazy plays on the blackboard. 'This is what we gotta do!' It'd be something like a tight end around double reverse. Madden would love to watch it happen—on paper. But he'd never use the plays."

Raiders guard George Buehler would sometimes be totally lost when talking with Casper.

"He'd frequently say things to you that you sort of wondered about. If you walked up to him and asked him a question, he'd ponder the answer for a second or so. Then he'd give you a series of confusing answers."

Defensive tackle Dave Rowe enjoyed conversations between Madden and Casper.

"Casper would purposely say odd things to John and get him started. One day we're about to go on the field for practice, and Madden was all pumped up, and Casper says, 'Hey, coach, did you ever notice that if you lost something you find it in the last place you looked?'"

"Madden looked at him and said, 'Well, yeah, that's just stupid. It's the last place you looked because after that you stop looking.' So Casper says, 'Coach, one time I found something in the last place I looked, but because I didn't want it to be in the last place I looked, I kept on looking.'"

"Madden goes, 'What?' Then he goes, 'But you found it, right?'

"'No,' says Casper. 'I kept on looking.'

"And he just walks away. Madden is dumbfounded. With Dave, everything he said was sort of rhetorical. There were no right answers."

George Atkinson called him "El Strange-o."

"A deep man from a different world. Trust me. Different world altogether."

"Dave was with us, but not really with us," said Dave Humm. "He was a part of it all, but he could also leave it all behind him. He was torn between being a professor and a really good football player."

DAVE DALBY: *DOUBLE-D*

When the great Jim Otto retired, Dave Dalby took over the center position. Dave was a product of UCLA and was drafted by Oakland in the fourth round of the 1972 NFL draft. Dalby was good size. He stood 6' 3" and weighed 247 pounds. His nickname was "Double-D."

In 1975, Dave started in every game of the season. Continuing this streak, he eventually played in 205 consecutive games.

As part of Dave's wedding vows, it was included that he would have Thursday night out—for every night of his life! Now how many wives would agree to that inclusion?

John Vella had numerous stories of Dalby, as he was his roommate for nine years.

"If you had to vote for the most popular guy on the team, Dalby would win hands down . . . and there wouldn't have been a close second. That's how much he was liked, how much people liked being around him.

"Dave loved beer. As roommates, we were going to split the cost of groceries. We're picking out groceries, and he picks up a case of beer. I didn't say anything. I'm not a big beer drinker. A case would have lasted me a month at home. But for Dave it only took two or three days for it to be gone. And during that entire time, I had only one. He had twenty-three. I said, 'Double-D, we're not splitting beer anymore.'

"Fifteen minutes before practice was over, he'd always start going around to his best buddies and say, 'Bamboo Room? Bamboo Room? Gonna have a beer?' He was already recruiting for the next good time; the next time for some camaraderie. The look on his face was like a little heartbroken kid if you said no, so you always wanted to say yeah, because you didn't want to see that look on his face if you said no. You couldn't say no to Double-D.

"Dave was not a fan of the press. He didn't want to explain himself. I remember a couple of times where he would be upset when the sports writers were inaccurately talking about us, putting blame on me or George for something that wasn't even our assignment.

"Double-D was the prime example of the guy who really understood that linemen don't get attention, and a guy who didn't care to have it."

RAY GUY

Ray Guy was a 6' 3", 195-pound punter out of Southern Mississippi. He was drafted in the first round of the 1973 NFL draft by Oakland and it was a steal! To this day, Ray Guy not only remains the only punter drafted in the first round, but is the first and only punter to be inducted into the Pro Football Hall of Fame.

"Al Davis was a risk taker." said former 49ers coach and general manager, Bill Walsh. "Al knew a player when he saw one."

When Davis drafted Guy he had a broken foot, but after his foot healed and the Raiders saw his 60 to 70 yard punts, they knew they hadn't made a mistake.

"Our punter for the last two years was Jerry DePoyster. He had three punts blocked in the '72 season and I feel it was because he had to catch the ball against his body, and you wondered if he was ever going to get it off. Every time you go to punt, you wonder, 'Is it going to be blocked, or dropped?' I said, 'I don't want to go through this again.'

"People said, 'How do you draft a punter in the first round?' Because every defensive guy wanted him because he helped the defense. Because every offensive guy wanted him because he helped the offense. And of course everyone on special teams wanted him."

Even though Ray was one hell of a punter, his nervous energy allowed him to practice with the safeties—"but just practice," as Madden put it.

"Ron Wolf told him [Ray] he could play safety when he signed him. The first day we practiced, I look up and we have Guy in at safety, and I tell him to get the hell out of there. He said, 'But Wolf told me that if I signed with you I could play safety, too.' I told him, 'Ron Wolf lied!' We never had another conversation about him being a safety."

"I used to let Ray practice with the safeties [during walkthroughs] because he was such a hyper guy," Madden continued. "He couldn't just stand around. He'd always want to jump in and help, play defense against the receivers when you were walking through practices. He could throw the ball farther and harder than any of our quarterbacks, so then we started letting him throw the ball, which was safe, and it got his energy out of him."

Ray could also drink beer with the rest of them.

"If he wasn't singing and playing guitar at Clancy's, he was hoisten' a few brews with the guys," said Banaszak. "Hell, you look alongside of you to see who had that pitcher of beer and Ray was right next to you slopping them down with everyone else."

It was also known that Ray loved to hit the Circuit.

"Yeah, it was fun. First we'd hit Uppy's then the Grotto, Big Al's—from Castro Valley to Walnut Creek to Jack London Square. We'd try to get to all of them. It'd take half the night to do it, but we would do it. Then always back to the Denny's at three or four o'clock in the morning. Boy, did you feel bad the next day at practice."

Ray was content with the simple life. And the Raiders treated him like family.

"I don't like complex things. Life's too complex as it is. But as soon as I got to the team, there was that family sense. After the first day, it was like I had been there all my life. They were just like me. It made me feel at home."

Even though Guy had done well during the preseason, he was still a little apprehensive about the first regular season game.

"I had a great preseason, but when I stepped onto the field for the first real game, I was nervous. I grabbed the ball and hit it, caught it good, but when I looked down the field, the ball wasn't there. It went about five or ten yards and about four rows into the stands. Talk about being nervous—I didn't even know which bench to go to."

"When I finally made it back to the Raiders bench, the first person I saw was George Blanda. He said to me, 'You messed up, didn't you?

What did they draft you for? To be a punter? Then go do it. Have fun.'

"That hit home. I got up, got over it, and started mixing with the players. It was always like eleven guys moving at one time, and they were smoking when they did it. We were kind of like those Transformers. You keep turning all those parts. You fold them in and out and suddenly it's one big man."

Ray described the nature of punting.

"I just learned that every part of your body has a natural process, and you just have to keep everything in a natural alignment. You have to have timing and rhythm. Specifically, you don't grip the ball tight. You drop it where your foot naturally wants to be. Then you trust your instincts.

"Where the power comes from, I haven't a clue. Maybe it's the long legs. Maybe it's the muscles. Maybe God gave me something a little bit extra.

"It was at the 1976 Pro Bowl in the New Orleans Superdome when people began to talk about me hitting the dome's hanging scoreboard on a punt. As the team was walking to the line, it just hit me right then. Why not? One of the officials, Jim Tunney was standing next to me when I heard him say, 'You're going to try it, aren't you?' I nodded my head. When the ball was snapped, I knew if I caught it right, and I had the right trajectory, I'd at least come close to it.

"Then when I kicked it, I knew I'd done it. When the ball left my foot, it was a perfect spiral. It just started rising and rising. If I'd been a yard further back, the ball would have gone over that thing. As it was, the back of the ball hit the top of the gondola, and the ball fell straight down.

"I had to re-kick the ball. This time I nailed it good; went just under the gondola. All I did was lower my drop a little bit. While practicing for the '81 Super Bowl, I nailed that sucker four times in a row. When we came out on Sunday, they had raised that sucker all the way to the top!"

After being a finalist in 1992, 1995, 1997, 1999, 2002, 2007, and 2008, Ray Guy would finally be inducted into the Pro Football Hall of Fame in 2014. His presenter: no other than his former coach, John Madden.

LESTER HAYES:
LESTER THE MOLESTER/THE JUDGE

Before he was known as the "Judge," Lester Hayes was affectionately nicknamed "Lester The Molester." If I'm not mistaken, I think it was me who came up with the nickname.

This 6' 0", 200-pound Texas A&M defensive back was drafted by the Oakland Raiders in the 5th round of the 1977 NFL draft.

In his junior year at Texas A & M, Lester was converted from linebacker to strong safety. When the Raiders drafted him, they made one more change. They moved him from strong safety to cornerback—a position he didn't really like.

"I was 6-2, 230 pounds, I was a linebacker and strong safety," Hayes said. "I'm thinking, You don't move All-Americans; you move other dudes."

While in rookie camp, Lester pleaded with John Madden to talk to Al Davis about his case—to leave him at strong safety.

After practice Hayes watched as Madden spoke with Davis.

"I'm hoping, wishing, praying that Mr. Davis would say something," Hayes said.

Davis smiled then walked away. Madden then confronted Hayes.

"Son," Madden told Hayes, "you can play bump and run and you can play cornerback."

"My face," Hayes said, "dropped to my knees. I was driving down Santa Rosa Boulevard, crying."

By being fearless, proud, and tenacious, Lester turned out to be one of the best corners in Raider history.

If any player was created to play a particular position, Hayes was born to be an NFL cornerback. He had the perfect body for a corner during the '70s and '80s when the "bump and run" defensive technique was allowed in the league. In addition to his size, Hayes could run like a deer and turn direction in an instant as he covered the best receivers of the day. His strong upper body and long arms allowed him to jam receivers at the line of scrimmage and most receivers never made it past 5 yards downfield once the Molester got his hands on them.

One of the best matchups on any given Sunday were Lester and Seattle Seahawk wide receiver, Steve Largent. They were both equally competitive as well as aggressive and would battle one another from the first down to the last.

Also during his rookie season, Lester was introduced to Stickum by Fred Biletnikoff.

"Try that, rookie," Biletnikoff said as he walked away leaving Lester confused. "I thought," said Hayes, "that Fred had put axle grease in my hands."

Hayes absolutely went overboard when he began using "Stickum" all over his uniform and body. That's right—his entire body! I followed and then running back Mark van Eeghan—"The Grass Monster" also started spreading it on his jersey. However, Lester took the use of Stickum to a level no one had ever seen before. Prior to every game, he would spread an ungodly amount of this glue to every part of his body and uniform that he felt could help him in intercepting a pass. In fact, because of his excessive use of this substance the NFL banned the use of Stickum in 1981 and the rule is now known as the Lester Hayes Rule! Did he need the Stickum to help him become a better player? Probably not, but then again any small advantage helps when every Raider played to 'just win.'

Lester now reflects back at his introduction to Stickum and laughs at what it did for his career.

TED HENDRICKS:
THE MAD STORK, KICK 'EM IN THE HEAD TED

Linebacker Ted Hendricks was a one-of-a-kind player. Even though he possessed an extremely high IQ, he was as crazy as they come. They didn't call him "The Mad Stork" for nothing!

Hendricks was 6' 7" and weighed only 220 pounds—light for a guy of that height. He was drafted out of Miami (FL) by the Baltimore Colts in the second round of the 1969 draft. Like other members of the team, Hendricks didn't find his niche in football until after he had completed five years with the Colts and one year with the Packers. In 1975, Green Bay, like Baltimore, had had enough of Ted and traded him to Oakland. It was the best move ever for Hendricks and, in 1990, Ted was inducted into the Pro Football Hall of Fame. His presenter: none other than Al Davis.

"The thing I couldn't figure out was why they wanted me when they already had Irons and Villapiano," said Hendricks.

The big event of Hendricks' career happened when the Raiders were at Denver and losing 17–7. In the third quarter, middle linebacker Monte Johnson was out with a back injury and was replaced by Mike Dennery. Dennery couldn't do the job, so Madden called upon Ted Hendricks. In the Raiders defensive system, the middle linebacker always called the defensive signals. Unfortunately for Hendricks, he didn't know the signals.

"In the first huddle, I asked if anyone else knew the signals. Everyone shook their head. I only knew two defenses—man to man or zone—so I used them for the rest of the game. We were able to shut down the Broncos offense and did not allow them to score again. We beat Denver, 42–17."

But Ted wasn't happy with the way Madden kept alternating he and Monte Johnson. Ted wanted more playing time but found himself on the bench more than on the field.

Hendricks purchased a harlequin mask to wear on the sidelines because he was sad.

"Madden was alternating the middle linebacker position between me and Monte Johnson. During the Denver game I was on the bench. I was very unhappy. I put on this harlequin mask that I had bought at a Renaissance Fair. It was a smile to show that I was sad underneath that I wasn't playing. The ABC cameraman captured it on national TV."

Against the Bengals in the division playoffs, Hendricks was magnificent. It would be his first full game as a Raider and with that he tallied up four sacks for the day along with a blocked punt. Al Davis was quoted as saying, "He played like a madman out there!"

Monte Johnson gave Ted a second nickname: "Kick 'em in the head, Ted."

"We're having a scrimmage. Ted is trying to vault over Hubbard's block, and he hits Hubbard in the head. Hubbard's laying knocked cold. The Ted kicks him in the head with his cleat. Not maliciously."

Villapiano said that Ted brought more than just his playing ability to the team.

"Teddy Hendricks brought the Miami spirit to the Raiders. Now, you try not to live by this, but you have to in a way. The Miami spirit is 'Help yourself and fuck the rest.' And what you mean by that is taking care of your own fucking job, and then help wherever else you can. And when you fucking dominate somebody, then you can help the linemen. But help yourself first. At the end of the day it's very true. And if anyone should know that, Ted should know. He fucking dominated."

Matuszak looked upon Hendricks as a master at clothes-lining players.

"Before it was outlawed, Teddy was a master at the clothesline tackle. One time Joe Kapp was running a naked bootleg when he encountered Teddy in the open field. Kapp tried to juke him but Teddy wouldn't bite. The clothesline went out and Kapp nearly lost his head. Kapp just looked up at him and said, 'Nice hit, kid.'" Then he stumbled back to the huddle shaking his head. Teddy took pride in his ability to clothesline."

Hendricks could also take food and drink orders.

"A bunch of Raiders were riding a bus to a golf tournament in the California desert," said Matuszak. "It was hot and dusty and everyone wanted a drink. When the guys asked the bus driver to stop at a roadside store, he kept on driving as though he never heard them.

They asked again and this time he refused. Teddy didn't appreciate his lack of concern.

"'You stop this bus right now,'" he screamed. "'Or I'll stop it because I'll be the one who's driving it!'

"When the driver stopped the bus, Teddy took food and drink orders for everyone."

MARV HUBBARD

Marv Hubbard was a 6' 1" running back who was drafted by the Raiders in 1968 out of Colgate. From experience, teammate Bob Moore describes Hubbard's street fighting techniques on the gridiron.

"He was unbelievable. He was just a street fighter. When he ran the football, he was looking for a fight. Marv probably ran all of a 5.5 forty at the time. He'd start the season at 250 and work his way up to 275—and his mission was to run right over you. You'd slip off your block, and he'd be running past you, right up your nose. He wasn't trying to avoid you. He was trying to run right through you! It didn't matter how big you were, he was going to make you pay."

Madden only needed a few words to sum up his running back: "Hubbard was tough!

"He was tough and he enjoyed being tough. He enjoyed a good fight. He said where he came from you could go to a bar, have a drink, fight a guy, knock him down, pick him up, dust him off, buy him another drink and you were buddies. He said, 'I come out here to California, go to a bar, have a drink, get in a fight, knock a guy down, they want to sue me! What the hell is that all about?'

"He was so proud of the technique where he could punch the window of an establishment, break it, and not cut his hand. He did this one time too many, and the owners of the establishment informed Marv that the next time he broke a window they were going to call the cops.

"And so I called him in and told him, 'You can't do that.' And he said, 'Yeah, but I pay. I'm not running away from anything.' I said, 'But you can't break the window of a business. You just can't do it.'

And he couldn't understand why he couldn't do it. I told him, 'Just don't do it.' And he stopped doing it. But he couldn't figure out why he couldn't do it. Or why he couldn't fight."

"He played real hard and partied real hard," said van Eeghen. "But a lot of people did. One night he rode his motorcycle through the Piccadilly Pub in Castro Valley."

"It was a straight shot back to front," said John Vella. "There was a long hallway from the back door before you got to the bar and you could go straight to the front with no tables or bar stools in between. So Marv rode his motorcycle from the back straight through to the front. I'm not saying people had to dive to get out of the way. It wasn't like he was going 100 miles an hour. But put it this way, though, he never stopped."

George Buehler talks about the physical toughness of Hubbard.

"Marv played the entire '75 season with a dislocated shoulder. We had to have a belt wrapped around his ribs tied to the belt on his pants so his arm couldn't go any higher because it would come out of his socket. He went to Stabler before one game and said, 'Snake, if you're going to throw the ball to me, it can't be any higher than this because of my arm.'" Ken looked at him and said, 'Marv, we're not showcasing you in our passing attack today.'"

On one play back in 1970 between the Raiders and the Chiefs, Marv Hubbard and Kansas City linebacker Willie Lanier hit the hole at the same time.

"When they hit, the whole stadium went silent," said Duane Benson. "I thought they were both dead. Then Hubbard jumps up and says, 'Is that the hardest you can hit?' Next thing you know, Hubbard is walking toward the other goalpost. He was so knocked out they had to escort him off the field."

"Marv loved to block," said Stabler. "He used to say, 'I get this nasty little thrill out of sticking my helmet into somebody's stomach.' Then he'd chuckle."

Stabler continues.

"He was also an emotional player who took losses harder than most."

"One night after a loss, a group of us were heading for Clancy's, a restaurant in Jack London Square. We had started at Al's Cactus Room and hit another bar or so before reaching San Francisco, and Marv was ready to break something. Loud music was pouring out of the open doors of a rock n roll club in the square, and Marv hollered, 'Turn that shit down!'

"The rest of us kept walking, thinking nothing of it. Then someone yelled, 'Fuck you!' and went at Marv—a big mistake on that man's part. Marv grabbed him by the throat, threw him up against the wall, and popped him. Another guy tried to sucker punch Marv, missed, and also got himself punched out.

"After that, his aggressions apparently all out [of his system], the man who had gone to Colgate on an academic scholarship joined us in Clancy's for a nice dinner.

"But Marv could get a little crazy on the field, too, particularly when we played the Chiefs.

"Kansas City was always the toughest competition in our division until the late 1970s, when Denver came along. Kansas City also had the best middle linebacker in the AFC, if not in the entire league. Willie Lanier weighed about 240 and hit like he weighed 260. Marv went to war with Lanier every time we played KC because our full-back plays were all off-tackle and up the middle.

"Marv would take a pill that we called 'rat turds' from a Coke cup, get that jaw working, get that glazed look in his eyes, and just hammer away at Lanier. And late in the games, when our running attack picked up a lot of yards because defenses tended to be beaten down from all the pounding by then, Marv would start yelling at Lanier when we broke the huddle. He would point at Willie and yell, 'Here I come! I'm coming right at you, Willie!'

"And that's where the play would be going! I'd scream, 'Shut the fuck up, Marv!'

"Marv got into it with another middle linebacker in one game after receiving a couple of cheap shots in pileups. He stood up and yelled, 'I'm gonna get you if I have to bomb the bus you're on!'"

DARYLE LAMONICA: *THE MAD BOMBER*

Quarterback Daryle Lamonica was drafted by the Buffalo Bills in the twenty-fourth round of the 1963 AFL draft. At 6' 3", 215 pounds, Daryle played four years with the Bills before being traded to the Raiders where he would finish out the next eight years before retiring at the end of the 1974 season.

Kenny Stabler and Daryle Lamonica were two different quarterbacks with two different styles of play. According to Stabler, Daryle didn't get the nickname "The Mad Bomber" for nothing.

"Daryle was known as The Mad Bomber—a big, strong guy who would throw the ball long and throw it often. He had come to Oakland from Buffalo in 1967, led the AFL in passing, and took the Raiders to their second Super Bowl. He played behind a good offensive line and had excellent receivers in Warren Wells, Freddy Biletnikoff, and Billy Cannon.

"Daryle was not as popular as George Blanda was with his teammates. Blanda was a man's man and everybody respected him. Lamonica was aggressive, had a tremendous ego, and was always talking about how well his outside business deals were going. His personality did not sit well with some of his teammates. I liked him because he always took time to answer any questions I had. But we had different styles of play.

"In my opinion, Lamonica was a good thrower, not a good passer. Up until 1970, most teams stayed in man-to-man defenses. But later, teams began mixing in zone coverage. Daryle could not adjust because he was not a touch passer.

"But Lamonica was the starting quarterback, Blanda was the backup, and I accepted the role of third stringer. The 1970 season was devoted to learning and getting to know my teammates."

JOHN MATUSZAK: *THE TOOZ*

Missouri defensive end John Matuszak was the first pick of the Houston Oilers in the 1972 NFL draft. The 6' 8", 280-pound Matuszak played one year with the Houston before spending a year in the WFL with the Houston Texans. From there he found himself with the Kansas City Chiefs, but that only lasted for two years. Like with other misfits and rebels, the Raiders signed John to a contract in 1976 (after the Chiefs had traded him to the Redskins where he didn't last through training camp)—even though he had a long list of former coaches, former teams, behavioral problems, and substance abuse issues.

A week following his release from Washington, Matuszak received a call from Al Davis.

"I received a call from the Raiders telling me that Al Davis wanted to meet with me. He was interested in signing me with Oakland. With all the crap Al had probably heard about me, I'm sure he wanted to see if I had three eyes and a pair of heads.

"I was a little nervous about meeting Al since I had had two previous encounters with the team: I bloodied one of their quarterbacks and cursed their sideline. In both incidents, I was playing for the Chiefs.

"In one game, I tackled Clarence Davis just as he was about to run out of bounds. It was a hairline call that could have gone either way. But John Madden went haywire. He started screaming at the refs, demanding that they call a penalty. If the hit had been obvious, I would have minded my own business. But I didn't think John had reasonable grounds for arguing so wildly on such a borderline call. Obscenities were exchanged between me and the Raiders and I ended up giving them the 'we're number one' sign—to no one in particular.

"My other run in with the Raiders was when they replaced Kenny Stabler with George Blanda. George was forty-eight years old and at the end of his career. When the ball was snapped, his O-line broke down and I busted through for a sack. The shot was clean—helmet to helmet—but George went down hard. There was blood running down his face and he had to be helped off the field. I was worried on how the Raiders and Al Davis would take that."

"Upon meeting Al, he said that whatever problems I'd had in the past didn't mean a damn thing as far as he was concerned. He knew I could play in this league and that's all that really mattered. He couldn't use me in that week's opener against Pittsburgh, but he would definitely find me a spot on the team. He shook my hand and said he was glad to have me as a Raider.

"I was flabbergasted, close to tears. I probably would have hugged him, but I didn't want to get fired before I was hired. I signed for eleven thousand, five hundred dollars."

John Madden asked Art Thoms what he thought about Matuszak as a player.

"Madden asked me about Matuszak. He asked if I thought John was any good. I said, 'Every time we see him play, we laugh at him. He just can't do anything.'

"I didn't recommend him. They signed him anyway. He didn't have a lot of moves, but he definitely had a lot of power."

"At that point, with all the injuries, we really needed a defensive end," said Villapiano. "Al kept bringing in these other people, and I kept saying, 'Al, they're horrible! I got a guy in Bowling Green named 'Mad Dog' MacKenzie. He's selling for Carnation Foods. He's as good as these guys. Can we bring in Mad Dog? Give me someone who can fuckin' play! I'm out there on an island!'

"So one day Al calls me and says, 'I got your guy: John Matuszak. But I'm going to get him a house next to your house. And I want you to watch over him. He's fucking wild.'

"And then we finally started playing some fucking football. And now we had a fucking defense. He was perfect for that team."

Matuszak never pulled punches.

"I'm the kind of guy who's all or nothing. I mean, if I'm going to go out and get screwed up, I do it all the way."

Dolphins' defensive tackle Manny Fernandez remembers an incident with Matuszak at a bar.

"It was in January of 1974. The Dolphins were in town (Houston, Texas) to play the Vikings in the Super Bowl, and me and a couple of other guys walked into a bar called the Sports Page. As we made our way into the darkened part of the bar, we heard a loud bang! It was Matuszak. He shot a hole in the ceiling to honor the entrance of the guys going to the Super Bowl."

When John Madden confronted Ted Hendricks as to whether or not Matuszak would be a good fit for the Raiders, Ted replied, "Look around you, John. What's one more going to hurt?"

"It's strange," said Matuszak. "When people expect you to be wild, talk about you being wild, encourage you to be wild, you begin to be wild. It's almost as if you become your image. There were times when I tried to live up to other peoples' expectations, be the life of other peoples' parties, and I wound up getting hurt for it.

"But I don't want that misconstrued. Ultimately, anything I did was my decision."

One of the linebackers on the team was Jeff Barnes. Like many others in the Raiders organization, he was a little strange. Matuszak recalls two stories about Jeff.

"Once there was a power outage at the Coliseum after one of our practices. The entire stadium went black, including the players' locker room. Everyone was bumping and fumbling around the locker room when a voice came out of the darkness. It was Jeff's.

"'Shoot.' He said. 'I wonder if the lights on my car are out.'

"Another story has to do with an airplane. On a flight to a road game, our plane had just landed when, all of a sudden, it was approached by a man driving one of those luggage trucks. This guy was coming up on one of the wings awfully fast, but we all figured he would brake in time. He didn't. He ran right into the tip of the wing. One of the guy's spoke with the pilot a few weeks later and the pilot said the driver had caused something like $75,000 worth of damage. He was also fired from his job. Just after the incident, Jeff put it all in his own unique perspective.

"'Boy,' he exclaimed, 'it's a good thing we weren't in the air when that truck hit us.'

"Another dancer, another different drummer."

* * *

When the Raiders broke training camp in 1979, Coach Tom Flores asked Stabler if he would room with Matuszak.

"I went over to his office, wondering what was up. I found Tom pacing around with his head down, looking concerned.

"'Must be serious,' I said.

"Tom looked up at me and asked, 'Who're you rooming with in Oakland, Snake?'

"'Just like last year, Tom,' I said. 'Nobody.'

"'Well, wound you mind rooming with Matuszak?' Flores said. 'We'd like him to move out of the trunk of his car.'

"I laughed.

"'It's no joke. Last season, when he wasn't living with some woman, I hear he actually spent some nights in his goddamn car. Now we need performance out of John this year and it'll help if he's settled in one place. Will you take him in?'

"'Will I qualify for hazardous-duty pay, Tom?'

"Flores smiled. 'You're about the only guy on this team who can handle him, Tooz.'

"'I don't know if anyone can handle The Tooz.' I said, remembering our loss to Denver in the 1977 playoffs."

"John had partied the pregame night away. When he got back to the hotel in the morning, he decided he didn't like the window draperies, so he tore them down—rod and all. A hotel employee tipped the Broncos that Matuszak was in bad shape and the Broncos ran out the clock over him. They had Tooz gasping for oxygen in that high altitude the whole final quarter. That wasn't the reason we lost, but John was real depressed on the flight home.

"I like John. He's basically a good guy," I said. "And I know he felt bad about that 1977 playoff game. I don't think that'll happen again.

"'We can't afford to have it happen again.' Tom said.

"'I'll see what I can do.

"I thought it might be kind of fun. I never had a 280-pound pet before.

"Although I'm obsessive about keeping my cars, duds, and living quarters organized, everything neat and polished, I told John he was welcome to join me in the condo."

"'Hey, Snake, that's damn nice of you,' he said, 'But I'll have to see the place before I decide.'

"'You have other offers?'

"'The Tooz always has offers for his person,' he said, pushing out his chest.

"The moment John looked through the sliding doors and saw the hot tub, he cried, 'Goddamn, Snake, this is me!'

"He got right on the telephone. And before we had even unpacked, The Tooz, myself, and three airline stewardesses were all cavorting naked in the hot tub.

"John began tossing a girl into the air and catching her in the water. He grabbed a second girl, who couldn't have weighed over 100 pounds soaking wet, which she was. When he threw her skyward, the girl must have sailed up about eight feet. The Tooz gave an appreciative roar, and the girl let out a piercing scream. An upper floor window came open and a woman yelled, 'A little quiet, please!'

"John hollered, 'Quiet this, you . . .' and I reached out and clamped a hand over his mouth.

"'Tooz, we don't want to get thrown out of here the first day,' I said. 'We can have fun without riling the neighbors.'

"He floated on his back and waved his dick at the upper window, whispering, 'Quiet this, neighbor.'

Matuszak craved attention—and he knew how to get it.

"Typically, John would go out wearing a flashy multihued shirt, red, white, and blue suspenders, tight jeans, flip-flops or cowboy boots, and a pair of New Wave wraparound sunglasses, usually chartreuse," said Stabler. The attention didn't stop there.

"I don't know how many times I've seen The Tooz walk into a bar, grab his shirt at the chest with both hands, rip it open to the waist, and growl like a lion at the top of his lungs. That tended to get everyone's attention.

"He particularly enjoyed stomping into the gay bars in San Francisco and scaring the shit out of everyone in them. Eyes glaring and muscles bulging, he would let out that roar and it would rattle glasses on the bar and just freeze everyone solid. He loved to see fear on people's faces.

"His favorite cry when he entered a bar with me was, 'Stabler will arm wrestle anybody in here for $5.00!'

"'You crazy bastard,' I'd say. '*You* arm wrestle!'

"He never did because nobody would challenge him.

"One night we went into a quiet San Francisco restaurant. An attractive and petite young woman wearing a tailored suit was seated at the bar near the entrance. As John walked by, he scooped her up onto his shoulder, saying, 'Get up there, little lady.' He kept walking until he reached another pretty and diminutive woman at the bar. 'You too,' he said and hoisted her onto his other shoulder. He carried them to a table in back and gently sat them down."

"'Now, what would you two gorgeous girls like to drink with The Tooz and his partner here, The Snake?' he asked, charming the women who ended up at the condo with us later that evening.

"At a disco one night, we met two young women and decided to take them to a quiet bar across Jack London Square. John picked both of them up on his shoulders and we walked down the street. Approaching the open door to the bar, John bent down and the girls ducked too. But they couldn't get low enough. One girl screamed as John crossed the threshold, bumping both girls' heads on the doorframe.

"'You big dummy! Couldn't you see we wouldn't fit?' one girl said.

"'And didn't you hear me yell?' said the other girl, holding her head.

"'I'm used to women yelling around me,' John said, rubbing her head. 'I'm sorry, but hey, you got to play with the small hurts, as Vince Lombardi used to say.'

I don't think that John and Vince Lombardi would have hit it off very well. John didn't go much for discipline and that included his eating habits.

Matuszak wasn't exactly what one would call a healthy eater. John may have put away copious amounts of liquor, but when it came to food, he wasn't a real big eater.

"We had to keep the condo liquor cabinet pretty well stocked, but luckily I didn't have to keep a wide variety of food in the fridge for The Tooz," said Stabler.

"His meals basically consisted of Cheese Whiz smeared on bagels. That's about what he lived on—Cheese Whiz, bagels, and Crown Royal. Not exactly The Breakfast of Champions.

"He used to tell me all the time that I shouldn't smoke. He once told me, 'It's a terrible habit. Take up pocket pool instead.'

New experiences were plentiful when The Tooz was in town.

Sadly, John Matuszak died of a heart attack on June 17, 1989. He was only thirty-eight-years-old at the time.

On Sunday, June 25, 1989, I was asked by the New York *Daily News* to write an article about how I remember John. Here is that article.

The Two Toozes: Fans Came First for Big John

It seems ironic that several months ago I sat watching my friend and former teammate John Matuszak on a TV show. He was playing the role of a veteran football player in the twilight of his career, trying to retain his position on the team by using steroids, who then tragically dies of a massive heart attack on the field.

John had become a fairly good actor. He made you believe in his character and that such a thing could happen in pro football. But that was Hollywood, that was make believe. If you don't get it right the first take, you film it again and again if necessary.

In real life, you don't always get a second chance. Such as a week ago, Saturday night, for my friend 'Tooz,' when he died of a real heart attack in Los Angeles.

Larger Than Life

My first reaction was disbelief. After all, how could such a huge, strong man succumb to a simple heart attack? He was in perfect physical condition and could have still invoked fear in opposing NFL quarterbacks.

But yet it was true. Big John Matuszak was dead at age thirty-eight.

It's difficult to speculate what killed John Matuszak. As it stands now, the county coroner's office is conducting tests to find answers.

Perhaps it was those years of hard living that had finally caught up to him. I'd known John for almost twenty years, first meeting him while playing against Tampa University my senior year at Villanova, then as an opponent and teammate in the NFL.

John was larger than life. He was an intimidator and, at 6' 9", 290 pounds, he was physically bigger than any man I had met or seen.

His mere presence attracted immediate attention, but he seemed to love the fame and notoriety, and perhaps that's why he chose Hollywood to live in and acting as his vocation after football.

But there was another side of Tooz. It was almost as though he were two different people.

The other Tooz was always the last player out of the stadium parking lot after a game because he could never say no to anyone seeking his autograph.

I can recall talking to John in Reno aout today's pro athletes earning huge sums of money and then charging kids for their autographs. I listened to the anger in his voice as he vehemently objected to the practice—he insisted pro players owe it to fans to oblige them with such a small token.

The other Tooz was a man who would go just about anywhere to appear at a charity event. He would travel for hours from Oakland to places like Sacramento, Stockton, Modesto, or Fresno to speak at Pee-Wee football dinners or Boy Scout luncheons. There were seldom any fees involved.

My most vivid memory of John Matuszak is of the Sunday night after we had just beaten the Vikings in Super Bowl XI, and were winding down from the greatest party ever thrown by Al Davis. It was 5 a.m. and I was walking through the lobby of the Newport Beach Marriott with a friend of mine, Dan Bruscella. There was Tooz—still signing autographs.

I introduced Dan to John and asked if he would sign a football for him. He obliged by signing the ball. The next thing I knew, Tooz makes like Kenny Stabler and sends Danny deep down the middle of the lobby for a bomb. He hit Danny with a perfect spiral, just missing a crystal chandelier by inches, in full stride in front of the elevator for an imaginary touchdown. Then John proceeded to high-five anyone still left in the lobby. As I got into the elevator, I turned and saw Tooz had gone back to signing more autographs.

JIM OTTO: *DOUBLE-O*

"Double-O," as he was called, was a 6' 2", 255-pound center out of Miami (FL). Otto joined the newly founded Oakland Raiders in 1960 and, for the next fifteen seasons, was the only starting center the Raiders ever had. He was one of only three players to see action in all of the Raiders' 140 regular season games over the AFL's ten-year history.

More than anything, Jim wanted to play for the NFL, but no offers came around. But in 1959, the AFL held its first draft and Jim was drafted by the Minneapolis franchise which later became the Oakland Raiders.

"I was notified by telegraph, and I had to ask where the hell was Oakland," Otto said. "I signed for $8,000."

Whenever we played the Steelers, it was always Joe Greene vs. Jim Otto.

Here were two men who defined the AFC title game's matchup at the line of scrimmage—Green at the top of his career and Otto, called "Pops" by his younger teammates—in his fifteenth season, 223 consecutive start, and his final game.

Greene tried to rally Otto on the field but Jim simply said, "How's your wife and children, Joe?" That was Double-O's way of saying, "Shut up and play!"

For six seasons, Greene had done battle with Otto.

"I mean, you hit him in the head and your helmet would just . . . ring!" Greene said. "You had to deliver a blow with your helmet, and hitting him with your helmet was not something that you cherished. First, you had to get your 'mind right' as we used to say."

Jim was taught to lead with his head, as did most of the players of that time.

"Well, in being taught to lead with your head and shoulders to make a tackle, and basically place your head to where it's going to hit the ball, because you get some good fumbles that way when you tackle and place your head and shoulders to where you're going to hit the side where he's carrying the ball. And then being in that position to hit the ball, the runner drops his head, the quarterback drops his head or whatever it might be, and you have head-to-head contact.

"You're the tackler, and *you* get fined! Now, I don't think that's fair. I think some of these below-the-waist blocks as well, sure, you stand to hurt a knee or stand to hurt something, I don't have knees anymore. And sure, this hurts, but you know, and it can hurt somebody, but I don't think a guy should get fined for doing something he was taught to do all his life. Uh-uh, can't do it, you know?"

Jim once returned to the sideline in 1973, his forehead oozing blood that streamed over the bridge of his nose; a screw inside Otto's helmet was the cause. The team trainer approached Jim to help stop the bleeding.

"Get away from me!" Otto growled. I thought, *Double-O likes it! He thinks the blood will intimidate his opponent!* He had no idea that it intimidated me!

Jim refused to listen to his body when it was telling him to stop.

"I was very physical and never cared how I came out of it," Otto said. "It was almost like being a kamikaze pilot, and I've been fortunate enough to have landed when my wheels were down."

Double-O retired in 1975 and was inducted into the Pro Football Hall of Fame in 1980—the first Raider to of many to come. And I'm sure I don't have to tell you who his presenter was . . . who else but Al Davis!

CHARLES PHILYAW

Charlie Philyaw was a one-of-a-kind guy and to say that he was different would be an understatement. He was a defensive end out of Texas Southern. At 6' 9" and 276 pounds, he was a giant of a man. The Raiders drafted him in the second round of the 1976 NFL draft. Though large in stature, it always seemed as though Philyaw was in a perpetual state of confusion.

"One day on his way to practice, Philyaw stepped in a hole and sprained his ankle," said Tatum. He limped his way through the day and later that night came over to our room to see the doctor. Philyaw was standing in the hallway outside our room, all six feet nine inches of him, explaining his problem to Skip. Philyaw was saying, 'Trainer say to get the whirlpool from you.'"

"What you talkin' about, Dummy?" Skip screamed at Philyaw.

"'Trainer say you have the whirlpool and I need it for my ankle,' Philyaw explained as he started taking off his shoe to show Skip his swollen ankle."

"Skip turned to me for help and asked, 'Tate, what's this big dummy talkin' about?'"

"I just shrugged my shoulders and rolled over in bed. I wasn't about to get mixed up in any of Skip's and Philyaw's communication problems.

"Skip slammed the door in Philyaw's face and stormed over to the phone. He called the trainer and cussed the man out. Skip wanted someone, anyone, to teach Philyaw the difference between the team's doctor and the team's cornerback. Skip didn't stop with a phone call to the trainer either. He called Big Red, El Bago, Tom Dahms, and even one of the owners. Skip cussed and screamed for over an hour, and that was the last time Philyaw came after Skip for medical attention.

"Next day at practice, Philyaw came over to Skip and said, 'Hey, man, you know, all this time I've been thinking you were the doctor. Can you believe that?'

"Skip had to hold himself back from killing him."

John Matuszak saw Philyaw as a one-of-a-kind man.

"Charles Philyaw was a sideshow by himself. But I want to make it clear that I am not trying to poke fun at Charles. He was one of the nicest people I ever met and I always considered him a friend. He was a good football player, and his unusual way of doing things kept everyone smiling.

"Charles weighed in at 276 pounds and was always hungry. One day he was complaining during practice that he was starving. Fred Biletnikoff heard him moaning and generously directed him toward George Blanda. This was near the end of George's career and he wasn't getting much playing time at games or in practice. Fred told Charles that George's sole function at practice was to take food orders for the rest of the guys. Charles walked up to George and put in an order for a hamburger. George nearly killed him.

"Another story involves Phil Villapiano. Phil would always look out for Charles and help him whenever he saw he was having problems. In one game, Charles was unexpectedly inserted into the lineup against the Steelers. As always, he was more than willing, but they ran a lot of traps and misdirection plays, and their offense could be confusing if you weren't familiar with it. Charles was falling for too many fakes. Phil used to have an uncanny knack for guessing the other team's plays. Right before each play, he began to whisper to Charles what he thought was coming. Phil was often right and Charles had a great game.

"The following week, Charles was back in the starting lineup. Before the first defensive play, Phil noticed that Charles was staring at him as they waited for the offense to break its huddle. When the offense got to the line of scrimmage, Charles was still staring. Phil didn't know what Charles was up to, but he had no time to worry about it. He had a play to stop. Finally, just before the ball was snapped, Charles cupped his hands over his mouth and whispered to him, 'Hey Phil, aren't you going to tell me what to do this week?'

When a player gets a minor injury, he's instructed to come and watch the other guys practice. Injured players always feel awkward and insecure, and they usually don't like to call much attention to themselves. Most guys dress accordingly, in some basic shorts or sweats, certainly nothing flamboyant.

One day Charles sprained an ankle and came by practice to watch. He had on skin-tight shorts with his car keys dangling from a belt. He was wearing a tennis shirt, a hat, and a pair of sunglasses. Over two different color socks, he had a regular shoe on his good foot and a sandal on his bad one. He was also sipping on a coke. Other than that, Charles blended right in.

Philyaw was a great guy, but sometimes he didn't have both oars in the water. Just ask Dave Rowe.

"Charlie was extremely naïve. One day, Charlie comes by and says, 'Hey, van Eeghan, how come you have both your names on your jersey?' Mark explains to him that van Eeghen is his last name and that his first name is Mark. But Charlie still wanted both names on his jersey like van Eeghen.

"One day he got towed into training camp. When I asked him what happened, he told me, 'I ran out of gas. I didn't have any money on me.'

"I asked him if he had a credit card and he said he had a Master Card. I asked him why he didn't use it to buy gas. He told me, 'You can use that to buy gas?'

"Charlie was a really nice guy. He had a world of talent. He just had a difficult time with learning defenses and utilizing basic, common sense."

Jack Tatum gave Philyaw the nickname, "King Kong."

"We named Charley King Kong. To say that Charley was sometimes a little slow catching on is an understatement. At practice, Charley hurt his hand and needed medical attention. He walked over to Pete Banaszak, holding his hand and asked, 'Hey, man, what should I do?'

"'Go see the doctor,' Pete told him.

"'The doctor?' Philyaw asked.

"'Yeah, the doctor,' Pete said.

"Instead of Philyaw walking over to the *team* doctor, he walked out into the middle of a pass defense drill and pulled Skip Thomas aside, saying, 'Man said I should show you this,' and he stuck his bloody paw in Skip's face. Obviously he had forgotten his last encounter with Skip.

"Coach Madden asked, 'Philyaw, what the hell are you doing?'

'Showing my hand to the doctor.' Charley answered. 'The man said that I should show it to the doctor.'

'Get that man the hell out of my sight!' Madden screamed.

"Every morning the offense and defense went to separate film rooms and view game films. One morning, Philyaw was sitting in the offensive film room ten minutes before someone said, 'Philyaw, you're in the wrong room.'

"Defensive coach Tom Dahms had a nice meeting going without Charley, and when someone said, 'Coach, Philyaw isn't here,' and he answered, 'Good!'

"During a morning practice session, Philyaw had hurt himself once again. He wasn't expected to practice for a couple of days, but that afternoon, like a good rookie, Philyaw was back on the field. Like before, Charley was wearing one shoe on his good foot and a sandal on the one he had sprained, but that wasn't all. This time Charley had on different colored socks, the wrong colored jersey, no belt, and his thigh pads were upside down. Everyone stopped and stared in disbelief. The coaches took Charley aside and started counting up the things wrong with his uniform. Philyaw set an NFL record with ten things wrong with his uniform."

ART SHELL

Shell was drafted by the Raiders in the third round of the 1968 NFL-AFL draft. The 6' 5", 265-pound guard turned tackle out of Maryland Eastern Shore (now University of Maryland-Eastern Shore) developed a great respect for the man who played opposite him on game day.

"I always felt that you didn't have to hate each other on the field," said Shell. "From high school to the pros, I always heard that I wasn't mean enough, but I sincerely mean it that you don't have to be angry to play football. It is a job, and you treat it as such. I think that during the course of my 15-year career, I was angry three times about something that someone on the other team did to me."

The one thing that bothered Shell the most was allowing his man to sack Stabler. He took it personally.

But it's something that didn't happen often. Kenny Stabler can attest to that.

"Art possessed natural strength," said Stabler. "He was very quick on his feet and could move accordingly to the oncoming pass rusher. He completely dominated the line of scrimmage and saved my ass more than once."

When Shell was ready to enter the NFL-AFL draft, he thought that the Chargers would take him.

"I drew interest from a lot of teams, and I really thought I'd go to San Diego. All I got from the Raiders was a questionnaire. But the Raiders drafted me in the third round. As I understand it now, the Raiders missed out the year before on drafting Kansas City linebacker Willie Lanier, who had played at a historically black, small school, Morgan State and they vowed that if a talented small school player was available, they weren't going to miss out on him. But back then, what got my attention about the Raiders was watching their games on television and seeing Jim Otto snap the ball without looking!"

Shell became a starter in 1970 and held the position until he retired in 1982.

"The coaches told me that if I didn't win a starting job within three years, I should quit," Shell said.

Against opponents Upshaw and Shell *were* the left offensive side of the line of scrimmage. They were two completely different men. Shell was quiet while Upshaw was loud and brash. Even though it was Gene who usually did all the talking, the players would come to Art in the huddle, knowing that when he had something to say, Stabler would listen.

"When Snake walked into the huddle, it was his, but if I had something to say, I'd catch him before the huddle. I used to be the carrier pigeon for Cliff Branch. Cliff would insist he was open and could go deep, so I'd talk to Snake about it and he'd tell me that Cliff thought he was open but he didn't see the safety rotating back. So I go to Cliff and tell him that he didn't see the safety rotating back, but it got to the point where Cliff was always open."

My most vivid memory of Art Shell occurred in my rookie season. It was my second, professional, regular season game and we were playing the powerful Green Bay Packers at Lambeau Field.

We had just lost our opener to the Steelers in Pittsburgh, however, in the fourth quarter I was able to get free for two long touchdown catches thrown by Lamonica. Since it worked with the Steelers, John Madden and then wide receiver coach Tom Flores decided we would continue bombing away with Lamonica.

Guarding me that day for the Packers was All-Pro cornerback Ken Ellis. We had never played against each other before and early in the game I was able to break free for a 56-yard catch. That didn't sit too well with Ellis and he began taunting me throughout the first half. Occasionally he would take a swing at me when the officials were not looking.

Enter Art Shell! Art saw what was going on and he wasn't about to let anyone cheap shot his teammate. So big Art got in between Ellis and myself during an altercation. He simply told Ellis to back off in so many words and waited for Ellis to turn and walk away—which he did.

From that point on and throughout my career, all I had to do was ask Art for a little help if I ever had a problem with a defensive back and the problem was solved quickly and efficiently.

As big as Art was, he was incredibly agile and mobile. I witnessed Art dunk a basketball from a standing position and as gentle as his demeanor was, he could seriously hurt you if he wanted to! I'm glad he was on my side and not my opponent!

In 1989 Art was inducted into the Pro Football Hall of Fame. His presenter, of course, was Al Davis. Along with Willie Wood of the Green Bay Packers, Art was enshrined with Pittsburgh Steeler foes, Mel Blount and Terry Bradshaw.

That same year, Al Davis named Art Shell the head coach of the Raiders. Art was the first black head coach in the NFL.

OTIS SISTRUNK

6' 4", 265-pound, defensive lineman Otis Sistrunk never attended college, but was discovered at a Los Angeles Rams tryout by Al Davis. Sistrunk was one of the first NFL players to sport a shaved head. He was also instrumental in helping the Raiders obtain their misfit image. He gained national attention on *Monday Night Football*, when commentator Alex Karras said of Sistrunk: "He's from the University of Mars."

The reason Karras said that was because when Sistrunk came over to the sidelines for an interview (it was really cold that night), steam was coming from his head. Otis actually like the nickname, "The Man From Mars."

Sistrunk arrived in Oakland in 1972.

"When I got to Oakland in '72, John told me later, they knew nothing about me. 'Did he just get out of jail, or what?' They were taking a chance. 'Who's this guy Treetrunk?' So you come in with your big cigar and your Dashiki, and you start doing your thing.

"When John asked me what position I played, I told him 'all four.' 'Which one do you want?' I said, 'I play all four. Just say the magic word. Whatever makes the Raiders win, that's what I'll play.' When you make a boast like that, you better back it up. So I played in the first exhibition against Baltimore, and afterwards Madden said, 'You proved it.'"

Madden agrees that he knew nothing about him.

"We had no background on him. We had no idea how old he was. And I never did know. He looked old then. When he played for us he could have been anywhere between thirty and sixty. But he was good—good enough to start the season. He was just a natural defensive lineman."

KENNY STABLER: *SNAKE*

Kenny Stabler, a product of Alabama's Crimson Tide, was drafted by the Raiders in the second round of the 1968 NFL-AFL draft. At 6' 3", 215 pounds, Stabler rode the bench during his first three years as a Raider. Game plans and playbooks were not a strong part of his vocabulary. *The Snake*, as he was nicknamed, would always be a sandlot type of player—in other words, if you got open, he'd find you.

Kenny got his nickname in high school after he zigged and zagged and snaked up the field for a 70-yard touchdown on a punt return. He was also a great pitcher. As a matter of fact, the Houston Astros drafted him right out of college.

But Stabler marched to the beat of a different drummer.

"I didn't study in front of film like a Peyton Manning. I went out and played the game. But remember, it was a simpler time and a simpler game. The defenses weren't sophisticated. John would give me the playbook at the Wednesday night meeting, but I didn't study the game."

Regardless of his style, Madden still thought that Kenny was an amazing quarterback.

"The whole thing is seeing it, reading it, deciding where you're going, and getting it on its way. It's something you can't teach; you're born with it, and Stabler had it. He was amazing."

"Kenny was the most accurate fucking thrower I've ever seen," said Pete Banaszak. "If you wanted the ball between the four and the zero, he'd put it there. If you wanted it in the ear hole, Kenny could put it there, too."

"The ball sure didn't have a lot of velocity on it, but I think accuracy is the thing that's overlooked and underrated," said Stabler, "That was my game. It's not just a high completion percentage or quickness of release. It's where you put the ball. I had a pretty good knack of putting the ball where ever I wanted."

"The bigger the situation, the calmer he got," said Madden. "That was a great combination with me, because I was just the opposite. I was intense. If everything was normal, and we were ahead, he'd get bored. He had to have his ass in the fire to get really focused in on something. Then, when he really got focused in, instead of getting excited and tight, he'd get calm."

John gave an example of how incredibly calm Stabler was.

"It was 1977 and we were playing the Colts. The game had gone into double overtime. I was thinking of a play to call, or three plays. 'We'll do this, or this.' So anyway, he was listening to me, he had his helmet cocked up, and he was taking a drink, and he says, 'These fans are getting their money's worth today.' I just looked at him in awe."

In sticking with his calm and cool demeanor, John Vella mentions how he never saw Stabler criticize a player.

"I want to tell you what I never saw him do. I never saw him chew guys out. He never once singled a guy out. It was always, 'We'll get 'em on the next play.'"

When the game was on the line, it was known how Kenny was usually pretty quiet in the huddle.

"He was usually the one guy in the huddle who wasn't talking," said Bob Moore. In the huddle, it was always Upshaw talking, or someone else—well, primarily, Upshaw talking and someone responding to Gene. Meanwhile, Kenny is as quiet as you can be. He calls the play in the same voice in the fourth quarter as in the first quarter. He's the same guy starting the game as he was at the end. Same guy as he was in practice. All kinds of things would be going on around him and he'd be just as calm as he could be. Strangely calm."

One reason that Stabler may have been so calm is that he always knew his offensive line would take care of him.

"In 1975 we beat Cleveland 38–17. I took several late hits from defensive ends Earl Edwards and Turkey Jones. On one play I rolled out to the left and threw a 22-yard pass to Branch. I was standing there watching the ball in flight when Jones came running at me from about ten yards away on the blind side and hit me in the back of the head. Gene Upshaw always arranged for turkeys like Turkey Jones to receive a message about their deportment, usually from a double-team.

"Look, this guy took a cheap shot at Snake. Let's take care of him," Upshaw said in the huddle.

"On the next play, Vella and Buehler dropped Jones. As he was getting up, Upshaw ran over and leveled him, and Turkey was carried off the field."

After the game, the Browns coach and former Green Bay Packers member Forrest Gregg said, "The Raiders remind me of the old Packers—nothing fancy. They just take a football and drive it down your throat the way we did in Green Bay."

Stabler quoted Kansas City coach Paul Wiggin in reference to his team's defense.

"The Raiders defensive players aren't really bad fellows; it's just that they're trained to kill."

While Stabler loved his teammates, he also had much admiration for some of the great NFL quarterbacks of the game.

"I think the quarterbacks I admired most after Bobby Layne were Sonny Jurgensen, Joe Namath, and Billy Kilmer .

"They all followed a similar pregame plan to prepare for games. I had to love Kilmer, who won a championship and led his team to the Super Bowl playing with one leg shorter than the other.

"And just for the record, all four liked to have a drink now and then. Hell, Bobby Layne was known for hoisting a few at halftime!"

Teammates John Vella can't understand why Stabler isn't in the Pro Football Hall of Fame.

"How could he not be in the Hall of Fame? Are stats everything? Ask the Steelers defense of the '70s. Who would they have not wanted to face? Ask the Dolphins 'No-Name Defense' who they would not want to face in the clutch. That says it all. They would say without a doubt, 'We don't want to face Stabler.'"

THE SOUL PATROL:
ATKINSON, BROWN, TATUM, AND THOMAS

The emergence of what would be dubbed "The Soul Patrol" began in 1974 and lasted through the Raiders 1976 season. It was comprised of the following Raiders players: cornerback Willie Brown, cornerback Skip Thomas (aka Dr. Death),, free safety Jack Tatum (aka The Assassin), , and safety George Atkinson (aka The Hit Man).

"That beard, the hair," said Atkinson. "That was part of our persona—part of our makeup. It was saying, 'Fuck you' more or less. We're here. We don't care. We're going to kick your ass and walk out of here, and we don't care whether you like us or not, but you're going to respect us and you're going to fear us."

"The Soul Patrol: I wouldn't trade them for any secondary in the league," said Stabler. "It's as simple as that."

SKIP THOMAS: *DR. DEATH*

A 6' 1" 205-pound defensive back out of USC, Alonzo "Skip" Thomas was drafted by the Raiders in 1972. Teammate Phil Villapiano talks about his overall toughness.

"He was the size of a linebacker and he could run like the wind. I thought Nemiah Wilson, whom Thomas replaced, was good, but he was so small he'd get outmuscled. Because Willie Brown had so many All Pros behind him, people would keep throwing at Skip, which was just stupid. Skip was as good as Willie. I wouldn't mess with Skip Thomas in a million years!"

Jack Tatum knew right from the beginning that Skip was Raider material.

"When Skip came to the Raiders, they made me his roommate. I knew from the beginning that he was Raiders material. He liked to beat people up, and he likes to be called *Dr. Death*.

"Skip never talked to reporters or let anyone take his picture. He said, 'Gettin' your picture taken steals part of your soul.' As far as reporters go, Skip just didn't like people. One time a reporter came up to our room to interview *me*. Skip didn't like the questions I was being asked so he threw the reporter out the door!

"The night before a game, Skip would eat four or five full-course meals, drink a bottle of tequila, smoke two packs of cigarettes, and watch TV for hours after all the channels had signed off.

"Skip also had a fascination for motorcycles and fast cars. When the motorcycle craze was going around, Skip had a dream of jumping the Golden Gate Bridge on a bike. He was going to build a ramp in the parking lot of our training camp and practice by jumping over a couple of hundred cars. Al Davis put a stop to Skip's dream.

"Another time Skip and one of our cornerbacks, Clarence Davis, got into a debate about which was faster, a Corvette or a motorcycle. Once again we were in the parking lot. Clarence was gunning his Corvette and Skip was on his bike. Al Davis didn't get there in time to stop the race and when they zoomed across the finish line, there wasn't enough parking lot left to stop the car or the bike. Davis banged off a few parked cars and slid into the practice field while Skip jumped off the bike and landed in a ditch. No one was hurt, but Al Davis sent the bike and car back to Oakland on a big truck."

Skip Thomas was given the name Dr. Death because of his tempestuous behavior on the field.

"They called me Dr. Death because I was so wild. They didn't know what I was going to do one minute to the next. I didn't know what I was going to do! I knew one thing: if I did something wrong, Willie [Brown] was going to get on my ass. George [Blanda] was going to get on my ass. John [Madden] was going to get on my ass. John was going to send Gene [Upshaw] and Art [Shell] after me. They went all the way to make sure I did what I had to do. So I kept it where it needed to be."

"Thomas used to check himself into the hospital on Sunday night after the game to make sure he was rested," said George Atkinson. "He'd do that after every home game—with his motorcycle. Can you image that? He had his motorcycle with him in his room."

Skip would *literally* ride his Harley through the front door of the hospital.

"I'd ride my Harley right down the hallway, ride it to the room, push the bed over and put it to the side. See, I'd go to the hospital after the game because I wanted to be ready to play the next Sunday. And I knew that once the game was over with I was going to do my thing. I was going to have fun. So if I go to the hospital, and then if I'm back for practice on Wednesday, I'm good to go. So I'd stay in the hospital 'till defensive day on Wednesday. On offensive day, John might even say, 'You look bad. Go back to the hospital.' They wanted to keep me out of trouble, but that didn't always happen. I had a bunch of nurses down there I'd play strip poker with. They'd have my liquor for me. They'd have a fifth of Crown Royal or a fifth of tequila, and they'd have it waiting for me."

John Madden was *comfortable* with Skip in the hospital

"I liked Skip. Skip Thomas had no one to take care of him at home. So he'd go to the doctor. Like if he had a cold or something, they'd just put him in the hospital. He started to enjoy it. Cause he was getting, like, service. So the doctor said, 'I don't think there's anything wrong with Skip. But he wants to be in the hospital.' I said, 'I'd rather have him be in the hospital than any place else he's gonna be. So just put him in the hospital. I don't give a shit.'"

Dave Rowe talks about Madden and his altercations about Skip wearing his helmet during Saturday practices.

"John Madden was like a father to Skip, and Skip would do anything for John—except put on his helmet.

"We were having a light Saturday morning practice before we left to play the Chiefs in Kansas City. Madden comes in and says, 'Get your helmets on.' Skip is looking at John. John says, 'Come on, put your hat on, Doc.'

"Skip says, 'I'm not putting my hat on. It's going to make my head look terrible. I just got my hair fixed.' Now, Skip's hair looks pretty good. He turns around and shows us, and it does look pretty good.

"'Everyone listen up,' Madden said. 'Skip just got his hair done. Skip, don't put your helmet on. We don't want to mess that hair up. Everyone, be careful. Don't run into Skip.'

"There's not any other NFL coach who would have done that. He would have walked right off the field, but that was John, and that was Skip."

WILLIE BROWN

Oakland's defensive captain Willie Brown came undrafted out of Grambling in 1963. At 6' 1", 195 pounds, Brown played tight end and linebacker for the great Tigers coach, Eddie Robinson. Denver picked him up as a walk-on but, in 1965, Brown joined the boycott in New Orleans and Coach Lou Saban traded him to the Raiders for his actions. It was the best thing that could have happened to Willie. Willie was moved to the defensive back position Upon his arrival in Oakland would end up being inducted into the Pro Football Hall of Fame in 1984.

Jack Tatum was amazed at Brown's work ethic.

"This is the truth. When I first got here, I saw Willie Brown working after practice, and I thought, 'This guy is All Pro, and he's still out here working after practice? I'm not going to let this old man outwork me.'"

Willie Brown credits that it was his teammates that made him what he became.

"They talk about how good I was, but I didn't see it that way. The things that happened in my career I attribute to the Raiders, number one—my teammates. They're the ones who helped me get into the Hall of Fame. I didn't look at it in terms of how great I was. I always wanted to be better than how great they think I am, you see? I wanted to be the guy on third down where if you threw the ball to my man, I know it's going to be incomplete. I didn't worry about how hard I hit them, because chances are I'm not going to have a chance to hit them anyway, because the ball is going to be incomplete.

"I wasn't a drinker. Didn't chase girls. I was a captain. I had to be at a higher level. I had to reel them in once in a while, because they'd get out of hand on certain days. But I didn't care what they did off the field. Come game time, my job was to make sure those three guys were focused. That's the way the secondary took it: that I wouldn't stand for any bullshit.

"You try to keep them calmed down some, make sure they're in compliance with the rules. We're not going to break the rules, but we're going to bend the rules as much as we possibly can."

GEORGE ATKINSON:
THE HIT MAN, THE PHILOSOPHER

George Atkinson was a 6' 0", 181-pound defensive back drafted by the Raiders in the seventh round of the 1968 NFL-AFL draft out of Morris Brown College in Atlanta, Georgia. Like father like son, George Atkinson III now plays for the same team his dad played for: the Oakland Raiders.

George Atkinson was also known as "The Philosopher."

"Yeah, we all liked to party, but we drew the line when we had to. There was a point, come later in the week, when you've got to gear down. To be human encompasses the whole thing—you know what I'm saying?

"You exist through a process you don't understand. You don't even know what is inside of you. And to not humble yourself and realize you were given a gift makes no sense; a gift not to be made a mockery of but to be displayed."

Madden looked to Atkinson as a leader.

"George was one of the best I ever had. He was the type of guy, if you needed something done, you could just call him in and say, 'Get this straightened out,' and he would."

Atkinson talks about how the Raiders loved to rattle other teams.

"Yeah, we had fun. We rattled other teams. Teams didn't rattle us. We had 'em scared—especially after the first quarter. We'd let guys catch a pass and jack 'em up. We intimidated people. We didn't sit back and wait. We initiated shit. We made shit happen.

"We had a special section of our locker room known as 'The Ghetto.' That's what we called it. You couldn't come down to our end of the locker room. We had a strip of tape laid down on the floor. Colored it black on one part, and colored the other part white. If you crossed that line, we'd put you I a trash can, upside down."

JACK TATUM: *THE ASSASSIN*

Jack Tatum was named "The Assassin" in a press release after a Colts game when he leveled Baltimore's future HOF tight end, John Mackey.

Tatum was a 5' 10", 200-pound defensive back who played for the notorious Woody Hayes at Ohio State. He was the 19th pick of the first round in 1971, but it would be a week before he contacted anyone from the team. He took a road trip to the beach with a couple of friends from Ohio State . . . another player who marched to the beat of his own drum.

"In 1971 I joined the Raider training camp," said Jack. "It was right after the College All Star Game. I was a superstar in high school and an All-American in college. At twenty-one years of age, I walked into training camp with an overconfident attitude, but the Raiders deflated that attitude and put things in proper perspective by introducing me to a former Raider, now retired, by the name of Fred Biletnikoff.

"Fred Biletnikoff was a balding but hippy-looking wide receiver for the Oakland Raiders. When I was instructed by my coaches to cover Fred one-on-one during a pass defense drill, I laughed to myself. red Biletnikoff had a great pair of hands and could catch anything near him, but he was slow by NFL standards. I've played against big receivers, small receivers, and fast receivers, and they couldn't burn me. Now, for my first test in an Oakland Raiders camp, they put me against a slow receiver.

"Fred ran his first pattern and I showed him why I was an All-American. Covering him like a blanket, I nearly intercepted the ball, and after the play I told Fred, 'You're lucky that we aren't hitting.'

"On the next play Fred drove off the line hard and made a good move to the outside. I was too quick for him though and reacted like an All-Pro. But then he broke back across the middle and left me tripping over my own feet. Needless to say, the quarterback laid a perfect pass into Fred's hands and he scored. On the way back to the huddle Fred showed me the football and asked, 'Were you looking for this, Rookie?'

"That got me upset and I started cussing. I told him, 'Try me again and see what happens, Chump!'

"Fred came at me again with about five different fakes and just as I went left, he went right and scored again. Biletnikoff started running patterns that quickly deflated my ego and taught me humiliation. He burned me time and time again so bad that I went back to the locker room feeling very uncertain as to whether or not I had what it took to make it in professional football. Deep down inside my pride was scorched.

"Later that evening I bumped into Fred and we began talking about practice. He turned out to be a pretty good guy and after a few minutes we were talking like old friends. After that I listened to everything Fred told me because he had the experience and wanted to help my career."

Pat Toomay knew Tatum as a quiet and soft-spoken guy (surprisingly)."

"Believe it or not, Jack Tatum was quiet and soft-spoken. He looked like Genghis Khan—he had an Asian feel to him, and he had a big afro, and he looked fearsome—but he was really a gentle presence."

Mark van Eeghen saw a different side of Tatum on the gridiron.

"He was quick to smile and so relaxed. Quick to giggle and laugh. Then he'd put his helmet on and, Jesus, the switch would turn. It was hard to think it was the same guy. Jack used to count how many knockouts he'd get on the field. Anyone who didn't get up in eight counts was a KO.

"You can't be off the field what people see on the field. That's a whole different world. It was a different person when you take the field."

Dolphins running back Jim Kiick never forgot how hard Jack would hit his target. "Tatum would hit you with all he had and do it every time. But everybody respected him."

"That's the way I learned to play from Woody Hayes at Ohio State," said Tatum. "He told me, 'You never make a tackle with a smile on your face.'"

"Pound for pound, Jack was the toughest football player I've ever seen. The only guy I could ever compare him to was Dick Butkus—as far as being ferocious. He would rather have a receiver catch the ball and drill him than try and knock the ball down. John had to tell him in practice, 'Don't hit your own players. Don't hurt your teammates!'"

While it's said that he was soft spoken off the field, Jack Tatum once got into an altercation during practice with John Vella, and just wouldn't let it go.

"We were at practice and I was hit. The hit knocked me into Jack. Now, I definitely wasn't going after a safety in practice. That was something none of us ever did. So we collided. I again told him that it was just an accident, but on the next play he said, 'I'm gonna get your ass, man.' I told him to forget about it.

"We get back to the showers and Tatum is standing six inches from me. He kept repeating the same thing, 'I'm gonna get your ass, man!'

Again, I said, 'Will you just forget it?' I turned my back and let it go.
"But Jack *still* hadn't let it go.

"We were having lunch when Jack, once again, told me that he was
'gonna get my ass.' By this time I had had it, and told John [Madden]
that there might be a fight between Jack an me.

"Madden got all fired up. 'Don't do anything! Don't get into it
with him! I'll take care of it!'

"I don't know what Madden did and I never asked him, but
Tatum didn't confront me anymore. But we didn't talk again the rest
of the year. Not a word. I saw him one time in the off-season and
we ignored each other. And then the next year, in training camp, I
thought, 'You know what? I'm going to see if he's ready to move on.'
I asked him how his off-season was, extended my hand; he shook it,
and we moved on.

"Put it this way: you were glad Jack Tatum was on your team, and
that's the highest compliment I can give any player."

"Yeah, John was a little concerned about what had happened
between Tatum and Vella because Jack is quiet, but you didn't know
what's underneath it all," said Bob Moore. "I know from *personal*
experience. When I was at Stanford in 1970, we were scheduled to
play Ohio State in the Rose Bowl.

"The week before the Rose Bowl, both Stanford and Ohio State
took their players to Disneyland. Both buses pulled up next to each
other in the parking lot. We had a receiver [from Stanford] by the
name of Randy Vataha (who would later play for New England)—a
little guy at 5' 10", 176 pounds who looked like he was fifteen years
old. Now, Jack gets off the Ohio State bus; he's about 215, big head,
huge shoulders, and he's pretty gnarly looking. Randy gets off our
bus, takes one look at Tatum, gets back on our bus and says, 'I'm not
going to that fucking place with this guy.'"

"Compared to Jack, I was Little League!" said Villapiano.

"He was a Jersey guy like me and the whole state had heard about
Jack. I thought, 'What the fuck is he?' I'm jealous. Then he goes to

Ohio State and I go to Bowling Green, and I'm still Little League compared to him. I get drafted, and I'm still behind him. Then once I got to play with him, I immediately understood why I'd been behind him."

"When you're a pro, you look for guys you can learn something from—guys you can say, 'Wow. That's what I want to be like.' I had my own way of hitting, and he had his. I liked his better.

"When Jack hit someone, it was a different sound. It was like a blow. I knew it was him just from the sound of his tackles. There was a different sound between everyone else's hits and Jack Tatum's hits. It was much more solid. Put it this way, it was like a pro golfer hitting the ball and comparing it to a guy like me hitting a golf ball."

Linebacker Ted Hendricks remembers the power and force of Jack's hits.

"I remember one specific game when Tatum had Earl Campbell on a fourth and one at the goal line. To this day Earl doesn't remember scoring. I thought for sure that somebody was really hurt.

"Another time Atkinson was getting beat by Denver tight end Riley Odoms. Odoms was running slants, and Atkinson couldn't get there in time. While talking about it in the huddle, Tatum said to Atkinson, 'Let's just switch. Take my guy and I'll take care of Odoms.' Tatum knocked him out of the game."

August 12, 1978—Exhibition Game—Patriots @ Raiders

"Tatum's most infamous collision occurred when he hit and paralyzed the Patriots 6', 194-pound wide receiver Darryl Stingley in a 1978 preseason game at the Coliseum.

"On that fateful night, Pats quarterback Steve Grogan threw to Stingley on a crossing route. The ball sailed incomplete. Tatum blasted Stingley head on anyway. Darryl never got up.

"The hit was considered legal at the time—the kind of vicious shot Tatum delivered on a regular basis. No flag was thrown. The NFL didn't discipline Tatum. That Darryl Stingley suffered two broken vertebrae and was paralyzed from the chest down was considered a risk of the game.

"In a 2003 *Boston Globe* story, Darryl Stingley said he still would welcome a visit or a call from Tatum."

"If he called me today, I'd answer," Stingley said. "If he came to my house, I'd open my door to him. All I ever wanted was for him to acknowledge me as a human being. I just wanted to hear from him if he felt sorry or not. It's not like I'm unreachable. But it's not a phone call I'll be waiting for anymore."

Stingley also claimed he harbored no hatred for Tatum.

"It's hard to articulate," Stingley said. "It was a test of my faith—the entire story. In who, and how much, do you believe, Darryl? In my heart and in my mind I forgave Jack Tatum a long time ago."

Tatum tells his side of the story on how this tragic mishap affected his life.

"On August 12, 1978, I was involved in a terrible accident with Darryl Stingley, a wide receiver who played for New England.

"On a typical passing play, Darryl ran a rather dangerous pattern across the middle of our zone defense. It was one of those pass plays where I could not possibly have intercepted, so because of what the owners expected of me when they give me my paycheck, I automatically reacted to the situation by going for an intimidating hit.

"It was a fairly good hit, but nothing exceptional, and I got up and started back toward our huddle. But Darryl didn't get up and walk away from the collision. That particular play was the end of Darryl Stingley's career in the NFL. His neck was broken in two places and there was serious damage to his spinal cord. "

"For weeks Darryl lay paralyzed in a hospital and there were times when, because of complications after surgery, he nearly lost his life.

"When the reality of Stingley's injury hit me with its full impact, I was shattered. To think that my tackle broke another man's neck and killed his future, well, I know it hurts Darryl, but it hurts me, too."

In one game Tatum didn't knock out his own teammate George Atkinson once, he did so twice.

"We were holding a 21–14 lead over the New Orleans Saints. Late in the fourth quarter, the Saints quarterback Archie Manning threw over the middle for his wide receiver, Danny Abramowicz, who was well covered by our strong safety, George Atkinson. In my eagerness to assist, I blasted in from the weak side and creamed everyone. It was a double knockout. I got Abramowicz, but I got George too.

Author's Note: Darryl Stingley died on April 5, 2007, from bronchial pneumonia, quadriplegia, spinal cord injury, and coronary atherosclerosis. Sadly, neither Tatum nor Stingley ever once spoke to each other since the tragic event had occurred.

"After that my play became sloppy. I'd go after the ball and slam into anyone that got in the way. It was early in the season and I had already knocked out seven men. That would have been a good start, except that four of those knockouts were Raiders. I knocked out Willie Brown, got Nemiah Wilson and cut his eye pretty bad too, and then there was George Atkinson. I knocked out George twice. It got to the point where our defensive people were starting to worry more about me than the real enemy.

"After George recovered from his second knockout, he took me aside and said, 'Dammit, Tate, are you colorblind or something? I wear the same color jersey as you do. I'm on your side and the deal is getting the other team.'"

Even though Jack knocked out George twice, Atkinson still took the time to teach Tatum the tricks of the trade.

"George started teaching me a few of his tricks. He said, 'I was going to teach you the hook when you first came into the league, but you were having identification problems. Now that you seem to know who's who, let me show you the best intimidator in the business, the hook. Of course, the rules governing the hook have changed, but back then it wasn't just legal but an important weapon in a good hitter's arsenal.

"The hook is simply flexing your biceps and trying to catch the receiver's head in the joint between the forearm and upper arm. It's like hitting with the biceps by using a headlock type of action. The purpose of the hook was to strip the receiver of the ball, his helmet, his head, and his courage.

"Another trick that George taught me was the groundhog." The groundhog is a perfectly-timed hit to the ankles just as the receiver is leaping high to catch a pass. The groundhog isn't as devastating as it looks on TV, but it does have a tendency to keep the receiver closer to the ground on high passes."

Following Atkinson's advice, Jack tried out one of his new maneuvers on Denver's Riley Odoms with a devastating hit to the head.

"If ever a man did have a reason to complain about my style of play, it had to be Riley Odoms, the 6' 4", 230-pound tight end with the Denver Broncos. During a game at Mile High Stadium, I leveled the best shot of my career against Riley. It was a clean hit, not a cheap shot, but I was upset because I really thought I had killed the man.

"When the play started to develop, I dropped back a few steps to give Riley the impression I was in deep coverage. Riley saw me dropping off and made a quick move over the middle and broke open. Denver's quarterback Charley Johnson wasted little time releasing the ball toward Riley. I zeroed in on Riley's head just as the ball arrived in his hands. It was a perfectly timed hit and I used my hook on his head. Because the momentum built up by the angles and speed of both Riley and me, the hit was extremely hard. I heard Riley scream on impact and felt his body go limp. He landed flat on his back and the ball came to rest on his chest for a completion, but Riley's eyes rolled back in his head and he wasn't breathing.

"Riley was scraped off the field and carried to the sidelines. He was shaken and hurt, but thank God he was still alive. After the game I went over to the Denver locker room and talked with Riley. He said, 'Damn, Tate, don't ever hit me like that again. You nearly killed me!' Then he laughed and I slapped him on the back and smiled with relief. Very few people understand the camaraderie and mutual respect professional athletes feel for one another.

"People called that hit everything from vicious to brutal but I never heard anyone say it was a cheap shot."

Tatum used his hook on Floyd Little, another Denver running back.

"I remember one game, again it was against Denver, when the Broncos' best running back, Floyd Little, took a hand off and swept around the left end with a herd of blockers leading the way. As he turned the corner, the red and blue jerseys of Denver had gone south and I was coming up fast. Floyd didn't see me coming and there was a collision at mid-field near the sidelines, right in front of the Denver bench. I whipped my hook up under Floyd's facemask and landed a solid shot flush on his jaw. Floyd looked like a magician practicing levitation just before the lights went out. His head snapped back, his feet straightened out, and the ball and one of his shoes shot into the stands. I was coming so hard that my momentum carried both of us into the Denver bench."

In Tatum's second year George Atkinson suggested that they start a contest for who would get the most knockouts over the course of the season. And you thought that *Bountygate* began with the 2009 New Orleans Saints.

"It sounded like a good idea, and we agreed on a set of rules," said Tatum "First of all, neither of us wanted to get penalties called against us so we agreed that our hits must be clean shots and legal. Next, the man you hit would have to be down for an official injury time out and he had to be helped off the field. That would be considered a *knock out*, and was worth two points. Sometimes, one of us would hit a man and he'd take the injury time out but would limp off the field under his own power. We called that a *limp-off*, and it was worth one point. When the season started, so did we. Actually, it was all part of our job, but we made a game out of it. Guess who won?"

Tatum pleaded guilty . . . but only to aggressive play.

"I came into the NFL wanting to be the most intimidating hitter in the history of the game. But some people considered me a dirty player and a cheap shot artist.

"After a few *questionable incidents*, everything began to mushroom into a serious problem—enough for Howard Cosell to dedicate one of his halftime shows on *Monday Night Football* to George Atkinson and me and our 'cheap shots.'

"It started in 1976 in a game against the Steelers, a few good hits, a knockout, and a certain coach's *criminal element* speech. From there it was picked up by the press and traveled into the office of the Commissioner, Pete Rozelle. From there some fines were issued, which I refused to pay. After that, every official in the NFL threw a quick flag in my general direction. I'll tell you like I told the Commissioner, 'I plead guilty, but only to aggressive play.'"

JACK TATUM, GEORGE ATKINSON, AND LYNN SWANN—1975 CHAMPIONSHIP GAME

"On the ice of Three Rivers Stadium, I caught Lynn Swan running a pattern across the middle. I hit him! I hit him hard and he went down. Then several plays later George just leveled Swann. He was knocked unconscious and suffered a severe concussion. Swann spent two days in the hospital.

"My collision with Lynn Swann was premeditated. I saw him coming across the middle for a pass, and even though Terry Bradshaw had thrown the ball in a different direction, Swann was still a fair and legal target.

"Later in the game, George and I smashed into Rocky Bleier and caused him to fumble. Everyone was scrambling for the ball except Steelers' center Ray Mansfield. He set his sights on me and speared me in my knees with a cheap shot in retaliation for my hit on Swann. No flag was ever thrown.

"The Steelers tried that same play again but Bleier wasn't in my area. This time I spotted Lynn Swann nonchalantly roaming over the middle, and I drew a bead on his rib cage. But then I saw George Atkinson homing in on Lynn, and with one quick swipe of a forearm, George sort of pulled Lynn down using a club-like action across the head and side of his neck. Lynn went down and George moved in toward the ball carrier. The shot to Swann was by no means an overpowering one. In fact, I thought that it had simply caught Lynn off guard and he had lost his balance. But Lynn needed some assistance getting off the field. The incident was so insignificant that George didn't even get credited with a *knockout* or *limp-off*. As the game resumed, I could see Lynn running back and forth behind the Steelers' bench.

"On the next series the Steelers' offense came on to the field, but without Swann. He stayed on the sidelines running lazy patterns behind the bench. He seemed perfectly healthy and I wondered why he wasn't in the game.

"On the next play I got John Stallworth. Stallworth caught the ball over the middle and a split second later, I hit him hard. As a result of the contact, John twisted his knee and had to be helped off the field. George gave me credit for a *limp-off*.

"When Swann was called up and told to go back into the game, he collapsed on the sidelines. One second he was perfectly normal and the next second he was supposedly out cold. It could be that it took George's shot a long time to register, but then again, I really wonder.

"The next day, I received a call from my attorney. He told me that Lynn Swann was in the hospital with a serious concussion and Chuck Noll was blaming the hell out of me and George. Noll had taken his complaint to Commissioner Rozelle. That same day, Rocky Bleier wrote a letter to Rozelle regarding our tactics. This is the same guy who tried to take my knees out. In that letter, Bleier stated that I was 'deliberately trying to hurt receivers and running backs.' In addition, I was accused of being a cheap shot artist and of employing tactics designed to seriously injure my opponents. The letter also implied that many players feared for their lives when playing against me. They demanded that some type of disciplinary action should be taken immediately.

"Several weeks later, I received a certified letter from Rozelle fining me $750. The fine was for punching Grossman, slapping Franco, and slugging Bleier. I was charged $250 for each incident. Because there was no hearing, I refused to pay the fines and filed suit against the NFL.

"At the hearing, the evidence was not conclusive, so Rozelle fined me $500 for 'unnecessary roughness' charges. Pete later dropped the fine to $250, but the money was not the issue. I wasn't guilty of unnecessary roughness or unsportsmanlike conduct. I was a victim of the system and resented it. I was even more resentful of Rozelle for not hearing my side of the story.

"I cannot stress enough the fact that football is a violent and brutal game. When people start pounding each other, they bleed. Whenever I step onto the field for a game, I expect to get knocked around, and I consider the possibility I will sustain a serious injury. If I get hit and injured, whether by a clean block or a cheap shot, I just consider it part of the game. I get hit and I hit because it is a part of football.

"The verdict was in and I was guilty regardless of favorable evidence or the NFL's lack of proof that a crime has been committed."

* * *

It only took one good hit to discourage a passive team.

"When I played, the Vikings, Browns, and Bengals were just a few of the passive teams that could hang in there for a quarter or two against the Raiders, but pain and punishment have a way of warping their will to win," said Tatum.

"When playing against a passive team, one hit—a good hit—will usually discourage the entire offensive team from getting fancy."

In terms of players who Tatum knew he could get an edge on, Hall of Fame Steelers running back Franco Harris was at the top of that list.

"On paper, running back Franco Harris was big, fast, and devastating. On paper his stats looked good, but in reality Franco was a big man who would sometimes back down. Franco lacked aggressiveness. He ran from sideline to sideline instead of aggressively straight forward.

"From my point of view, a running back is paid to carry the ball forward, and if that means running through, over, or around the defense, he ought to make the effort. Franco either ran for the sidelines when it got a bit sticky or he gave way to one of his patented slips. This made him a target for me and the entire Raiders defense.

"In one game, the Steelers were driving for a touchdown. Franco took the ball and tried [to go up] the middle. There's wasn't a hole, so I knew he would either fall down or run for the sidelines. Since the last few attempts on Franco's part had been no gain slips in the backfield, he moved outside and made a straight path for the sidelines. I had a good angle, and Franco was going to get busted before he reached safety. He realized the fact, too, and before I could get within five yards of him, Franco slipped and fell to the ground. I was mad. Damn! If a man is going to put on a uniform and play football, he should at least play it like a man!

"Under the NFL rules, a ball carrier isn't officially down until a defender either has made the tackle or has physically touched and downed a man. Franco still had the chance to get up and run because no defensive man had yet touched him. I realized that Franco wasn't going to attempt to get up and I really wanted to blast into him. I wanted to stick my helmet in his ribs or face or anything. I just wanted to hit him, but instead, lazily downed him with a *light* slap on his helmet. I didn't give the incident a second thought until I got up and saw the penalty flag.

"Once again I was the villain. The official felt that I had hit Franco too hard and he flagged me for unnecessary roughness and a fifteen-yard penalty. What a fucking, ridiculous call!"

According to Tatum, Harris wasn't the only Steeler on offense that played cautiously. "Swann looked for the easy way out.

"Lynn Swann, although a great receiver, lacked consistency on patterns over the middle. Against the Raiders, he rounded everything off and looked for openings in the zone rather than making those bold dashes across the middle."

But it wasn't only the Raiders who played above the rules. Steelers defensive back Mel Blount tried to use Cliff Branch's head for a pile driver.

"Early in a game against the Steelers, our wide receiver Cliff Branch caught a short turn in pass and was quickly scooped up by Steelers defensive back, Mel Blount," said Tatum. "Cliff wasn't a very physical receiver and when Mel had him shackled, that should have been the end of the play . . . unfortunately it wasn't.

"Instead of just making the tackle, Mel grabbed Cliff, turned him upside down, and then tried to pile drive his head into the ground. It was obviously a deliberate attempt to hurt the man and it got some of our defensive people talking about payback to the Steelers' receivers."

GENE UPSHAW: THE GOVERNOR

Gene Upshaw was drafted out of Texas A&M Kingsville (then known as Texas A&I). The Raiders drafted the 6' 5", 255-pound guard in the first round of the first combined 1967 NFL-AFL draft. Just for the record, Upshaw is the only players ever to start on championship teams in both the AFL and NFL. Gene was inducted into the Pro Football Hall of Fame in 1987.

"Gene was my roommate," said Willie Brown, "and sometimes he would talk so much I'd fall asleep on him. I'd wake up three minutes later and he'd still be talking."

"Upshaw was talking 100 miles per hour all the time, pumping you up, pumping himself up, but that was part of his leadership role," said Pete Banaszak. "His mouth was going all the time, but he played all the time. He never dogged it. That's what a leader does. Shit—if you can walk it, you can talk it."

Quarterback David Humm quickly learned *never* to tell Upshaw to shut up.

Quarterback David Humm quickly learned *never* to tell Upshaw to shut up.

"One day in the huddle [during a game] I said, 'Gene, would you shut up!' He came across and grabbed me around the throat and walked me out of there right past the ref. He said, 'Rookie, I'll tell you when to talk.' He was shaking me like a rag doll. Madden's going crazy. I get to the sideline Madden says, 'Can't you handle that damn huddle?' I said, 'I'm having a few problems.'"

Gene wasn't just the spokesperson for the team, but he was also the spokesperson for his coach, John Madden.

"Upshaw handled me like butter. We'd start off with a big argument. He was a great politician, not in a negative way. He knew how to manipulate and get what he wanted. He'd come in and say, 'The guys could use a day off.' I'd say, 'The way they're practicing today, they're not doin' piss anyway.' But I wouldn't do it then—I'd do it two days later. But I'd do it.'

"Or, I'd want him to talk to the team. I would say, 'There's something going on, and guys are doing this or that, and if you're really the captain, get it knocked off,' and he would. We had a really good relationship, because he could get stuff done. He was such a good guy."

It was known that, whenever Madden and Upshaw would argue, Gene always won.

"During one of our games," said Madden, "Stabler was constantly getting sacked. I went nuts on the sideline. I screamed at the offensive line, 'Do anything you have to! Hold them! But, I don't want goddamned Snake to get hit!' A few players later, Gene got hit with a holding penalty.

"A few days later we were watching game films when I made the remark, 'We've got to cut down on the holding.' All of a sudden a voice rang out from the back of the room, 'You said if we can't block them, we got to hold them,' said Upshaw.

"I didn't mean you got to *hold* them," said Madden.

"Upshaw responded with, 'Oh, no, I remember exactly what you said. You said, *If you can't block them, hold them.* You didn't want Snake to get hurt. So I held him.'"

"How do you respond to that? You don't!"

Willie Brown remembers the confidence that Upshaw possessed.

"When I think of Gene, I think of his confidence. He not only had confidence in himself, but in the teammates around him. He played at such a high level with such confidence in everything that guys couldn't help but rise to the occasion with him."

Raiders 6' 4", 270-pound guard Mickey Marvin commented on Upshaw's blocking techniques.

"What can I say? Gene had holding down to a science!"

Banaszak concurred with Marvin's statement.

"Upshaw was the greatest holder on our line. You'd have to get an ice pick to get the thread out from underneath his fingernails after a game because he was grabbing so much—red thread if it was Kansas City, black if it was Pittsburgh.

"But what he really had was speed. He was quick, real quick off the ball. Shit, he was fast. I had to run my balls off just to keep up with him on a sweep, and he knew that. He'd say, 'Rooster, we got to get out of there quick.' I'd say, 'Holy shit, I just gotta try and get behind him and try and hold on to him.'"

Defensive tackle Kelvin Korver remembers what Gene used to do after the ref's warm-up check before a game.

"Not only did he tape and wrap each forearm, he would soak them! The refs would check your arms during warm ups, right? Then Gene would come back and put them under hot water, and if you took that tape and put it under hot water, it'd set up like a cast . . . then he'd hit you with that."

John Vella called him "The Michelin Man."

"He looked like the Michelin Man, but I'll say this about Gene, players know when other guys are exceptional. We knew he was great. You knew he was a special guy. I would say that if there was one constant, it was Gene Upshaw."

MARK VAN EEGHEN

The Raiders opened the 1975 season in Miami on Monday night and devastated the Dolphins with a 31–21 win. During the game, Marv Hubbard separated his shoulder and had to be taken out of the game. Madden replaced him with second year players, Mark van Eeghen.

Van Eeghen was a 6' 2" 223-pound running back out of Colgate. He was drafted by the Raiders in the third round of the 1974 NFL draft.

Mark found his first training camp to be a little chaotic.

"That first training camp couldn't have sucked worse. Whatever I thought it was supposed to be it wasn't what I was doing on the field. It was just a battleground with rookies and free agents. It was chaos.

"So one day I'm sitting there in the shower, and I'm thinking, *I don't have to do this. I didn't go to school to do this. It was never my goal to play professional football. It was never my dream.* But when the veterans returned in August, Marv Hubbard took me under his wing. It was then that I realized that we had a real football team. But I also found out that I was a choirboy compared to most of them. You couldn't have found a more bizarre group of people!"

Dave Rowe remembers van Eeghen looking like a Chia Pet.

"He put Stickum on his arms 'cause he thought it'd be better to hold the ball. By the end of the first two series he looked like a Chia Pet. He has grass all over him. We started calling him 'Grass Monster.'

In my opinion, Mark was the last, true fullback. I thought he was the most underrated fullback in the history of the game. He wasn't the type of player to run around anybody. He wasn't going to put a move on anyone. His weapon was a stiff-arm and he'd just run over you, pound you, and then get up and do it again.

PHIL VILLAPIANO: FOO

When they made Phil Villapiano, they broke the mold. Phil was a one-of-a-kind player who will never again be replicated on the gridiron.

Phil came to the Raiders from Bowling Green University. The 6' 2", 225-pound linebacker was drafted by Oakland in the second round of the 1971 NFL draft.

Phil had played defensive end in college and had to learn the line-backer position.

"As the opposing quarterback called signals, Phil would look over at Dan Conners and say, 'Where do I go?'" said Stabler. "Dan would tell him, and Phil would go to it. In between getting burned, he just knocked the shit out of people. He was one tough wild man from the beginning."

Matuszak and Villapiano got along famously. Matuszak once said that Phil was "all heart."

"He would pump me up before a game by pulling me to the side, looking me straight in the eye and saying, 'Tooz, I was talking to that fucking quarterback the other day. You know what he said? He said you weren't worth shit. That's exactly what he told me.'

"I would play along by saying, 'This guy thinks I'm shit, huh? We'll just see about that.'"

John and Phil were well known for their pranks. Tooz describes what he and Villapiano did to offensive lineman, Steve Sylvester.

"One night at the Bamboo Room we got Steve Sylvester and totally took advantage of him. First we grabbed him and tore off his shirt, but that only wetted our appetites for more. Next, we ripped off his sweat shorts. Next we began spinning the 6' 4", 260-pound guy around like a top. I don't know how much fun it was for Steve, but Phil and I enjoyed it immensely!"

After summer practice, the players would shower, change, and stop by the Bamboo Room. Phil and Matuszak decided to go in full uni-form—including cleats.

"One sweltering afternoon, Phil and I were badly dehydrated. We walked right from the practice field to the Bamboo. We were fully dressed—cleats, pads, jerseys, everything but our helmets. We told the patrons we wanted to be just like any other working class person—right from the job to the tavern. Phil was in the middle of a story and it was loud in there. He felt he was having some trouble getting his point across. So he decided to stand up on a table so he could be heard. Phil is Italian and likes to speak with his hands. He was on the table, swinging his hands around, when his metal cleats began to slide from beneath him. He fell to the floor with a crash. Drinks and pretzels flew across the room. Phil banged up his elbow. Case in point: Never let a 220-pound Italian linebacker climb up on a table with his cleats on a sweltering day in Santa Rosa.

This next story has to do with Phil, Jim Otto, and some "free" turkeys.

"One Thanksgiving, Phil told some rookies about a local meat market that was giving away free turkeys to all the Raiders," said Matuszak. Phil laid it on thick. He told them that these guys really loved the Raiders and if the rookies didn't go and get some turkeys, we'd probably lose some extremely devoted fans. This was an old Raiders routine. Rookies being rookies, these guys bought it hook, line, and sinker."

"Unbelievably, so did our veteran center, Jim Otto. He overheard Phil and figured it was a pretty good deal. Even though he'd already ordered his own turkey for the holiday, Jim cancelled it to get the free one. It gets worse. Phil had found a meat market in one of the seediest, most dangerous sections of Oakland. You wouldn't go there on a dare. I can imagine the look on Jim's face as he drove there. When Jim walked in and asked for his complimentary turkey, the employees thought he was nuts. They shooed him away like they would any other freeloader. Phil thought he was done for but, because Otto was a peaceable man, he decided to spare Phil his life."

Phil may have been a prankster off the field, but on the field he tallied a lot of hits while with Oakland, but his most important hit came in the 1977 Super Bowl.

The most important hit I ever saw Phil make was in the 1977 Super Bowl against the Vikings," said Villapiano. "It was scoreless in the opening quarter when Ray Guy had the first punt of his career blocked. When Minnesota recovered all the way back to our three, it looked as if the Vikings would take the early lead.

"Chuck Foreman ran the next play down to the two. Then the Vikings tipped their hand. They inserted Ron Yary, normally a tackle, as an extra tight end. Phil knew the next play was coming his way.

"Slipping beneath Yary's block, Phil stuck his helmet directly in the vicinity of Vikings running back Brent McClanahan's heart. McClanahan fumbled and we recovered. The offense drove to the other end of the field for a field goal. The momentum of the game swung to the Raiders and we beat the Vikings, 32–14 to win the Super Bowl."

As you can see, tight ends and linebackers are like oil and water, according to Matuszak. "They just don't mix!"

"The worst shot Phil ever took was from a 49er tight end by the name of Ted Kwalick, who would later play for the Raiders."

"Tight ends and linebackers have never cared for each other anyway. When a tight end goes out for a pass, it's the linebacker's duty to bottle him up at the line of scrimmage. This leads to encounters you'd normally find in professional wrestling. Kwalick's and Villapiano's dislike for each other went far beyond this. They would go looking for each other.

"It was one of those shots you never see coming. It came on a reverse. Phil had changed directions and was running full speed in pursuit of the wide receiver. Running from the blind side, Kwalick struck Phil's helmet with his own. Phil was a bloody mess, his forehead cracked down the middle. John Madden had to run on the field and literally pull Phil to the sidelines. Phil could care less about all the blood. He just wanted to discuss the matter with Kwalick."

In a game against Kansas City, Phil had no choice but to take the guy out.

"George Atkinson handed a vicious blow to the head of Chief's running back Ed Podolak," recalls Matuszak. "They rolled through Kansas City's sideline. When one of the Chiefs came rushing at

Atkinson's blind side, Phil had no choice but to take him out with a flying block. The opposition's sideline is the one place you don't want to be at a football game. Phil somehow wound up beneath the Chiefs' bench, where the Chiefs were kicking his ass—literally. I ran over to their bench and threw three or four guys out of the way. Then I picked Phil off the ground and carried him back to the playing field."

One night Phil returned the favor to John. They were together at a local bar when Matuszak cracked a joke that the bartender did not find very funny.

"Phil and I were with a couple of the Raiders and we walked into a bar that was normally popular. That night, the place was nearly empty. We were standing around when I looked at the bartender and made a joke.

"'Hey, this place is really jumping tonight, isn't it?'

"Not hysterically funny, but a harmless statement, right? Apparently this guy didn't agree. He reached behind the bar and pulled out a 9mm pistol. He aimed the damn thing about twelve inches from my head and looked crazy enough to shoot me!

"'There isn't a judge in the world that would convict me for blowing away an asshole like you,' he said

"I literally started to sweat. The last place I wanted to die was some bar in Oakland but I wasn't about to let this guy get away with this. Just as quickly as he'd blown up, the maniac suddenly cooled down. When he lowered the gun, Phil said, "John, it's not worth it. Let's just go." "Thanks to Phil, I lived to see another day."

CARL WEATHERS

Before he was known as Apollo Creed from the *Rocky* movies, Carl Weathers was a 6' 2", 220-pound linebacker out of San Diego State. Undrafted, he tried out with the Raiders in 1970 and made the team. Even though he only played for two years, he made his mark with the franchise.

"One night at Al's Cactus Room, I got talking to a fellow rookie named Carl Weathers, a linebacker from San Diego State," said Sta-

bler. He was 220 pounds of sculptured muscle. Carl, a reserve linebacker, was real quick and a really tough hitter on special teams.

"'Carl, you're doing a helluva job on kick coverage,' I said.

"'That's my game for now,' he said. 'I like to be the first one downfield.'

"'A tough job.'

"'Yeah, and I'm only gonna do it one more year if I can't play linebacker,
too'" he said. 'This game is not my life's work. I'm gonna be an actor.'

"Carl Weathers gave us one more year, then went into acting and
finally hit it big playing Apollo Creed in the *Rocky* series. It's no doubt
his height helped him win the role opposite Sylvester Stallone, who
is only five-eight or so. I just wish he had a better shot at linebacker
with us because he had that mean streak in him that you need to be
a good ball player."

NEMIAH WILSON

Nemiah Wilson was a 6' 0", 165-pound defensive back out of Grambling State, who was traded by Denver to the Raiders in 1968.

Monte Johnson was just a clean-cut kid out of Nebraska.

"I was drafted in the second round of the '73 draft. Coming in
from Nebraska, Bob Devaney was my coach and Tom Osborne was
an assistant. Our team was disciplined and structured. You said 'Yes-
sir' to the coaches.

"I remember one day sitting in the Raiders training room and one
of our defensive backs, Nemiah Wilson, was on the phone cursing
the person he was talking to. I asked someone, 'Who in the world is
he talking to?' They said, 'Al Davis.' I practically fell off the bench!"

RON WOLF

In 1963, Ron Wolf began his career as a scout for the then AFL's Oak-
land Raiders. In 1972 he was the Player Personnel Manager for the
Oakland Raiders of the NFL. According to Wolf, "The 1972 Oakland
Raider draft was the best by far.

"We never had any restrictions on what program they would come from. We were trying to find football players. It didn't matter where they were or what their level of competition was. It was how good they were."

Coach Tom Flores had heard about Wolf long before ever seeing him.

"In camp, I'd walk by this one room where he hung out. It was always dark. All I could hear was the sound of this old Bell & Howell projector. I'd think, 'Who's that guy?' No one knew what he looked like. You just heard about him. But you never saw him."

According to John Madden, Ron Wolf was a one-man, full time, personnel staff.

"And he was the one man who could be a one man staff. I mean, Ron Wolf knew every player everywhere. Ron Wolf's mind was amazing. You could ask him, 'Ron, there's this junior wide receiver someone told me about at Alcorn,' and he would know him. He didn't have to go through notes and read stuff. He'd say, 'This is who he is, and this is what he does.' He truly had a photographic mind."

Wolf just considered himself lucky.

"I was just one of those guys lucky enough to be along for the ride and you are welcome to believe John if you want.

"Al had this desire to always find a sleeper. Someone no one really knew about. We hit with a couple of them. We always tried to pick the best player for the Raiders. There wasn't anything like need for position or that type of thing. To be perfectly honest, what Al Davis did was design that team in his mold. Those of us who were there can take some credit, but really and truly, with the exception of Lamonica, those were all his trades—from Willie Brown to Ted Hendricks. I look back at the moves he made, and they were remarkable moves."

NICKNAMES

Nicknames were an important part of Raider life.

"Getting your nickname was a sign that you'd finally been accepted into the club," said Tatum. "For example, most of the guys called Coach Madden 'Big Red.' Madden was a burly guy with red hair, but for some reason Skip called him 'Pinky.'

"No one is given a nickname; one must earn his title, even Skip. Most of the time we let ourselves go at training camp. We hardly shaved and we never wore fancy clothes. After all, nobody was going to see us except the coaches and maybe the Queen. And who wanted to look good for her?

"One day, Skip was walking over to the practice field looking the way he thought a Raiders athlete should look. His appearance was bad even by Raiders training camp standards. Someone said that Skip looked as though he was coming back from one of his frequent trips to Mars and all points beyond. Bob Brown, our big offensive tackle, saw Skip coming up the path and jumped back ten steps and said, 'Damn, Skip, you look like death warmed over, swallowed down whole, and spit back out.' Skip looked terrible, but the next day he looked even worse. After a week of letting himself go, Skip earned the nickname 'Dr. Death.'

"Everyone who's been through the wars has a nickname. My friends called me 'The Reverend,' not 'The Assassin.' They knew that I was a saintly person off the field.

"George Atkinson was 'The Weasel.' George got himself into impossible situations but had a knack for weaseling his way out.

"Some of the guys liked to use their mouths a lot. Gene Upshaw, our All-Pro guard, was 'The Pelican Jaw.' He fancied himself a politician and kept his jaw moving while talking about the issues. Dave Rowe liked to hear himself talk, too. We called him 'Radio Rowe.'

"All-Pro wide receiver Cliff Branch ran the hundred in 9.2 seconds. Naturally, Cliff was 'The Rabbit.'

"Neal Colzie, our punt return specialist, thought he was a ladies man. We called him 'Sweet Pea.'

"Dave Casper was 'The Ghost.' Dave was the whitest white person I had ever seen. At the opposite end of the color spectrum was 'Black Angus.' Football fans knew him as All-Pro tackle, Art Shell.

"Mark van Eeghen isn't black, but his kinky Afro hairstyle started the rumor about his mother running off with a black man. Most of the time we called Mark 'Black Blood,' but if he didn't crack a smile with that nickname, we came back with 'Bundini Brown, Jr.' Skip said that Bundini and Mark looked alike.

"Clarence Davis is another man with two nicknames. Most of the time, we referred to him as 'C. D.,' but the bigger guys on the team called him 'The Militant Midget.' C. D. is only about five-feet nine, and when people get on him about being short, he started making threats about the little people taking over the world and shooting everyone over five-feet ten.

"If you're going to have nicknames, you must hit Al Davis with one, too. Everyone did call Al a variety of different names behind his back, but no one said anything to his face.

"As the general manager, Al was the man who controlled the contracts and the money. It's not that anyone treated Al like a special person, because he really wasn't, and never put on any airs, but the players had this unwritten law to simply ignore the man. Treat him like he wasn't there until it was time for contract talks.

"But one night Skip forgot his wallet in the locker room and we drove back to pick it up. Al was in the weight room working out with his skinny arms. Skip started blasting on Al's physique and it was a heavy scene. Al responded with, 'Skip, we're both the same size. You wear a size 44 suit and so do I.'

"The next day at practice, to prove his point, Al came out dressed in a suit, size 44. Seeing how Al is more at home in a size 40, the jacket and pants fit a little loose. That's all Skip needed. Skip ran over and grabbed Al by the seat of the pants and started poking fun of the baggy suit. Skip was carrying on something terrible, and before long everyone was on the ground laughing, including Al.

Finally, after Skip had nearly tugged Al's pants off, he blurted out, 'El Bago!'

"And that's how Al Davis got his nickname."

SUPERSTITIONS

Superstitions are a part of every Superstitions NFL team. The Raiders were no different. Here Jack talks about the superstitious nature of the team, their coach, and their owner. The Raiders were strong believers in 'luck'.

"I knew that coaches and players alike believed in luck, and Al Davis, John Madden, and the Raiders were no exception to that rule. The only trouble was that the Raiders carried their luck charms and superstitions a little too far. I'm talking about Coach Madden and Al Davis for the most part, because they really seemed to sail off the deep end when it came to mumbo-jumbo.

"The superstitious phases of Raider mania hit the hardest in 1973, when fifteen or sixteen of the guys wanted to play in a golf tournament instead of practicing. Coach Madden understood, I guess, because the guys went golfing. Then, on Sunday, we smashed the New York Giants, 42–0. That just happened to be the most points we scored all season and the only shutout our defense recorded. After that, Coach Madden encouraged the guys to go golfing and even started a special team golfing tournament.

"The golf tournament was simple compared to the many other superstitious beliefs the Raiders held on to. It's just throwing salt over your left shoulder for good luck (Al Davis did it all the time) or the team not traveling on the thirteenth day of the month. As time went by, superstitions included eating the same pregame meal (if we won the last game), staying at the same hotel, and coaches wearing the same clothes. If we lost, then everything changed.

"In Denver, we always stayed at the Continental Hotel and we always beat Denver and we always won our division championship. I guess the Denver management also has some superstitious blood in them because they took over the Continental and moved us out. The team never really liked staying there anyway. It was an old, cinder block building, drafty and cold, and not my idea of upper-middle-class living.

"But Al Davis insisted that we beat Denver because we stayed at the Continental. Al fought to keep us there, but the management of the place said we had to go. In 1977, Denver beat us twice and won the division title for the first time in the history of their club. Al Davis went around growling at everyone and saying, 'I told you so!'

"I didn't believe in that sort of witchcraft, but then we went to San Diego for a game, and strange things started to happen. In the past we'd stayed at the Stardust Motel and the Chargers hadn't beaten us in eighteen games. As a matter of fact, San Diego couldn't muster enough points on the scoreboard to make the games respectable. But just before we played the Chargers for a second time in 1977, their management decided to move their team into the Star Dust and shifted us over to the Hyland. I don't know if superstition spurred the move or not, but we were quartered on the other side of town and San Diego had our winning motel.

"Al Davis and John Madden were upset over the deal, but it didn't shake up any of the players. We still went on with a normal pregame night (five wild parties) and showed up at the stadium early Sunday afternoon in time for kick off. The game was simply unbelievable. The Chargers won, 12–7. After that experience, every member on the team started to avoid stepladders, black cats, and new hotels. Every pregame burp and sneeze became a new ritual."

John Matuszak was fascinated with the superstitious rituals of his teammates. Here he talks about the crazy and bizarre rites they would perform before a game.

"Football is a funny game, all right, and one thing I always found amusing was the superstition. I, personally, didn't have many, but if a player did something a certain way and his team went on to win, he usually did it that way forever—or at least until a loss.

"When we were on the road, Mark van Eeghen would climb on top of his TV set, and then dive off it onto his bed. If he didn't do that, he couldn't fall asleep. But that was only one of his habits.

"He and Dave Casper would get back-to-back, drop their pants, lock their elbows together, and lift each other off the ground. You won't find it in many astronomy books, but it was the rarely sited *double moon*.

Jack Tatum had his own unique way.

"Dressing for a game, any game was a ritual with him. He took great care with his shoes. He made sure his cleats were tight and new because he didn't want to slip. Next he put on two pairs of socks and jammed his foot into the shoe. He wanted a tight fit. Then he taped his shoes on tight so there was no chance of the shoe giving way under the stress of starting and stopping."

"After that, he taped his wrists and forearms. Once all the gear and tape was in place, he channeled all his attention to the game and the people he'd be going up against."

"Lester Hayes always wore the same chinstrap he bought in junior high school for a dollar. He used to wear a towel hanging from his uniform belt, and he'd always have to have it taped exactly seven times. If the trainer didn't tape it exactly seven times, Lester felt naked out there. If that weren't enough, after every coin toss, Lester would touch the helmets of one of the veterans, usually Hendricks or Upshaw. Since they had been through the wars so many times, Lester wanted to soak up some of their aura."

THE TWO COKE CUPS

The use of performance enhancing drugs in the NFL has been an ongoing issue since the late 1950s. It wasn't until 1987 when the NFL finally began to test for steroid use.

But up until there was reported drug abuse on the San Diego Chargers in the early seventies and the league tried to cut back on the use of amphetamines, there was always a big jar of them in the

Raiders' dressing room. Players who wanted some extra energy could just dip in.

Stabler describes the effects of the amphetamines.

"The big Raiders' candy jar contained gray colored amphetamine capsules that the players called 'rat turds.' I had taken some speed in college when I was seeing a girl in Mobile and staying up all night. Typically, it would make my brain race and my mouth so dry I couldn't even spit. I'd feel like I was so wired with energy that I could go forever and do anything I wanted without having to sleep. As I was a hyper, high-energy guy anyway, I had to be careful with speed.

"I hadn't seen myself on speed, but I did see my teammates on the sidelines before and during games. Their eyes would get real big and they would have a kind of wild, distant look to them. They would be so wired they couldn't stop moving their jaws and grinding their teeth. I was standing next to Blanda before one game in early 1970 watching guys seemingly grinding their teeth down to nothing, and I said, 'They're gonna have to wear a mouthpiece out to dinner.'

"'I know. I would never take that shit,' George said.

"The guys were constantly downing Gatorade because of the chronic thirst from the pills. Everywhere you looked you'd see wild eyed guys guzzling that yellow liquid and moving their jaws like an old man gumming food—but you knew they were ready to play.

"It was all part of the game. If it made a guy play better, or made him *think* he played better, fine. The team owners and the league itself didn't care how much speed was taken until the Chargers headlines appeared. Then there was an outcry in the media, public opinion turned against the league, and that worried the TV networks that paid the NFL millions of dollars every year. The networks feared advertising would withdraw from NFL telecasts if the drug situation was not cleared up. So the NFL said it was policing the situation and, therefore, only team doctors could dispense amphetamines and other medications.

"But I played over ten years after the so-called NFL crackdown on speed, and it was always readily available to players. Guys took it for diet reasons, for hangovers, and for that extra jolt they liked to bring with them into games."

Linebacker Monte Johnson was used to a different kind of performance enhancer.

"It was my rookie year, one of the first games we had. When I was in college, I had a habit of taking salt tablets. So I walked into the training room and I asked someone where the salt tables were.

"'They're on that table in the Coke cups,' someone said.

"I walked over there and grabbed a handful. I'm moving my hand up to my mouth to pop them in, when all of a sudden someone reaches out to grab my arm. My hand opens up and the pills go everywhere. The guy says, 'The *other* Coke cup.'

"The amphetamines were nicknamed rat turds and they were just in a jar (or Coke cup) sitting there," said guard George Buehler. "You could take all you wanted."

Pete Banaszak doesn't believe that there were steroids available.

"Sure, there was some of that taken. I ain't gonna deny that. But steroids? I really doubt it. Hey, our steroids came in a brown bottle. It was Budweiser we loved. Kept your weight up, too. The trainer always said, 'Instead of Coca Cola, have three or four beers.' We had to listen to the trainer, right?"

"We didn't use performance enhancers," said Atkinson. "I smoked a little weed, whatever, you know, but not none of that steroid shit."

THAT INCREDIBLE 1976 SEASON AND SUPER BOWL XI

THE MYSTIQUE BEHIND the Raiders organization was, of course, Al Davis. But before the 1976 season, Oakland had never won when it mattered most.

Between 1968 and 1975, the Raiders played in six AFL/AFC Championship games and lost all six—each time to the eventual Super Bowl Champions.

Kenny Stabler talks about the frustration of not winning the big one.

"When you get as close as we had gotten and you're still not able to get it done, and then to get so close time and time again, the frustration becomes insurmountable.

"Tough guys are tough guys on the field, but football players are no different than anybody else. You really feel bad when you lose. Maybe guys have too much pride or have an image of being too tough to cry outwardly, but I've seen guys break down because of the hurt of not winning and I've been one of them. We had been bridesmaids far too many times."

While the Raiders could not get past the championship game, the Pittsburgh Steelers spent much of the '70s raising the Lombardi trophy.

Pittsburgh's victories were usually controversial; but that still spelled trouble for head coach John Madden. Since his hiring in 1969, Madden had won more games than any NFL coach but had failed in taking his team to a Super Bowl. Here he repeats what Chuck Noll had said.

"You did hear that Madden couldn't win the big one. But I used to say, 'Hey, before the game, tell me when there's a little one.'

"We won a lot of big games, a lot of regular season games, a lot of big games to get to playoffs, and a lot of playoff games."

When the Raiders ended Miami's two-year reign as World Champions in the "Sea of Hands" game, we did it for our coach.

After the win, Villapiano was so happy that he gave Madden the game ball.

"When we beat the Dolphins, I went right to the sidelines and gave John that football because he deserved it.

"It bothered me if I read something about myself but it bothered me even more if I read something about John. He was our man. We as players loved him and you had to watch John operate. On the sidelines he was a maniac—and that was beautiful. But during the week the Xs and Os had to be perfect. He prepared us so well and when we lost it wasn't John Madden's fault—I guarantee it."

"I don't believe in that thing that eighteen men can't win the big one," said Madden. "We have been in playoff games, we've been in championship games, but for some reason, we still hadn't won it all.

"I was really frustrated because I knew we were good. I knew we were close. We never lost to a bad team. We lost to some of the greatest teams in the history of the NFL. The worst thing you could do is get into the playoffs, lose a championship game, and panic. 'Cause all we did was maybe need a first down here, a call here, and we would have been there. The guys who have to be frustrated are the guys who only won two games all year."

The 1975 season ended with another crushing defeat. Once again, the Raiders lost the AFC Championship to the Steelers.

"We were a great team that year," said Villapiano. When we lost to the Steelers, I just couldn't believe it. Then I started actually getting a little spooked."

"There was a lot of hard hitting by both sides," said Madden. "I think it was a very emotional game and there was a hell of a lot of meaning to this game as you know. The winner goes to the Super Bowl and the loser goes home."

Losing was not an option at this point. The Raiders needed to win it all in 1976, or history would remember them as a team that couldn't win the big one.

If the Raiders were ever going to become champions, they were going to have to beat the Steelers. In the first game of the 1976 season, with the opener against the Steelers, Pittsburgh led by two touchdowns with five minutes remaining.

"They came right at us and got ahead of us, but we did have one of Kenny Stabler's great comeback games," said Villapiano. "We took them down. Kenny to Casper, Kenny to Branch—once we got going we could score quickly. Give Kenny an inch, he'll take a yard."

In true Raiders fashion, Oakland's defense ran all over Bradshaw and his Steelers. Final score: Oakland 31, Pittsburgh 28.

Oakland's victory was overshadowed by an escalating controversy. In the 1975 AFC Championship, George Atkinson had knocked Lynn Swann out of the game. In the season opener, Oakland's hard-hitting safety had done it again, and Pittsburgh's coach launched a media offensive.

"Chuck Noll said that we were the criminal element of the NFL, but that was the way that those guys played," said Stabler.

He continued: "George clubbed with a forearm and knocked him out of the game. Maybe a little outside of the rules, but that was George's way of setting the tone for the game."

"When we played Pittsburgh it was a physical game," said Madden. "Those things are going to happen. It wasn't only George Atkinson and Lynn Swann."

"Pittsburgh was just like us—very tough and very intimidating," said Stabler. "I've seen Joe Greene kick guys and stomp on guys. He's a Hall of Fame player. I've seen Mel Blount grab Cliff Branch and pick him up and shake him like a rag doll and dump him on his head. Our team played within the rules. We were just so physical that a lot of people always accused you of these things because they couldn't beat you."

As the Swann incident magnified, the Raiders' reputation as outlaws and the legend of Atkinson only grew. If the Raiders were above the law, it was because Madden refused to lay down one. Just ask Villapiano.

"We had no rules. Just show up and play your hardest. John would preach that and we would do it."

Madden saw his players' style of play as *creative*.

"These are the greatest athletes in the world. They are like artists, and if you take their creativity away from them by making them robotic, then they are going to play like robots. But if you give them individuality and some freedom then they can be and play the way they are."

In the opening weeks of the 1976 season, the Raiders mauled their competition. Oakland tallied three consecutive victories, but domination of the regular season, which was a Raiders tradition, would prove nothing as New England manhandled the Raiders 48–17 in their worst defeat since 1963.

"We got the hell kicked out of us," said Stabler. "Looking back on it, to go up there and get thumped the way we did. Maybe it's a little bit of a wake-up call; maybe it's a little bit of a blessing in disguise. Maybe you're not quite as good as you think you are."

According to Madden, "It was just one of those things."

But that would be the final loss the Raiders would face the rest of the season. Oakland's vertical passing game was devastating, and no amount of penalties could stop the Raiders' march to the top of the NFL . . . but that doesn't mean they didn't try.

"The referees got a pat on the back if they could throw more flags on us than the other team," said Villapiano. "Maybe they were coached to do it. Don Shula at that time was in charge of the Competition Committee and the lily-white Miami Dolphins were as nasty as anyone else, but they never got penalties called on them. It was like 'let's get these Raiders out of here and make everyone else's lives easier.'"

"The League just didn't like the Raiders," said Stabler. "It was speculated that a lot of people didn't like Al, they didn't like John, and they didn't like our players. They could throw as many penalties as they want, as long as you win, it's no big deal."

In week seven, when the Raiders hosted the Green Bay Packers in late October, they were flagged thirteen times and accumulated more penalty yards than rushing yards (115 rushing yards to 119 penalty yards).* But the Snake threw three touchdowns in nine minutes to beat the Packers, 18–14.

"Ever since the Atkinson and Tatum incidents, the officials had been watching the game closer and were calling more penalties than ever before," said Otis Sistrunk. "Any little thing that a guy did, they would call a penalty."

But nobody played the game quite like Ken Stabler. The Snake succeeded "Broadway" Joe Namath at Alabama and learned from the master how to score on and off the field.

"Everybody's metabolism is different," said Stabler. "Some people need eight hours, some people need three hours. I don't really need an awful lot of sleep. Sometimes I would read the game plan by the light of the jukebox. How many hours do you need to go play three hours?"

"When the going was easy, Snake would get bored," said Madden. "When the going was tough, he was ready to play. He would be better in the fourth quarter if it was a tight game and we were behind. If we were ahead by twenty or thirty points, he could call a play in the huddle and by the time he got to the line of scrimmage, he would forget what he called."

Despite Stabler's short attention span, Madden still delegated the play calling to Snake.

"John basically pitched the playbook to me and told me to go in. It made me a better player to have that responsibility. What comes out of your mouth is going to dictate a lot of success."

---

* The Green Bay Packers were also flagged thirteen times in that game for a total of 151 yards.

Madden enjoyed the fact that his players became involved in the play calling.

"I liked it when the players were in the huddle and they said, 'OK, this is what we want to do. This is a play *we're* calling.' Rather than a play being sent in and saying, 'Hey, this is what *they* want us to run.' When you put the word *they* on it then you separate it as to say, 'We're not responsible for this.' When you put the word *we* on it, then we are all in it together."

Fred Biletnikoff often had his number called in Stabler's huddle, even though his nerves couldn't stomach the pregame anticipation.

"All the time he would be smoking a cigarette," said Stabler. "He was a two-pack-a-day guy since he was ten years old. And he would push his helmet back on his head and go into the john and throw up for twenty minutes in there. And then go to the edge of the tunnel and take one last drag of his cigarette, flick it, and pull his facemask down and go make the Hall of Fame."

Stabler's other wide receiver, Cliff Branch, was anything but nervous.

"When he was a young player, he would maybe in the third quarter tell me, 'Hey, Coach, I can beat my guy deep,'" said Madden. "After he'd played for five or six years and the National Anthem would just finish, he would say, 'Hey Coach, I can beat my guy deep.' I said, 'Cliff, we haven't even played a down yet. How do you know who your guy is?'"

After a 7–1 start, everyone was pulling for the Raiders.

In Chicago, Stabler was sidelined with a concussion. But the Snake came off the bench to knock out the Bears with a pair of bombs.

The winds of fate were finally blowing in the Raiders' direction. Final score: Raiders 28, Bears 27.

"Because of the Bears missing a field goal and the wind and weather conditions playing in our favor that day, we were lucky to get out of there [with a win]," said Stabler. "I don't think you ever felt that this was our year because we caught a break in Chicago; no, we needed to catch a break in Pittsburgh!"

Since the mid-1960s, the Oakland Raiders had won more games than any other organization, and the hallmarks of Raiders football had become legendary: physical, dominant blocking, the vertical passing game, and a relentless assault on the quarterback. But the greatness of the Raiders came from their attitude. Al Davis once said, "I will do anything to win." And he wanted players who would win at any and all costs.

"The type of player that Al brought in had that type of attitude," said Stabler. "We wanted to be tough and we enjoyed being disliked. I think half our team was on a work-release program just to play."

The media called the Raiders a lot of names, but whatever they called Oakland, the team belonged to Madden.

"People said we had renegades, but they were *my* renegades. I didn't think they were renegades. If that's the way they are going to portray you, I just figure you should just take it. If that's what they want to say that we are, and we're really not, then we'll be it."

"As they say, 'If the shoe fits . . .' Oakland was a very tough, blue-collar city with a very tough blue-collar team. Al Davis was as tough as they come as far as owners go, John was definitely a blue-collar type of guy, our logo was a pirate, and our main color was black," said Stabler.

"Nobody in the league was wearing black and flaunting black like our owner, Mr. Davis, and then on game day he would wear lily white," said Villapiano.

Madden talked about a trick of the trade in terms of getting an "upper hand."

"Any time you were playing a team with a dark jersey your protective hand or arm gear color would be dark. When we were playing a team with a white jersey, the protective hand or arm gear would be white so you couldn't see them holding."

The Raiders were always looking for an edge. Fred Biletnikoff had his Stickum and Phil Villapiano had his pads. Phil gives a much more comprehensive evaluation of how those pads were used.

"As I had mentioned before, our trainer George Anderson was an expert when it came to pads. Probably most of them were illegal, but what the hell. I could take my opponent down if I hit them just right. Right from the start it became my weapon of choice.

"After much experimentation, I began to call it 'the rake' and 'the can opener.' When you had them in the throat [raked them in] you could pop the helmet off and that would be the can opener. It was so fucking great!

"One time I hit O. J. Simpson perfectly, and they showed that tackle of me all year. Juice's helmet went flying and he fell to his knees. I attribute that to our wonderful trainer who was definitely the master of illegal pads!

"Look at John Matuszak's arms or Gene Upshaw's arms—the pads on those arms were incredible! Look at Bob Brown's thumb. He had a fake broken thumb for like seven years, but what he used to do is come up and deliver this blow into L. C. Greenwood's stomach and he could drop Greenwood with one thumb. Amazing! Is that fucking great or what!"

By Week 11, Oakland had won seven straight games. They beat the Eagles in Philly 26–7 and clinched their fifth straight division crown.

To Madden, clinching the division wasn't that big of a deal.

"When you clinch your division, it doesn't mean anything. If you can't win the big one, and there is only one big one—the Super Bowl. And if you can't win that one, none of this other stuff means anything!"

The Raiders' thirteenth game of the season meant a lot. Oakland's 11–1 record guaranteed them home-field advantage throughout the playoffs, but the fate of the Steelers and Bengals would be determined on Monday Night Football.

"The scenario was like this," said Villapiano. "We beat the Bengals, the Steelers are in and the Bengals are out. We lose to the Bengals, the Bengals are in and the Steelers are out."

Madden describes the thinking of how to approach this "situation."

"So the thinking was, 'They don't want to play Pittsburgh, they want to play Cincinnati, so they are going to go lose.' That's the worst thing you could say about someone [a team], that they lost on purpose.

Just for the sake of the organization, just for the sake of football, just for the sake of what's right. You gotta go win!"

The Raiders were definitely a collection of renegades, but while some might accuse them of cheating an opponent, they would never cheat the game.

Villapiano believed that no NFL team would ever lose on purpose.

"I couldn't even think of an NFL team ever lying down—especially on Monday night—especially a team like the Bengals. We hated them, but then we hated everybody.

"We just kept pounding these guys. Coach wanted us to annihilate them and we did!"

After that Monday-night game, Madden was proud of his team.

"We knocked Cincinnati out of the playoffs and we put Pittsburgh in. That Monday-night game was the proudest game I ever coached in my life! I don't know any other way to play, and thank goodness my players didn't either. It doesn't get any better than that."

Final score: Raiders 35, Bengals 20.

The Raiders entered the divisional playoffs against New England with a 13–1 record. The Pats were the only team who had beaten them, and when New England raced to a 21–10 lead, Oakland needed a miracle . . . and that miracle was Ken Stabler.

"Whatever that thing was, that focus, that concentration, Stabler could just step it up a notch when you needed it," said Madden. "We needed it right now. Either do it and go on, or we're done."

"Kenny didn't get the name Snake for nothing," said Villapiano. "He was as cool as a cucumber. He wanted that ball. He knew he could do something. He just knew it."

But Stabler's final drive stalled on the New England 29-yard line.

"Third and eighteen," said Stabler. "That's a long way. Too many third and longs will make you sleep on your side of the bed. You're gonna get knocked around."

For years the big games had turned against the Raiders on big calls. But seconds from defeat, the silver and black were saved, ironically, by the men in black and white.

Pittsburgh's nose tackle Ray "Sugar Bear" Hamilton hit Stabler in the head with a forearm just as he was releasing the ball. Madden was not happy about that.

"He said that he didn't mean to, but he hit him in the head and they don't allow that. Hamilton got the roughing the passer penalty he deserved."

"I had looped to my right and had a clear shot at the left-handed Stabler," said Sugar Bear Hamilton. "In an effort to change Stabler's ball flight, I had his hands high. After Stabler released the ball, I hit him on the helmet. Back in 1976, that was not considered to be roughing the passer, but referee Ben Dreith threw a flag anyway, giving the Raiders a first down. They went on to score the winning touchdown with seconds left on the clock."

That hit on Stabler made this one of the most controversial games in NFL history.

The Raiders capitalized on their second chance and stormed into their seventh AFL/AFC championship in the last nine years.

"It was a great comeback for us and we did what we had to," said Madden. "Sometimes the only thing remembered is the Sugar Bear Hamilton controversy—like we didn't do anything and they called roughing the passer on Hamilton and that gave us the game. That's just not true." Final score: Raiders 24, New England 21, and on to the Super Bowl!

Only one team stood between the Raiders and the Super Bowl: their rival and nemesis, the Pittsburgh Steelers. For the third year in a row, Oakland was pitted against the Steelers for the AFC Championship. All the hype was meaningless; this was the big one and the Raiders had to win.

Madden knew his Raiders had to play a near perfect, if not perfect game.

"We're going to have to play our best next week cause we've been here before and, dammit, this is a hurdle we have to get over.

"Swann, Atkinson, the Pittsburgh rivalry meant nothing at this point. But when you are this close to the Super Bowl, we can't let this one get away from us."

The Steelers, however, were not at full strength. Their two best running backs had been injured the week before against Baltimore.

Stabler didn't want to hear any excuses.

"Their excuse was not having Franco [Harris] or Rocky Bleier. Coulda woulda shoulda. Take the guys you got and go. The game we lost, we didn't have any excuses. They beat us—they beat the devil out of us. You gotta dance with the girl that you brought. No excuses!"

While having Harris and Bleier out gave the Raiders an advantage, Villapiano *wanted* them both to be available.

"A lot of people were saying that we were lucky we didn't have them there. I wanted Franco and I wanted Rocky. I wanted them all. I wanted the coach to suit up. I wanted to get them all.

"All of a sudden Mr. Bigshot, Frenchy Fuqua, wasn't good enough for them anymore. He was good enough when Jack Tatum nailed his ass and the ball bashed over to Franco, but now he wasn't good enough. They had their people and we stuck it to them.

"I wish that game could have gone seventeen quarters. The Steelers got what they deserved. They got a good and well-deserved butt kickin' that afternoon."

Madden had this to say at the press conference after the Raider win:

"There was a time when we took over, there was a time when Miami had taken over, and there was a time when Pittsburgh had taken over. Now it was our time to take over and dominate them all."

"No one can criticize us now!" said Stabler after the win.

"We had been criticized for not being able to win the big one. John and I had been criticized for not winning the big one. After the game was in hand it was like a piano falling off your back."

The Raider crusade had ended like it had begun sixteen games earlier: with George Atkinson crossing paths with Lynn Swann. But this time the only casualty was the Steelers' reign as World Champions.

Final score: Steelers 27, Raiders 24.

"Beating Pittsburgh was one thing, but the biggest thing was us going to the Super Bowl, and it was in California—in Pasadena!" said Madden. "And we're gonna win it!"

"We were so excited and having so much fun!" said Stabler. "We had finally accomplished what we had wanted to. Cigars and back-slapping, high fives and throwing the coach in the shower were all part of the locker room celebration."

Madden was overjoyed, but he knew it meant nothing without a championship.

"You're just so happy that you can't wait to be in this position and you finally get there and you do a lot of stupid things. But I remember saying, 'Hey, we haven't done anything yet. If we get this far and don't finish the job in Pasadena, we haven't done anything this entire season.'"

* * *

The Oakland Raiders arrived at Super Bowl XI on the brink of greatness. A victory would cap one of the most remarkable seasons in the history of the game. Standing between the Raiders and their destiny were the Minnesota Vikings. Like the Raiders, the Vikings were another team who had been unable to win the big one.

John Madden's short, pregame speech to the team will live forever in Villapiano's memory.

"I'll never forget what he told us in the locker room before the game. Coach Madden said, 'This will be the single biggest event in your whole life . . . as long as you win.'"

The Raider offensive line never had a finer hour. Upshaw and Shell chewed up Minnesota's "Purple People Eaters" and Oakland rolled up more rushing yards (266) than any other team in Super Bowl history.

Behind a wall of silver and black, the Snake was flawless—picking Minnesota apart, piece by piece.

For the Raiders, Super Bowl XI was never a contest. It was instead total domination.

This Super Bowl Sunday had been a long time coming. After sixteen victories and just one defeat, the greatness of the Raiders was indisputable. And to make this special day even more perfect, the ageless Willie Brown carried them into the history books.

"With less than five minutes to go in the game, the Vikings were on the Oakland 28-yard line when Fran Tarkenton threw a short pass to the left sideline," said Brown. "I cut off the receiver's route, drove to the ball, picked it off, and headed down the right sideline.

"I ran 75 yards for the score and that run turned out to be a Super Bowl record interception return."

Final score: Raiders 32, Vikings 14.

Like all other winning Super Bowl coaches, John Madden would be carried off the field by his adoring team. John was no different except for one thing: he was a little bit heavier than most.

"John was not the smallest coach in the league, and carrying him off the field was kind of a big task even for our biggest guys," said Stabler. "It was such a great sight to see him smile that way."

"I was surprised they could get me up," said Madden. "To make matters worse, the guys who were carrying me tripped over a photographer. Then it was just like an avalanche—we all fell down, which was kind of fitting. Carry the coach off and you drop him. I wouldn't be surprised if I was the first and only coach in Super Bowl history to be dropped by his players."

"The biggest kid of all was John and he had a whole bunch of reasons to win that Super Bowl game," said Villapiano. "He got it done and became one of the few great coaches to be enshrined into the Pro Football Hall of Fame. He's a terrific coach, and a great guy to have as a friend."

After a decade of dominance, the Oakland Raiders had finally earned a championship ring. Madden wanted this Super Bowl ring to be different than that of any other Super Bowl team.

"Myself and the team wanted it in silver and black with a football that had more diamonds than any other team had had before and, most important, we wanted it to be bigger than the Steelers' ring."

"The ring was really impressive!" said Stabler. "The big stone in the middle represents Super Bowl XI and the sixteen stones that make up the football represent our sixteen victories. It has the score of the championship game with *Pride* on one side and *Poise* on the other."

"To me," said Villapiano, "this ring is probably the closest thing [as an object] that's me. This ring, I'm sure, means the same thing to all of my teammates."

Coach Madden said it all when the rings were presented to his players.

"No one can ever take it away from you. In 1976 we won this ring and it will always be ours. But bigger than the ring are the memories. You look at it and you remember all those players; not only the big stars, but all of them, and you remember how they sacrificed and what they did. You earned it be playing hard, by winning, and by being a champion."

And that's exactly how it was. A Super Bowl championship, a ring, and a season's worth of memories that no one can ever take away from you.

MORE UNFORGETTABLE GAMES
SEA OF HANDS, GHOST TO THE POST, AND THE HOLY ROLLER

WHEN IT COMES TO professional football lore, momentous events such as "The Immaculate Reception," "Sea of Hands," "Ghost to the Post," and the "Holy Roller" are few and far between. For a team to experience even one of these bizarre plays would be considered incredible, but for a team such as the Oakland Raiders to experience four bizarre events, well that's phenomenal . . . but then so were Raiders of the 1970s.

SEA OF HANDS: DECEMBER 21, 1974

AFC Divisional Playoff: Miami @ Oakland

NBC Sports' top play-by-play telecaster, Curt Gowdy, called the 1974 AFC playoff game between the Oakland Raiders and the Miami Dolphins "the greatest game I have ever seen."

The 52,817 present in the Oakland Coliseum knew they had witnessed an extraordinary event. Forty million television viewers shared their view.

In the early '70s, the Miami Dolphins were as close to perfection as any NFL team could be. Following two consecutive Super Bowl titles in '72 and '73, the Dolphins were intent on capturing a third. However, in 1974, Miami wasn't the only team flying its colors proudly.

The radio station that carried the Raider games in the Bay Area had promoted the game as one for which fans should wear black, carry black, and wave black. The Coliseum was transformed into an ocean of black.

"I have never heard any louder cheering in the Coliseum than when we came out to be introduced," said Raider executive Al LoCasale. "The stadium left the ground."

"When we came out for that game there was more excitement in the stadium than I had ever heard before," said Madden. "Everyone had a black handkerchief and they were waving them. They were wired. We were playing the Dolphins. I'm excited and the team's excited.

"We kick off, they get the ball, and the Coliseum went silent in an instant.

"Miami's wide receiver Nat Moore received the short kick at the Miami 11-yard line, started up field, broke to his left and went unstopped and untouched 89 yards to the end zone for the score.

"So it's 7–0 with only fifteen seconds off the clock and the fans haven't even sat down yet!"

The Raiders' fortunes went from bad to worse when their explosive passing attack failed to ignite. But while the offense let opportunities slip away, the Raiders' defense took a firm hold on the Dolphins' elusive running game. And when the first quarter ended, the opening kickoff return remained the only score.

The Raiders stuck with their passing game and the all-out assault from the end zone eventually paid off. Charlie Smith pulled clear of Miami's man-to-man coverage, reached up, and pulled in a perfect pass from Stabler to complete a 31-yard touchdown play. The score was now tied at 7 apiece. And as the game wore on, the Raiders continued to focus their attention on the Dolphins' secondary.

Miami came right back to put three points on the board on a 33-yard field goal by Garo Yepremian with 1:01 remaining in the half. Miami left the field leading 10–7.

With 11:43 remaining in the third quarter, Stabler went long to Biletnikoff from 40 yards out, but Freddy's circus catch along the right sideline at the goal line was signaled by the referee to be out of bounds.

Madden then called for a repeat performance and this time Bilet-nikoff scored. Raiders 14, Dolphins 10.

"Freddy's catch was the best catch I've ever seen!" said Stabler

Biletnikoff relished the pressure.

"The ball's not always going to be perfect. The whole thing about being a receiver for me was: you gotta keep going. You may not be successful that one time. You may have to wait to make up for a mistake. Being either a success or a failure in a matter of seconds was always intriguing for me."

Trailing for the first time, 14–10, Don Shula refueled his team's competitiveness.

A 29-yard interference call on 3rd and 7 aided Miami and allowed a Paul Warfield TD to put the Dolphins back on top, 16–14. However, in the fourth quarter, the Raiders answered the score with a 72-yard touchdown reception by Cliff Branch. This gave Oakland the lead once more but, with time becoming a factor, Miami called upon its punishing running attack to eat up both the yardage and the clock while on its way to the Raiders end zone.

With 4:54 left in the game, Stabler threw to Cliff Branch, who was on the Miami 27. Branch dropped to the ground to make the catch, but because he was untouched by Dolphin defenders, he got up and ran from the surprised defensive backs to complete a 72-yard score. George Blanda kicked the extra point, and the score was now Raiders 21, Dolphins 19.

But with 2:08 to play, the game was far from over.

Larry Csonka muscled his way to the Oakland 23 and, on the next play, rookie running back Benny Malone ran 23 yards into the end zone to give Miami the lead once again, 26–21.

Just two minutes remained after Malone's touchdown.

Miami fullback Larry Csonka knew just how dangerous Stabler could be.

"I was concerned because there was so much time left. I knew that Stabler had the capacity to take the ball down the field . . . and he did."

Madden knew that Stabler thrived in pressure situations.

"When you get in a pressure situation where everything is riding on a single player, there's no one that you'd rather have involved in that play than Kenny Stabler. He has the uncanny knack of putting the ball between people and between hands and just being able to slip things in there from all different angles and that's just what he did."

With time running out, Stabler dashed Miami's hopes of a third consecutive title in dramatic fashion.

The following is an excerpt about what happened next from announcer Bill King's broadcast of that game.

> Here he is, fading, looking, looking, looking, he's under the gun, he throws . . . it is caught! Touchdown, Clarence Davis! Unbelievable! Davis took it away from the Miami defenders with 26 seconds to go. What a finish! Stabler had to loop the ball up because he was hit as he threw. It looked like he had lobed it into the promise land for Miami. But no! Davis got their first and it was the Raiders' promise land!

With Oakland now ahead, it was Villapiano who put the nail in the coffin.

"There was still enough time for Miami to score. Griese began to move his team down the field. With 13 seconds left in the game, and on second down from his own twenty, Griese threw a 30-yard pass to midfield and I intercepted. I ran over to John and gave him the game ball."

Oakland's 28–26 win brought out emotions characteristic of only the greatest of games.

Carl Taseff was a Miami assistant coach at the time. He remembers Shula's response to the loss.

"After the game, Don just cried. He said he was so disappointed for the guys' sake."

For guard Bob Kuechenberg, it was the most bitter loss of his career.

"This game was the toughest loss I have ever had to endure. It's the game I sleep with almost every night, and will forever."

Jim Langer, the Dolphins' center, shared his feelings about the loss.

"That was the toughest game I've ever been in, and the toughest loss I've ever been through. It was a kick in the balls."

"We were stunned and disappointed," said halfback Jim Kiick. "They were like enemies. Everybody disliked Oakland as a team. Basically the Raiders were disliked by everybody. But we had mutual respect for them. Yeah, they were all crazy, but I guess that's why they were so good."

On the final Oakland score, the ball was supposed to go to tight end Bob Moore.

"The ball was supposed to go to me. It was a tight end delay. I banged against Miami linebacker Doug Swift, but he just grabbed me—a very smart guy. I'm trying to slap him, get rid of him, fight him off, but he figured it out. So Snake had to go the other way."

Jim Kiick was watching from the sidelines.

"It was one of those freak things. From where I was standing I was sure that Stabler was going down."

"I think that play represents the attitude of that team," said Stabler. "You find a way to win. It doesn't matter how, it doesn't matter who, as long as you get it done. You trust that somebody will make a play—and they did."

GHOST TO THE POST: DECEMBER 24, 1977

AFC Divisional Playoff: Raiders @ Colts

It was the last great game in one of the last original pro football stadiums.

On a warm Christmas Eve, 60,000 Colts fans postponed holiday travel to see their team play football in a decaying shrine to fan loyalty in Baltimore, Maryland.

And if you ask anyone who was there in 1977, they might swear they saw the last autumn sun shine across Memorial Stadium. And they'll remember the game: 76 minutes, 68 points, and nine lead changes. They will remember the last great Colts battle before everything changed—a time that will live forever on the gridiron of Baltimore past.

It was the 1977 AFC Divisional playoffs, where the Raiders and the Colts slugged it out for nearly four hours. The contest would be decided in double overtime, and would be forever remembered for one critical play: "The Ghost to the Post."

Just before the game Madden said, "We have our work cut out for us. We have got to be solid. This tournament thing is so final, there is no tomorrow. It's just one day, one game and that's the way it has got to be."

Colts coach Ted Marchibroda said, "I think we are as ready to play this one as we ever have been. It will be the type of game that will take a total team effort. They [Oakland] are the type of club that can beat you on offense, they can beat you on defense, and they can beat you with their specialty teams. They are just an excellent football team in all aspects of the game. They do not have any weaknesses."

In 1975, the Colts had emerged from the AFC's cellar to become one of the league's most talented teams. Led by quarterback Bert Jones, their offense was one of the game's most powerful while their defense featured a young and formidable pass rush.

Though Baltimore captured three consecutive division titles, by 1977 both the Colts and their fans were eager for the team to ascend to a World Championship.

Championship games were one thing the Oakland Raiders were familiar with after topping Minnesota in Super Bowl XI the previous year. For Oakland, winning was second nature.

Wanting to prove themselves once and for all, Baltimore was eager to face the defending champs.

Colt's safety Bruce Laird said, "The stadium was absolutely electric and for us in the locker room, we really felt we could beat those guys."

"We felt like we could be able to set up good second down situations with good running plays, but to my surprise, and to our surprise, we weren't as effective running the football as we hoped to be," said quarterback Bert Jones.

Baltimore's inability to run the football sidetracked their attack, but Oakland fared no better against the Colts' front four.

Midway through the first quarter, a game that many thought would be a shootout was shaping into a defensive battle, with the offenses struggling as they did anything they could to show their resiliency.

This instance is where Coach Madden took what he had previously learned from studying the great Vince Lombardi.

"I know people used to say we ran to the left because Kenny Stabler was left handed. That had nothing to do with it. It was because Gene Upshaw and Art Shell were over there. I remember I learned this from Vince Lombardi that, if you are fundamentally sound and you work on your fundamentals and you do what you do best and practice it more than they practice against it, you'll have success even if they know it's coming."

Amid a defensive struggle, the Raiders struck first with a touchdown by Clarence Davis.

"It was what we called back then a 15-L," said Art Shell. "The read was off of my block. Whatever way I ran my guy, Clarence would counter off of that. I remember him breaking through the line of scrimmage and he broke a few tackles getting into the end zone. As a matter of fact, there was a facemask there that they probably should have called but wasn't. He was determined to get into the end zone and, of course, I was pretty excited, too."

With nineteen seconds left in the first quarter, Bert Jones threw two passes—one was almost intercepted and the other was deflected by Oakland. At that point he was 0–5 in pass completions.

Former Raiders tight end Raymond Chester had been traded to the Colts in 1973, and saw that his quarterback was struggling.

"It was probably the biggest game that Jones had been in," said Chester. "He was probably just a little hyper and a little nicked up. We all were."

Early in the second quarter, the Raiders gained possession near midfield with a chance to extend their 7-point lead and take control of the game. But fate didn't see it that way. On 3rd and 6, Stabler went back to pass and it was intercepted by Bruce Laird, who ran 61 yards untouched for the Colt score to tie the game at seven all.

"With a quarterback of that experience and caliber in those games, we always try and give them different looks," said Laird. "So what I did was cheat out a little bit and, when the ball snapped, I kind of flew to the sideline and just kind of made them think that that gap there in the flat would be open. And as soon as I saw him set, I just broke back and made a great jump on the ball. I stepped in front of van Eeghen and I took it 61 yards for a touchdown."

Stabler commented on Laird's intelligence.

"He was not a great cover guy, but he was a smart guy. Not tremendous speed, not big, not strong, not fast, but smart. And they sat in zones back there, in disguised zones. He sat back there in one of those zones, and I didn't see him."

After that play, Colts running back Don McCauley knew that the team had come together.

"I just remember what a lift it was for the team. It was a 61-yard score and I think what it showed the rest of the team was that everybody came to play—special teams, defense, offense—everybody."

With Laird's interception providing a sudden surge of adrenaline, the next six minutes turned into a defensive war of slow destruction.

For the Raiders, every yard, every completion, had become a struggle against this rough and tumble Colts defense.

"They didn't give you very much," said Gene Upshaw. "It was always very tough. Stan White was probably one of the smartest linebackers to ever play the game. And I can still see his number 53 standing out there trying to get that edge. You had Fred Cook. You had Joe Ehrmann. You had John Dutton. You had all of those guys that you knew very well."

"In the first half, we never had field position," said Ted Marchibroda, the Colts head coach. "We were always deep inside of our 20, and to go 80 yards against the Raiders is a tough assignment."

"We weren't doing much," said Colts running back Lydell Mitchell. "The Raiders really weren't doing much. The defenses were kind of dominating. And usually that's a sign of a pretty good football game."

Surprisingly, it was the Colts' defense and not the swaggering attack of the silver and black that had changed the tempo of the game.

In the second quarter, Bert Jones's completion to Freddie Scott was the spark that the Colts' offense needed. Baltimore then began to successfully pound the ball with Lydell Mitchell. Later in the series on a key third down, Jones shrugged off his slow start and seemingly willed his way to a first down.

"Bert, to me, was such a competitor!" said Colts running back Don McCauley. "And that's what I loved about playing on the same team as Bert. He was a fierce competitor with the strongest arm that I've ever seen."

Lydell Mitchell even compared Bert Jones to John Elway.

"Bert was very brash, very confident. He reminded me so much of John Elway. Same type of body, built basically the same way. I always said if you took the numbers off their backs, you might not be able to tell the two apart."

With 1:53 left in the half, Stabler led the Raiders downfield with a flurry of passes while taking advantage of the Colts defense. Mark van Eeghen's 16-yard catch and run put Oakland in position to tie the game. But a handoff to Davis resulted in a fumble with the ball flying out in midair and the Colts' John Dutton recovering. The half ended with the Colts leading, 10–7.

At the half, Madden wasn't thinking speeches. He was just visualizing the adjustments needed for the team to win.

"I think the game was shaping up the way we kind of expected it to," said Colts tight end Raymond Chester. "We were kind of a no-mistake team, you know, and bend, bend, bend, but don't break and then wait for an opportunity."

Upshaw felt the same about his Raiders.

"We left knowing that we had a lot of time to play. We could still score. We had Stabler back there that could find people and get things done."

According to defensive back Bruce Laird, the Raiders were loaded with talent.

"There's Art Shell. There's Gene Upshaw. There's Snake. There's Branch. There's Biletnikoff. There are all these great players. We're hanging in there. We're playing well. We gotta do a few things better. We gotta stop some of the big plays. And I kind of think the defense kind of looked over and said, 'Offense, you gotta get off your duff and start making some first downs.'"

"First half didn't matter," said Jack Tatum. "Second half didn't matter until it got to the end of the game, what was on the scoreboard. So we're trailing at halftime. It was no big deal. Just had to give us time to work it out."

Casper felt that the Raiders would stick to the running game.

"I think the game plan was still gonna be Branch, Biletnikoff, and the running game. We had a couple of little plays in there for down inside the 20 that when we got in there which we thought could be effective. But I don't really think that I was a big part of the game because of the fact that they're gonna play zones. The way they played, I don't think the Raiders looked at me as a big part of that game."

Following the second-half kickoff, Stabler marched the Raiders downfield and capped off the drive with a pass to Casper in the end zone for the score and the lead. Raiders 14, Colts 10.

"I had to step up in the pocket, if memory serves me well," said Stabler. "Somebody was hanging on my legs as Dave cut across, and I flicked the ball to him for the score."

The Colts, however, responded quickly.

On the ensuing kickoff, Colts wide receiver Marshall Johnson ran the ball 87 yards all the way back for the score and the lead. With 10:59 left in the third quarter, the score was: Colts 17, Raiders 14.

Once Baltimore provided Johnson a perfectly formed wedge to follow, Colts tight end Jimmie Kennedy paved the way further by not only taking out Pete Banaszak, but Randy McClanahan as well.

"We knew Jimmie had speed but we didn't know he had *that* kind of speed," said Bert Jones. "I think there was almost divine intervention for him to make that play the way that he did."

Upshaw remembers Madden's reaction to that play.

"What I remember about that play is Madden. I mean, that was, to him, a nightmare. Just being on the sideline and just to see his reaction of, 'How can you allow that to happen after we have so much momentum?'

"Other than John, nobody got really excited—as though it were the end of the game. It's something that happened, and we had to score and get the lead back."

Once again, the Colts kicked off and Stabler marched his team toward the end zone. On 2nd and 8, Stabler set up and threw downfield, but it was once again intercepted by Bruce Laird.

"We were just saying to ourselves that this is our time," said Laird. "I think defensively our feeling was, 'Okay guys, it's time for you to start playing. Start making some plays, and let's get this thing done.'"

The Colts ended up punting and Oakland rushed ten men on the play. Because of that, David Lee's punt was blocked by Ted Hendricks. Linebacker Jeff Barnes recovered for Oakland around the Colts 16-yard line.

"That wasn't one of my most classiest blocks," said Hendricks. "That particular one, I only had one hand out and hit the ball, slapped at it, and it hit my hand and dropped down. That was a pretty big play in that game because we got the ball back at that time."

A few plays later Stabler hit Casper in the end zone for the touchdown. Oakland 21, Baltimore 17.

"You go out, play, and do what they tell you to do," said Casper. "You run back on the sidelines and you sit down and get on the oxygen tank. It was a regular defense. They played normal coverages with good players. And you line up and get in your position. You get your right split, your good stance. You do your assignment, and you play like hell, and you've got a chance."

"We knew later in the game that we weren't gonna be as effective on the ground as what we had hoped," said Jones. "And so the natural thing to do was to utilize the run pass, or play-action."

On their first drive of the fourth quarter, Jones and the Colts put their new strategy in motion and began piling up the yardage.

With their passing game established, the Colts now found the running lanes open for the first time all day. By changing up from Mitchell to McCauley to Lee, the Colts staged an 80-yard drive, moving to the Oakland 1-yard line with four chances to retake the lead.

On third down with one yard to go for the score, Don McCauley dove for the end zone but ran into Raider Monte Johnson, who ended up cracking a vertebra in his neck. Johnson was taken out of the game, but didn't find out about the injured vertebra for about six months.

While the Raiders tended to Johnson, Baltimore tended to a fourth and goal situation just three feet from the end zone.

"There was never a whole lot of conversation about whether or not we should kick a field goal," said Jones. You don't get there by kissing your sister."

On fourth and goal, Jones handed off to running back Ron Lee who dove into the end zone for the score. Colts took the lead, 24–21.

"Obviously they had some reads on us and they were clogging up our strong points," said McCauley. "And thank God Ron got in. I know it was questionable by everybody whether he was in or not, but I say he was in. I'm sure Ron will give the same answer."

Once again, Stabler moved his team downfield. Following an interference call on Baltimore in the end zone, the Raiders were first and goal on the one. Stabler gave the ball to Banaszak for the score, and Oakland took the lead, 28–24, with 9:12 left in the fourth quarter

"That's the best part of a football game," said Art Shell. "Your adrenaline's flowing and now you got to make plays. Defense got to make plays. Who's gonna make the play? So you're gonna try to make sure that your team is the one making the plays."

"These guys act like they're home," said Lydell Mitchell. "But they just wouldn't go away. And I guess right then, you say to yourself, 'Man, this is the makings of a great game.'"

Jones moved his team right down the field, capping the drive with another touchdown by Ron Lee. With 7:54 left in the fourth quarter, the Colts once again took the lead, 31–28.

Jones knew that the Colts could not give the Raiders any opportunities to score.

"Oakland is a team that you want to hold the football on. You don't want them to have any more opportunities with the ball than what they have to have because they will score on you."

After the constant back and forth, the Baltimore defense fell like a blanket over Stabler and the Raiders. For the first time since the first quarter, Oakland was held without yardage and gave the suddenly red-hot Bert Jones the football in good field position with a chance to widen their lead.

"We felt great!" said Bruce Laird. "We said, 'You know, Bert, couple first downs, this and that, you know, maybe another three points. That's when winners are born.'"

With the lead, Baltimore could either stay with the successful passing game or try and run out the clock. The Colts decided to go back to the run and had their momentum stolen by John Matuszak and the Raiders defense.

"It was almost as though they were playing not to lose rather than trying to play to win," said Monte Johnson.

"It was not an independent thought of mine. We felt like we needed to eat up some time and move the ball.

"Ted Marchibroda called me and Lydell over and said, 'Let's run the football.'"

With another shot to put the Raiders away, Baltimore kept the ball on the ground, running twice and then again when Jones was flushed from the pocket.

"They don't get a first down then our side of the football started to get a little bit antsy," said Laird. "I can remember conversations going back and forth with us going on the field to our offensive team. And it wasn't pleasantries. We were telling them to get a gosh-darn first down, and let's get out of here."

Former Raider, now Colt Raymond Chester knew what the Raiders would do.

"I was scared because I knew we were gonna be in the prevent defense and I knew, basically, the kind of coverages our guys were used to playing and how they cover. And I just knew Snake."

With 2:55 left in the fourth quarter and trailing by three, Stabler and his offense took the field. Stabler hit Davis for 14 yards and a first down at the Oakland 44. After an incomplete pass, history was about to be made.

"We have a pass, and it was called "91-In," said Madden. "For a 91-In, the two outside receivers, the 'X' and 'Z,' both ran in patterns. And then on that, the tight end would run a post, which was kind of a clean out. In other words, he would go deep and clean out the middle. And then the two outside receivers would come to the inside of the middle."

"That play—if you look statistically—that was the most successful play the Raiders ever ran," said Casper. "Every time we called that play during the season, we gained over nine yards just for calling it.

"So Tom Flores, who was an assistant at that time, noticed when we would throw to the end zone that the safety would be sneaking up on the end and getting awfully close. So that would tell us if the safety was coming up to take away the end, which we could get by him to the post. So what he said was, 'On 91-In, take a peek at Ghost to the post.' And Dave Casper's nickname was Ghost."

With 2:11 left in the game, Stabler dropped back with Branch wide left and Biletnikoff wide right. Stabler threw long and hit Casper on the Baltimore 15-yard line.

"I don't think I caught a pass on that play all year," said Casper. "They weren't gonna let Branch get deep, so they put two guys short and deep on him. And they weren't gonna let Fred get open. And I'm supposed to run to the post pattern, but he came from the inside covering me. So I did some maneuvers to set him up, and I faked an out and I went underneath him to the post. And I had him going the wrong way, and I was open but by that time, because I was late, Snake had already thrown the ball guessing where I was gonna go.

"When I looked up over my shoulder, I took one look and said, 'The ball wasn't going where I was going.'

"I played a lot of outfield as a kid. So I just put my head down real quick, looked to a spot, ran to it, and quickly looked back up. Thank God the ball was coming right down into my hands. If I had looked up a second later, I wouldn't have seen it."

The play gained 42 yards to the Colts 14-yard line, but the Raiders had to settle for a field goal by Errol Mann to tie the game. The score was tied at 31, and the game would go into overtime. After sixty minutes and 62 points, nothing had been settled.

Baltimore would win the toss, with the first team to score would win. Jones moved his team down field, until they reached a 3rd and 8.

"I dropped back and everything was perfect," said Jones. "Raymond Chester's route was perfect. My throw was perfect except that it was a little early, and it was about two feet farther than where Raymond was."

"You know, nobody guarding me but God and the air," said Chester. "And I remember the pass leaving Bert Jones' hand. And I looked at it, and it literally was, I don't know how far over my head it was, but it was like, 'Wow.' I remember that feeling of frustration!"

"I don't know if he would have scored on that play," said Stabler, "but he would have put us in position to kick for the win. There are a lot of things that will haunt you and that one pass, I think, I will take to my grave wondering, *Why didn't I wait one more second before throwing to him?"*

The Raiders received possession and started to move the ball on the Colts, going 41 yards in nine plays and putting themselves in position to win the game on their first drive of overtime . . . but it was not to be. The field goal was blocked by defensive tackle Mike Barnes and the Colts took over on the Raiders' 32.

Unfortunately for the Colts, their offense remained stagnant. Since taking the lead midway through the fourth quarter, they had run 17 plays for just 27 yards, while being held to just one completion and one first down.

Baltimore once again punted. Stabler chipped away the yardage, was sacked for a major loss, and then on 3rd and 19 at the Colts 45-yard line, Stabler hit Branch on the 26-yard line for a first down.

"That was the real backbreaker because without that 19-yard reception, they would have had to punt and it would have given us another possession," said Don McCauley.

Oakland worked their way down to the 13-yard line when time ran out and the game would now go into double overtime.

"I knew that we could kick the field goal because we were in field goal range," said Madden. "But if we kick the field goal then we have one chance to win the game. If we throw a pass, if it was a play pass, a pass to Dave Casper in the end zone in the corner, we have a chance there because if we complete that, then we win the game. If we don't complete it, then we have another chance to kick the field goal. So it just made sense to me that before we settled on the field goal to try a shot at the end zone."

At the start of the second overtime, Banaszak bulldozed his way for three yards. On the next play, Stabler dropped back and threw his forty-second pass of the day to Dave Casper—a 10-yard touchdown to give the Raiders a 37–31 double-overtime victory over the Baltimore Colts.

"We go into the locker room and in the locker room, we're watching to see who we were going to have to play," said Madden. "And Denver won. So we started thinking right away about Denver."

Against the Broncos, Oakland's reign as champions came to a close. But within three years the Raiders would reload and in Super Bowl XV, Oakland captured their second of what would be three world championships in a eight-year span.

As for the Colts, the decline was swift and devastating. Injuries and contract disputes decimated the '78 season. Crowds began to dwindle, and on March 28, 1984, what once seemed unthinkable became real. The beloved Colts left Baltimore for Indianapolis.

For the men who played and the fans who watched it, the battle on Christmas Eve was the last great moment before everything changed.

New rules regarding pass blocking would alter the way the game was played, and franchise movement would affect where it was played. The how remains constant, though. And the desire brought forth through 76 minutes of football on that day is a tribute to a game sometimes forgotten, sometimes ignored, but forever remarkable.

HOLY ROLLER: SEPTEMBER 10, 1978

Week 2: Raiders @ Chargers

From 1968 to 1977, the Chargers went 18 straight games without beating the Raiders. Finally, in their second meeting of the '77 season, San Diego broke the streak. And in '78, when the breaks started going their way, it seemed certain that the Chargers were about to win their second in a row over the Raiders.

But if one were to review the stats of the game, there would be no doubt that Oakland was on the losing end. Generally, if your quarterback throws for three interceptions, you're going to lose. Typically, if your opponent's time of possession doubles your time of possession, you're going to lose. And more often than not, if you fumble on the last play of the game, you're going to lose.

This was not the case with the Raiders.

The Raiders' opening drive showed promise until Mark van Eeghen fumbled and Chargers defensive tackle Louie Kelcher recovered the ball on the San Diego 10-yard line.

Even though Chargers quarterback Dan Fouts managed to march his team down the field, the 28-yard field goal attempt was blocked by the Raiders, who then took over at their own 20.

The Raiders went three and out and the game seemed as though it would turn into a punting contest, as neither team was having success in moving the ball down the field.

When the Raiders got the ball back late in the first quarter, Stabler was picked off and the interception was returned to the Oakland 35-yard line. A few plays later, six-four tight end Pat Curran caught a deflected pass from Dan Fouts for a 14-yard score. The extra point was good, and San Diego led 7–0 early in the second quarter.

Stabler hit Casper for a 6-yard touchdown and Mann's PAT was good. The Raiders tied the game at 7–7 with a little over twelve minutes to go in the first half.

The ball continued to change hands several times before Chargers running back Hank Bauer ran the ball up the middle from the one for a score. The extra point, however, was missed, which would prove to be a critical mistake. Score: San Diego 13, Raiders 7.

The third quarter proved uneventful for both parties. A holding penalty shattered the Chargers' first possession of the second half and Stabler's second interception of the game ended a Raiders drive.

Stabler was picked off once more in the third quarter but thanks to a strong defense, the Chargers were forced to punt.

In the fourth quarter, Hank Bauer rushed for two yards into the end zone to give San Diego a 20–7 lead with just over twelve minutes left in the game.

A few possessions later, Stabler hit wide receiver Morris Bradshaw for a 44-yard score, shortening the Chargers' lead to 6 with a little over eight minutes left in the game.

The teams traded punts until Stabler started hitting his targets. Marching down the field, Bradshaw, Banaszak, Chester, and Biletnikoff all did their part. Finally, an incomplete pass from Stabler to Chester stopped the clock with 10 seconds left to play.

What happened next was best described by Raiders announcer Bill King. His call would become legendary.

> Stabler back, here comes the rush, he sidesteps, can he throw? He can't! The ball, flipped forward, is loose, a wild scramble, two seconds on the clock, Casper grabbing the ball, it is ruled a fumble, Casper has recovered in the end zone, the Oakland Raiders have scored on the most zany, unbelievable, absolutely impossible dream of a play!
>
> After linebacker Woodrow Lowe hit Stabler and the ball flew forward, and Banaszak flipped it ahead, Casper fell on the ball in the end zone after bending over and kicking it while trying to pick it up. As the referees signaled "touchdown," Casper stood up with the ball in his arm, practically devoid of emotion, stunned.
>
> Madden is on the field, he wants to know if it's real, they said "yes, get your big butt out of here," he does.
>
> There is nothing real in the world any more, this one will be relived . . . forever.

Despite a protest from the Chargers sideline, referee Jerry Markbreit ruled it a legal play.

But the game was *not* over. It was tied and the extra point still had to be kicked.

Mann's kick was good, and the Raiders were victorious by a score of 21–20.

"We played lousy," said Madden. "We should have never been in that position. I was mad at the team. I just thought we were terrible. We stunk out the joint that day."

"We had beaten the Raiders up and down the field all day," said Chargers linebacker Jim Laslavic.

"They get down to the final seconds and in typical Raiders fashion they're still in it. There was a feeling on the sidelines to get these final ten seconds out of the way and begin celebrating. But it didn't happen that way."

Banaszak's responsibility was to block the linebacker.

"On that particular play I do remember that my responsibility was to block the linebacker if he blitzed."

"Linebacker Woody Lowe beat whoever was supposed to block him," said Stabler. "He came pretty clean and he got to me just as I began to set up. And that's when everything took place."

"I was able to get my hand on Kenny," said Lowe. "Kenny was backing away. I thought he tried to flip or throw the ball underhanded. I thought it was an incomplete pass. I thought I was the hero of the game to be honest, but it was just the opposite."

"I remember looking back at Kenny and Woody Lowe had him around the arms," said Banaszak. "Kenny couldn't raise his arm up to throw the football and I hollered, 'Snake! Snake!' So he kind of flicked it. I couldn't get to it but it was rolling end over end in front of me."

"Pete goes to pick it up, but if he picks it up and gets tackled, the game is over," said Madden. "So he can't get tackled with the ball."

Ted Hendricks watched the whole thing.

"Banaszak picked up the ball and started to get tackled, so he just launched the ball up in the air."

"At the time, I thought it was a smart thing to do to just get my hands on the ball and push it forward and keep it alive," said Banaszak. "If I would have jumped on it, the Chargers would have jumped on me and that would have been the game."

"Now Dave Casper comes in the front," said Madden. "The ball is now on the two-yard line. Dave knows if he recovers the ball on the two-yard line and is tackled the game is over!"

But Casper was just trying to pick up the ball.

"I'm on the two- or three-yard line and the ball comes, so I just ran out there and try and pick it up, and I flub that. Now I'm scrambling on the ground watching the ball underneath me and I see a white stripe go by and I actually just fell on top of it. I didn't dive on it. Actually my greatest contribution was standing in the middle of the field."

Chargers quarterback Dan Fouts can't believe that the referees didn't see what *really* happened.

"It still blows my mind how the referees could not see what it was or see exactly what happened. But Woody Lowe clearly got a sack on Stabler and he shoved the ball forward. It wasn't a fumble; he threw the ball. If you ask Banaszak what he was doing, he was advancing the ball illegally. If you ask Casper, he had to push it across the line and fall on it for the touchdown."

"I would assume, with Banaszak, Kenny, and Casper that they wouldn't pass a lie detector test!" said Biletnikoff.

"I fumbled it on purpose," Stabler admitted honestly after the game. "Yes, I was trying to fumble."

In the locker room, San Diego's Jim Laslavic had this to say about the Raiders.

"In typical Oakland Raiders fashion, if you can't beat somebody the right way, you cheat!"

And according to George Atkinson . . .

"That play was well within the rules."

But Madden said it all.

"And it was one of those things that maybe you can't do that. But the rules say that you can do that, so you can do that, and

> **Note:** During the off-season, the league added a provision to the rulebook about fumbles after the two-minute warning that allows only the player who fumbled the ball to advance it. As such, the rule change will forever prevent the Holy Roller from happening again.

if you don't want to do that, then go change the rule, and that's what they did, they changed the rule. Now you can't do that anymore."

Markbreit's decision to uphold the play was absolutely correct by the rules in place at the time. However, that would soon change.

OAKLAND RAIDERS HIGHLIGHTS
1975-1979

1975 SEASON (11-3-0)

On January 4, 1976, the Steelers and Raiders met once again for the American Football Conference Championship. This title game matched the two best teams in professional football, and would be the toughest playoff test under the worst possible conditions.

Two feared and respected football giants hunted and hit for sixty furious minutes. Two champions entered the frozen confines of Three Rivers Stadium. Two champions would leave the dark and frozen battlefield three long hours later. But only one was destined for the Super Bowl and World Championship.

Safety Jack Tatum and linebacker Monte Johnson made key plays, but the Raiders trailed in the fourth quarter. Defying the elements, the odds, and the tough Steelers defense, Oakland stormed goalward.

After Mike Siani scored, Pittsburgh came back and the icy carpet again spelled trouble. Trailing 16–7 with time almost gone, Coach John Madden electrified players and fans alike with innovative strategy. Needing ten to win, he had George Blanda quickly go for three. And with only seven seconds left, the Raiders continued their heroic efforts . . . but it was not to be. The final words on this fiercest football battle in years were indelibly etched on the scoreboard. Suddenly another memorable year of glory ended in a single day of defeat.

But despite pain and heartbreak, these 1975 Oakland Raiders had added much to the organization's already unrivaled record of accomplishment with another year of triumph and tragedy.

Week 1 @ Miami

The new season opened on a Monday night in Miami, with a classic cross-country challenge—a renewal of the unforgettable 1974 playoffs.

But this was 1975—the Orange Bowl—with the mighty Raiders determined to again establish mastery by snapping Miami's 31-game home win streak. With Mark van Eeghen and Pete Banaszak leading the charge, the silver and black crashed the end zone with 31 points.

Tony Cline added a sack to Bob Griese's four interceptions. Then Harold Hart ran a punt back 102 yards to seal the 31–21 win.

Week 2 @ Baltimore

In Baltimore, the Raiders faced the playoff-bound Colts.

Art Thoms led the defensive line with six sacks. And behind explosive blocking by offensive captain Gene Upshaw, the Raiders scored on the ground.

Showcasing three proven wide receivers—Mike Siani, Fred Biletnikoff, and Cliff Branch—the Raiders' precision passing overpowered Baltimore. A touchdown by tight end Dave Casper helped Oakland rack up 31 points. Meanwhile, the Colts' hopes were shattered with great plays by rookie cornerback Neal Colzie, another product of great Raider drafting.

In the end, Baltimore was defeated. Final score: Raiders 31, Baltimore 20.

Week 3 @ San Diego

In San Diego, the Chargers were held to just five first downs by the likes of an aggressive Otis Sistrunk. Ray Guy, again the NFL's leading punter, kept the Chargers down deep all afternoon. With quarterback Kenny Stabler hurt and Fred Biletnikoff sidelined, the offense relied on George Blanda's field goals with a 6–0 victory.

Week 4 @ Kansas City

While the Raiders were flying high, they were brought down to earth with the Chiefs racking up 42 points against them. And with only one touchdown by Cliff Branch, the silver and black suffered their first loss of 1975. Final score: Kansas City 42, Oakland 10.

Week 5 @ Cincinnati

In rainy Cincinnati, the weary Raiders were on the road for the seventh consecutive weekend (including the preseason). Defense owned the day, and Raiders left linebacker Phil Villapiano owned one of four Raider interceptions, but the Bengals brought one of their own back all the way to squeak out a 14–10 victory.

Week 6 vs. San Diego

Finally the Raiders were back home. With San Diego in town, the Oakland defense raced out bound for glory. This would be the very first time that the Raiders registered two shutouts in one season.

It began when Mike Dennery and Ted Hendricks sacked the Chargers punter for a safety. Hendricks, Sistrunk, and Horace Jones also added a two-pointer, which would be the final points of the game. The spirited Raiders were on their way.

They even relied on dazzling deception, as Ray Guy found Louis Carter on a punt formation pass. Finally, behind blocking by John Vella, Upshaw, Shell, Buehler, and Dalby, Ken Stabler triggered the feared Raider bomb to Cliff Branch as the Raiders celebrated their homecoming, 25–0.

Week 7 @ Denver

In Denver, loyal Raiders boosters saw their conference-leading defense cut down the Broncos. With center Dave Dalby offering protection, Stabler hit Fred Biletnikoff for six of Oakland's amazing 35 second-half points. Neal Colzie returned three punts for 127 yards en route to an all-time NFL record 655 yards in that category.

Raider depth again overcame a wave of injuries when Marv Hubbard polished off a towering 42–17 conquest.

Week 8 vs. New Orleans

When the Saints came marching in, they ran into a poised Raiders offense primed for points. With Clarence Davis powering for tough yards, the silver and black poured over, around, and through the shocked Saints.

While the offense swiftly moved down field, the defense dealt out mayhem. Relentless pressure on Saints quarterback Archie Manning forced this breakdown.

Versatile special teams captain Warren Bankston scored his first Raider touchdown as one of nine different receivers who contributed to a spectacular 523 yards of total offense.

The afternoon's two big strikes went to deep threat Morris Bradshaw, as a sellout home crowd cheered a club record 34 first downs and a devastating 48–10 Raiders triumph.

Week 9 vs. Cleveland

When the Cleveland Browns visited the majestic Oakland Coliseum, they found Clarence Davis on the run. He ran for 64 yards on the opening kickoff and added 120 yards rushing to help set up scores like this one broadcasted by Bill King:

"Branch slots left. Stabler back, looking, looking, going to Branch wide open. Touchdown Raiders! Branch committed highway robbery without a gun."

When Stabler wasn't hitting passes, Horace Jones was hitting runners. In the air, the Browns met disaster against defensive captain Willie Brown as the Raiders thundered to victory. With the score tied at 17 in the third quarter, Stabler hit Biletnikoff for the score, and then handed off to Davis for two more touchdowns. Final score: Oakland 38, Cleveland 17.

Week 10 @ Washington

Next on the schedule for the Raiders were the Washington Redskins. The huge national audience knew about the pride and poise, drama and excitement that are Oakland traditions. And they saw Oakland roar back like a mighty train with three rushing scores from Pete Banaszak.

With little time left, Oakland led 23–16. However, a last-ditch Washington effort tied the score at 23 and put the Raiders into the first overtime game in their remarkable 16-year history.

When the Redskins won the toss, the Raiders defense responded to pressure and overwhelmed quarterback Billy Kilmer's attack. The Raiders continued to march goalward. Finally, it was time for ageless marvel George Blanda and the field goal team to clinch the Raiders' momentous 26–23 triumph, ensuring an eleventh consecutive winning season for the silver and black.

Week 11 vs. Atlanta

A Raiders victory against Atlanta would mean an unprecedented eighth division championship in nine years.

Despite Oakland's deluge of points—three touchdowns by Branch and one by van Eeghen—Steve Bartkowski brought Atlanta to the front, 34–31. With just six seconds left, a Blanda field goal tied the game, and this time even the extra period was a nail-biter.

But once again George Blanda was called in. The 36-yard field goal was good, and Oakland beat Atlanta, 37–34.

Week 12 vs. Denver

The following week, a Monday-night TV audience saw the Oakland Raiders, reigning AFC Western Division champions, go for seven wins in a row. The defense was superb as second effort had become first nature.

Rookie Charlie Phillips started for the injured Jack Tatum and grabbed a record-tying three interceptions. Ken Stabler guided the offense for two scores—one by Harold Hart and the other by Pete Banaszak. Final score: Oakland 17, Denver 10. The Raiders record now stood at 10–2.

Week 13 vs. Houston

The rejuvenated Houston Oilers were in Oakland for a game that was fiercely contested. With impenetrable protection from Art Shell, Henry Lawrence, and George Buehler, left-handers Ken Stabler and

David Humm hit Branch and Bradshaw for touchdowns and drilled the Oilers for 26 points and a narrow Raiders lead.

But the Oilers rallied and threatened to go ahead. A Raiders victory seemed assured when Skip Thomas intercepted in the end zone, but a phantom call away from the ball nullified the celebration and Houston went on to win a heartbreaker in the last seconds, 27–26.

Week 14 vs. Kansas City

In the season's final week, top rusher and scorer Pete Banaszak won the coveted Gorman Award as Most Inspirational Raider. Pete then scored three touchdowns against the Chiefs, bringing his season's total to a club record 16.

Tight end Bob Moore caught a Ken Stabler pass, which was his eleventh completion in twelve attempts. George Blanda then became the only player in pro football history to score 2,000 points.

Near the game's end, Jess Philips ran 66 yards to help capture Coach John Madden's 70th win in seven Raiders seasons.

A defense led by Villapiano, Thoms, Gerald Irons, and Horace Jones scalped the Chiefs, 28–20, for win number 11.

Ahead lay the AFC playoffs against the Cincinnati Bengals. There was no doubt that the proud Oakland Raiders were ready.

AFC Divisional Playoffs vs. Cincinnati

As Paul Brown coached his final game, he saw his Bengals overshadowed by an aggressive band of hunters in silver and black.

When the offense took over, Stabler followed Coach Madden's game plan and went right for the jugular. Mike Siani's touchdown was only the beginning, as the classy Raiders dominated scoring time after time.

Behind intense power blocking, Raider supremacy was apparent to all.

The Tiger was virtually caged when Dave Casper scored the last of Oakland's 31 points. The Bengals closed at 28, but the rugged Raider defense met the challenge and brought down the curtain. Final score: Oakland 31, Cincinnati 28.

AFC Conference Championship @ Pittsburgh

On January 4, 1976, the Raiders met their longtime foes, the Pittsburgh Steelers, for the AFC Conference Championship. With no score until the second quarter, the Steelers struck first with a field goal and a 25-yard rush from Franco Harris in the fourth. Later that quarter, George Blanda kicked a 41-yard field goal and Mike Siani scored the only touchdown for Oakland. But the Steelers came back with a John Stallworth touchdown to end the Raiders' Super Bowl hopes. Final score: Pittsburgh 16, Oakland 10.

In 1975, the Raider organization maintained its total commitment to excellence, winning 12 games in league and postseason play.

In terms of consistent victory, the Raiders continued their complete domination of professional football since 1963, when owner/managing/general partner Al Davis rescued a faltering franchise and pledged to build sports' most successful organization.

Since 1967, when Oakland won the first of eight division championships, the record was incredible. Now only a World Championship remained to crown this awesome record of achievement; to add the ultimate triumph to professional football's winningest team.

1976 SEASON (13–1–0)

The Raiders banner had proudly flown atop the sports world throughout an historic decade. And in 1976, the silver and black completed a decade of destiny, adding a crowning glory to their already unrivaled record of excellence.

Week 1 vs. Pittsburgh

On opening day, the Pittsburgh Steelers found the Raiders long on injuries, short on excuses, primed and ready. Ken Stabler's touchdowns to Dave Casper and Fred Biletnikoff helped earn 440 yards against the Steel Curtain. Still, Oakland trailed by 14 with only 5:35 remaining

Without standout vets Art Thoms, Horace Jones, Marv Hubbard, and others, able Coach John Madden's Raiders fought back courageously, defying adversity, time, and the Steelers.

Dave Casper capped a brilliant drive with a 10-yard score. The defense controlled Pittsburgh, forcing a punt that special teams captain Warren Bankston blocked and Charlie Phillips recovered.

The great Oakland fans had learned to expect heroic rallies from their Raiders, for these men of the silver and black were veterans of pressure situations and at home with dramatic last-minute victories.

Stabler bootlegged, tying the score at 28 with just 59 seconds left, and then Dave Rowe deflected a pass that linebacker Willie Hall intercepted, bringing on rookie place kicker Fred Steinfort with the go-ahead score.

The 1976 campaign began with another remarkable chapter in the history of daring Raider comebacks. Final score: Raiders 31, Steelers 28.

Week 2 @ Kansas City

In Kansas City for a Monday-night game, the Raiders special teams led the charge. Punter Ray Guy, Neil Colzie, Terry Kunz, Jack Tatum, Ted Kwalick, Rik Bonness, Mike Siani, and Herb McMath relentlessly shadowed the Chiefs.

On offense, Mark van Eeghen and Pete Banaszak surged for big yardage. With overpowering protection from offensive captain Gene Upshaw and Art Shell, Stabler coolly completed 22 passes, but in the fourth quarter, Stabler was hurt after drilling Mike Siani for the final Raiders touchdown in a 24–21 win.

Week 3 @ Houston

Houston gets hot even indoors, but more fired up was a fierce Raider defense that burned the Oilers.

Newcomers John Matuszak and talented rookie Charles Philyaw, products of football's premier scouting operation, were overwhelming.

The undefeated Oilers had not yielded a touchdown in 1976, but rookie Mike Rae, playing for Stabler, changed that with scoring passes to Cliff Branch for a 14–13 Raiders triumph.

Week 4 @ New England

A long Raiders trip to New England found the Patriots inhospitable. With scores by Fred Biletnikoff, Mike Rae, and a single field goal from Fred Steinfort, it was too little too late. Final score: New England 48, Oakland 17. But one taste of defeat was all this 1976 Oakland Raiders team would tolerate.

Week 5 @ San Diego

In San Diego, the Chargers challenged the first-place Raiders. Neil Colzie's punt returns gave Oakland favorable field position. Then Ken Stabler unfolded the game plan developed by head coach John Madden. Cliff Branch scored from 74 and 41 yards out, and Dave Casper scored from 4 yards—as did Pete Banaszak—as Oakland roared back, 27–17.

Week 6 @ Denver

In Denver, punt coverage corralled the Broncos. Van Eeghen powered toward his 1,000-yard season while Fred Steinfort kicked a 34-yard field goal. In the third quarter, Branch and Banaszak each scored a touchdown to seal the Oakland win, 17–10.

Week 7 vs. Green Bay

Home at last. The Raiders hosted Green Bay. A scoreless battle exploded after linebacker Phil Villapiano made a key interception.

In the NFL's 57-year history, no team ever had a better-completed pass percentage than these 1976 Raiders.

Though Ken Stabler quickly went airborne—striking for three scores in nine minutes—this lightning attack included an 88-yard pass to Cliff Branch, the most feared deep receiver in football at the time. Then a clutch interception by Skip Thomas preserved an 18–14 victory.

Oakland now stood at 6–1.

Week 8 vs. Denver

When Denver invaded Raiders country, Coach Madden's defensive aides, Tom Dahms, Don Shinnick, and Bob Zeman, unleashed an awesome pass rush that sacked Broncos quarterbacks ten times.

Behind textbook blocking, Clarence Davis went for one score. On third down, Stabler hit Biletnikoff on a leaping catch in the end zone. Then, behind textbook blocking, Clarence Davis went in for another score. Final score: Oakland 19, Denver 6.

Week 9 @ Chicago

Despite bitter cold, the Raiders' passing stayed hot. Stabler hit Dave Casper on 17-yard score followed by a 75-yard touchdown to Branch with a bomb in the end zone for the second score.

Though held to under three yards per carry, Chicago's Walter Payton found the end zone three times and the game rocked back and forth. Tough defense made big plays. A Sistrunk deflection and a Hendricks interception set up a 28–27 Raiders lead and victory.

John Madden epitomized coaching greatness. His foresight in taking the win in the fourth quarter helped preserve victory.

Week 10 vs. Kansas City

Oakland, now at 8–1, was at home against Kansas City where Ken Stabler utilized Dave Casper and Fred Biletnikoff for scores, and Pete Banaszak added a third with a one-yard rush as the silver and black thundered toward the playoffs. Final score: Oakland 21, Kansas City 10.

Week 11 @ Philadelphia

In historic Philadelphia, the Raiders rang the bell on both offense and defense to give Coach Madden his 80th win and capture their ninth division championship in ten years.

With touchdowns from van Eeghen, Biletnikoff, and Clarence Davis, a field goal by Errol Mann, and a safety by Hendricks, the Raiders flew by the Eagles, 26–7.

Week 12 vs. Tampa Bay

At home against Tampa Bay, the Raiders rolled to victory number eleven, their eighth in a row. Scores by Pete Banaszak, Warren Bankston, Cliff Branch, Carl Garrett, and two from Mark van Eeghen were scored in the first three quarters alone.

In the fourth quarter, Mike Rae to Mike Siani closed out the Bucs permanently. Final score: Oakland 49, Tampa Bay 16.

Week 13 vs. Cincinnati

In Week 13, a huge TV audience learned an unforgettable lesson about these mighty Oakland Raiders. By losing, Oakland could deny Pittsburgh the playoffs, but the Raiders know only one way to play—to win. Victory is a way of life for the silver and black.

Rick Jennings's kickoff return started it off. The rest was pride and poise, preparation and performance. There would be no stopping Oakland. These combat-ready Raiders had grown stronger through challenge and adversity. Stabler and Branch connected from 42 yards out which gave Oakland a 28–13 lead and the critics went silent. Two interceptions by Monte Johnson, and one by Jack Tatum destroyed Cincinnati's offense.

And then the Raiders calmly shattered the Bengals' playoff hopes as Stabler and Biletnikoff clinched win number twelve. Final score Oakland 35, Cincinnati 20.

Week 14 vs. San Diego

Prior to the game against the Chargers, Ken Stabler was named Most Inspirational Raider. This final game showcased Mike Rae, Dave Humm, Hubert Ginn, Carl Garrett, Manfred Moore, Rodrigo Barnes, Floyd Rice, Steve Sylvester, Henry Lawrence, Dan Medlin, Morris Bradshaw, and others as Oakland triumphed to a 24–0 victory, finishing 13–1 with the best record in football.

The Raiders had proved again that their commitment to excellence was no idle phrase. Together, these gallant Raiders and their magnificent fans were now bound for glory.

AFC Divisional Playoffs vs. New England

Against the Patriots in the AFC playoffs, Stabler received solid protection from Dave Dalby, John Vella, and George Buehler as Oakland marched for an early field goal.

The Raider defense alertly matched razzle-dazzle with readiness and reaction. Trailing 7–3, Oakland forged ahead on a catch by master craftsman Fred Biletnikoff, but the Pats regained the lead 21–10 late in the third quarter.

The valiant Raiders stormed goalward in classic drives. First van Eeghen scored, but Oakland still trailed by four. With only four minutes left and 68 yards to go, every Raider dug deep for that something extra that marks champions.

Then New England was caught belting Stabler in the head. The Raiders relentlessly closed in as the game drew to a dramatic finish. On second down, Stabler rolled to the left and took the ball in himself. Final score: Oakland 24, New England 21.

AFC Conference Championship vs. Pittsburgh

Against Pittsburgh, Ray Guy was fearlessly protected; the Steelers punter was not and Hubert Ginn's partial block set up a Raider field goal. But then the defense rose up tall. Hall intercepted a deflected Bradshaw pass and ran all the way to the three-yard line as he was run out of bounds.

Behind devastating blocking, Clarence Davis put the determined Raiders ahead, 10–0. The Oakland defense played with controlled fury, growing stronger and tougher as the game went on. Every play was a challenge to be met and conquered. Raiders execution and emotion were at a level that Pittsburgh found unstoppable.

With Pittsburgh's league leading defense on the ropes, Coach Madden went for the clincher, ensuring the Raiders' Super Bowl date with destiny.

The Raiders never faltered, casting a giant silver and black shadow across the Steelers' hopes, No team could deny these Raiders their place in the sun. Final score: Oakland 24, Pittsburgh 7.

Super Bowl XI vs. Minnesota

From the onset, there was never a question about the Super Bowl. This game, this season, this league, this decade belonged to the silver and black.

The Raiders might was undeniable early, but Minnesota got life blocking a punt deep in Oakland territory. But there was no panic, no break in the Raiders' concentration or intensity. Just stop them now and get the ball back.

Next, Fran Tarkenton handed off to Brent McClanahan, who fumbled the ball, which was recovered by Oakland.

Then 125 million people saw Clarence Davis follow guard George Buehler on route to a 137-yard rushing day.

The Raiders drew first blood after Dave Casper's catch was ruled out on an Errol Mann field goal.

Next, Oakland boldly drove 64 yards to gain a 10–0 lead. Carl Garrett contributed key yardage and Fred Biletnikoff took the Raiders to the one-yard line. Then a quick throw from Stabler to Casper in the end zone for the score.

The worldwide audience now realized that time alone stood between these Raiders and complete domination of Super Bowl XI.

Meticulous design coupled with devastating blocking by backs and linemen alike powered the Raiders down the glory road.

In the third quarter, Oakland moved farther ahead, 19–0, with an Errol Mann 40-yard field goal. Magnificent special teams, offense and defense, and an electrifying intimidating force in silver and black now stood as history's best.

After a Minnesota touchdown cut the lead to 19–7 and Oakland punted, Willie Hall intercepted on the Oakland 30, and the turnover turned into a Stabler to Biletnikoff touchdown.

Pete Banaszak scored again as the Raider assault rolled on relentlessly. Then defensive captain Willie Brown finished the scoring avalanche with an interception and a 32–14 Super Bowl win.

Together with their loyal fans, the Oakland Raiders—number one for so many years—now stood alone as the world champions of professional football.

1977 SEASON (11-3-0)

In 1977, the dynamic Raiders organization and their great fans shared a season that began with them as World Champions of professional football—a crowning glory for an already unrivaled record of excellence.

Week 1 vs. San Diego

A thunderous ovation greeted each of the world-champion Raiders as they came out for their season opener. Once the game started, the special teams—led by Lester Hayes and Randy McClanahan— swarmed the Chargers.

Ray Guy's booming punts set up coverage by Charles Phillips and Morris Bradshaw. Pat Toomay and Otis Sistrunk also limited San Diego's offense. Ken Stabler hit Cliff Branch and Dave Casper, while Pete Banaszak rushed in from two yards out and the confident Raiders opened with a 24–0 shutout.

Week 2 @ Pittsburgh

The spotlight shifted to Pittsburgh for the rematch of the 1976 AFC Championship. Prior to this dramatic Raiders–Steelers confrontation, two healthy squads calmly exchanged greetings, but hostile Steelers fans wanted no gestures of friendship, for they were on a wartime alert—and war they got.

Rowe, Toomay, Rice, Hall, Kwalick, and Atkinson helped shatter Pittsburgh in a performance labeled "Arson" by the press.

Oakland's famed precision passing was firing on all cylinders. Stabler's protectors included Mark van Eeghen and Clarence Davis, while kicker Errol Mann with David Humm holding added ten points and the mighty Raiders never trailed.

On defense, linebacker Monte Johnson delivered headaches for the Steelers. Defensive captain Willie Brown became the first player to ever intercept passes in fifteen consecutive pro seasons. Final score: Oakland 16, Pittsburgh 7.

But tragedy marred triumph. Outstanding starters Phil Villapiano and John Vella were lost for most of the season to injuries.

Week 3 @ Kansas City

In Kansas City, the Raiders were short six key players, but alert safety George Atkinson and a combat-ready defense gave Oakland room to operate.

A huge Monday-night national audience saw a Raiders offensive mastery as the silver and black scored 24 points in thirteen minutes. Touchdowns by Biletnikoff, Banaszak, and two by Davis along with three field goals by Errol Mann routed the Chiefs. Behind crushing blocking, van Eeghen and Davis each topped 100 yards as the defending world champions beat Kansas City, 37–28.

Week 4 @ Cleveland

In Cleveland, 80,000 saw Neil Colzie and the Raiders playing with controlled fury despite a short week and a third consecutive road game.

All scoring was from short yardage. Van Eeghen again rushed for over 100 yards and a pair of touchdowns while kicker Errol Mann scored on four consecutive field goals for the 26–10 romp, which was the Raiders' 17th consecutive win over two seasons.

Week 5 vs. Denver

When the undefeated Denver Broncos visited Oakland, their league-leading defense proved formidable. After an early score by Dave Casper, the Raiders were denied the end zone. Turnovers became touchdowns as Denver went on to win, 30–7.

Clearly 1977 would severely challenge the class and courage, leadership and loyalty of every member and fan of this Oakland Raiders organization.

Week 6 @ New York Jets

In New York, two ex-Alabama quarterbacks met, but Raiders assistants Tom Dahms and Lew Erber knew well that the Jets provide competition—not conversation.

Stabler to Casper put Oakland up 14–7, but the Jets roared back on an 87-yard score from Richard Todd to Wesley Walker.

The Jets increased their lead to 27–14 and held on till the fourth quarter. Calmly and deliberately, Raiders coach John Madden responded.

Stabler to Fred Biletnikoff brought the Raiders within six with time running out.

This seesaw struggle brought back memories of the Raiders' last New York visit: in 1970, with seconds to go, Oakland was trailing 13–7. Daryle Lamonica to Warren Wells defied all odds with a last second score to win the game.

Now as then, the Raiders' come-from-behind tradition would be tested, and once again the Raiders would pull another one out of the fire, as Stabler hit Siani in the corner of the end zone to beat the Jets, 28–27.

Week 7 @ Denver

In Denver, the Raiders, now 5–1, met the undefeated Broncos on "Orange Sunday," but Oakland would be the top dog today.

John Matuszak led the charge as Toomay and Sistrunk helped record eight sacks. Then the Raiders offense went to work—a pass from Stabler to Branch in the end zone drew first blood. Following an Errol Mann 42-yard field goal, the Raiders struck again with an eight-yard score by Clarence Davis and a one-yard score by Mark van Eeghen. Behind offensive captain Gene Upshaw, Clarence Davis ran for 105 yards as Oakland controlled and conquered, 24–14.

After five road games in seven weeks, the Raiders returned to the Coliseum, hopeful their roster would stabilize for the coming playoff drive.

Week 8 vs. Seattle

Against Seattle, Oakland's special teams were quick and deadly and Lester Hayes was lethal. On defense, Willie Brown, Skip Thomas, and Jack Tatum helped ground the Seahawks.

Van Eeghen followed Henry Lawrence en route to an AFC rushing title. With precision passing by Stabler to Siani, Biletnikoff, and Casper, rushing scores by Clarence Davis and Terry Robiskie, and three field goals from Errol Mann, Oakland triumphed, 44–7.

Next, assistants Oliver Spencer and Tom Flores prepared for Houston.

Week 9 vs. Houston

The Raiders defense pressured early with Dave Rowe and Otis Sistrunk in the forefront. The alert silver and black intercepted four passes as the defense created all the necessary breaks.

Stabler completed 23 passes as the explosive Raiders flashed toward a record 13th consecutive winning season.

But the Oilers hung in and trailed by only five points despite a swarming Raiders secondary. Neal Colzie's interception stopped one drive, and then safety Jack Tatum ended the drama. Final score: Oakland 34, Houston 29.

But there was no relief in San Diego the following week, as Ken Stabler joined the team's already lengthy injury list.

Week 10 @ San Diego

Inspired defense allowed the Chargers only 12 points, with Tatum and Thomas teaming up on an interception.

Quarterback Mike Rae scrambled for the Raiders' only score, as Oakland suffered their second loss of the season. Final score: San Diego 12, Oakland 7.

Week 11 vs. Buffalo

Buffalo was next, and the Monday-night crowd and television audience alike learned again that pride and poise is no idle phrase to the silver and black. Losses and injuries were forgotten, as brilliant Coach John Madden rallied his troops.

Three times Stabler threw for touchdowns—twice to Branch, once to Biletnikoff, and two TD rushes by Banaszak. There could be no doubt why these Oakland Raiders were feared, respected, and imitated.

The disciplined offense planned well and executed perfectly, completely dominating the Bills.

The defense led by Toomay, Matuszak, and Hendricks intimidated, controlled, and established superiority. Lawrence and Buehler sprung van Eeghen.

When the smoke cleared, the Raiders were victorious, 34–13.

Week 12 @ Los Angeles

In Los Angeles, photographers and fans awaited the Raiders.

The playoff-bound Rams excelled on defense, but the Raider offense—number one in the AFC—chipped away. Always productive Pete Banaszak scored once and Mark van Eeghen surpassed 1,000 yards for the second straight season.

Late in the game, Casper put the Raiders ahead, 14–13, but the Rams struck back against an Oakland secondary thinned earlier by the loss of George Atkinson with a broken leg.

The Raiders valiantly fought back, but their heroic efforts came up short. Final score: Los Angeles 20, Oakland 14.

Week 13 vs. Minnesota

Week 13 brought the Minnesota Vikings in for a rematch of Super Bowl XI, but Oakland needed victory now to make the playoffs.

Superb blocking by Dalby, Upshaw, Buehler, Shell, and Lawrence enabled Stabler to find Cliff Branch.

Special teams led by captain Warren Bankston, Ray Guy, Steve Sylvester, Terry Robiskie, and Jeff Barnes stunned Minnesota.

Linebacker Willie Hall's fumble recovery broke the dam and a tidal wave of Oakland points poured through.

Aggressive defenders were everywhere and linebacker Floyd Rice pounced on another Minnesota fumble. Raider fans were ecstatic, but there was still more to come.

With big Art Shell riding the rush harmlessly away, Ken Stabler hit for three scores in the devastating 35–13 win.

Once again the Oakland Raiders had clinched a playoff berth—their tenth in eleven years.

Week 14 vs. Kansas City

Prior to the final game of the season against the Kansas City Chiefs, Mark van Eeghen received the coveted Gorman Award as Most Inspirational Raider.

Despite the three field goals from Errol Mann and a touchdown by Carl Garrett, the Raiders trailed the Chiefs throughout the game until the fourth quarter, when Mike Rae threw to Carl Garrett to give them a 20–18 lead. Mann's 28-yard field goal gave them the 21–20 victory.

The Raiders were now headed for Baltimore and an unbelievable AFC playoff game.

AFC Divisional Playoffs @ Baltimore

This game would be played before the largest home crowd in the Baltimore Colts' history. The game itself would soon make history as one of the longest and greatest ever played in fifty-eight years of professional football.

From the beginning, the Raiders' execution was impressive as Stabler began a classic shootout that would total 345 yards passing as just one phase of a thundering assault.

While Davis left tacklers clutching at air, Baltimore quarterback Bert Jones was sacked by Matuszak. Like a great silver wall, Rice, Matuszak, Hendricks, Johnson, and others rose up.

Then the Raiders struck again with a deep bomb to Branch to the 20-yard line. A few plays later he lobbed one to Casper for the score.

Every play was big. Ted Hendricks got a hand on a Baltimore Colts fumble and Jeff Barnes recovered. The Raiders converted the blocked punt into points and led midway through the third quarter, 21–17.

But the Colts fought back, going ahead 31–28. Time became crucial. The Raiders had to stop the Colts right now, and they did exactly that.

They calmly sent "The Ghost to the Post." Casper's catch was a work of art. And then Madden called on Errol Mann to send the game into overtime.

This AFC playoff would go into a fifth period—a period of magnificent defense. In the final 23 minutes of this incredible game, the towering Raider defense did not allow a first down.

Tension and exhaustion tapped the last resources as the fifth period became the sixth. Desire and determination were stretched to ultimate limits, but these Raiders made one more gallant effort.

First it was Stabler to Branch for 19. Then on 2nd and 7, a beautifully conceived pass play brought down the curtain. Dave Casper's touchdown gave Oakland a 37–31 victory after 75 minutes and 43 seconds—the longest game in Raiders history.

AFC Conference Championship @ Denver

In the conference championship against the Denver Broncos, Dave Casper scored both touchdowns on passes from Stabler and Errol Mann kicked a 20-yard field goal. But the 17 points were not enough to stop the Broncos, as Oakland was defeated, 20–17.

1978 (9–7–0)

Week 1 @ Denver

The opener in Denver before a sellout crowd of 75,000 saw the silver and black clash angrily with the Orange Crush.

With linebacker Jeff Barnes and rookie defensive end Dave Browning seeking action, Denver was held to just five pass completions. But all the Raiders could muster that day were two field goals by Errol Mann. In the end, it was an incompletion that would hurt Oakland the most. A questionable interference call set up a Broncos touchdown and Oakland turnovers proved costly.

For Coach John Madden, the 14–6 loss was especially troublesome with the Chargers up next.

Week 2 @ San Diego

Despite over 700 yards total offense in San Diego, unique scoring plays still captured the headlines. Instead of a Raider interception came a Charger touchdown. But Ken Stabler hit Dave Casper and Morris Bradshaw as Oakland trailed, 20–14.

The Raiders stormed goalward again. Action peaked with only ten seconds to play. The ball was fumbled, bobbled, and kicked. And when play ended, Dave Casper had the winning touchdown. The silver and black had their 160th league victory (including playoffs) to add to the legend. Final score: Oakland 21, San Diego 20.

Week 3 @ Green Bay

Green Bay was the third consecutive road game and Mark van Eeghen rushed for a career-high 151 yards. With Clarence Davis on injured reserve, Terry Robiskie started and found pay dirt.

A pass from Stabler to Casper and then a hand off to Terry Robiskie put the Raiders up 14–0.

With Dave Dalby firing off from center and rookie Arthur Whittington following the silver and black convoy to two more scores, the Raiders destroyed the Packers. Final score: Raiders 28, Green Bay 3.

Week 4 vs. New England

For the NFL's first Sunday-night national telecast against New England, Steve Grogan's evening wear featured Ted Hendricks and John Matuszak.

Ken Stabler hit Dave Casper for one score, then Whittington followed Pete Banaszak and Gene Upshaw for another as Oakland exploded for 14 points.

A third Raiders score was called back. The Patriots had rallied to gain a winning position. Final score: New England 21, Oakland 14.

The rugged 1978 schedule would severely test the Raiders' will to win.

Week 5 @ Chicago

In Chicago, the fourth road game in five weeks would soon become the fourth overtime struggle in Raiders history. Chicago had won nine of their last ten, but tenacious defense led by Monte Johnson kept them in check. Terry Robiskie scored the first Raiders touchdown, but the Bears rallied for a 19–16 lead.

With Chicago threatened again, they were forcefully denied. With 60 seconds left, Cliff Branch grabbed his eighth pass of the day. Then when Morris Bradshaw's TD was called back, Errol Mann kicked his fourth field goal to bring the game into overtime. The Raiders had never lost in overtime, and they weren't about to start now.

Neal Colzie intercepted a Bears pass and ran it down to the three-yard line. On the next play, Whittington ran it in for the score and the win. Final score: Oakland 25, Chicago 19.

Week 6 vs. Houston

Oakland hosted the playoff-bound Houston Oilers and the NFL's MVP Earl Campbell.

First-year starters Dave Browning and Rod Martin and the entire defense rose to the challenge. Johnson, Browning, Matuszak, Otis Sistrunk, and company slowed Houston down.

Then Arthur Whittington took the long way around to put Oakland up 7–3. The Oilers fired back to lead 17–7, but their next drive backfired when Browning jarred the ball loose and safety Charles Phillips returned it 96 yards for a score.

Ray Guy's sky-high punts were skillfully covered by Booker Russell, Larry Brunson, Steve Sylvester, Derrick Ramsey, Joe Stewart, and John Huddleston, and the Oilers found themselves deep in the well with the Raiders relentlessly coming on.

With only 50 seconds to go, Ken Stabler rolled left and fired to Dave Casper, whose one-armed catch meant victory. Final score: Oakland 21, Houston 17.

Week 7 vs. Kansas City

The Kansas City Chiefs came to Oakland for their 39th meeting (including playoffs) and a rivalry dating back to 1960. But this October day, the Chiefs were no match for the Raiders' precision passing.

Cornerback Monte Jackson led a young secondary in scalping the Chiefs. Two scores by van Eeghen and one each by Casper and Phillips spelled doom for KC. In the end, Kansas City stumbled and Oakland alertly responded for a sweet 28–6 conquest.

Week 8 @ Seattle

In Seattle, things went sour for Oakland. Robiskie and Browning were injured early and versatile Seahawks quarterback Jim Zorn lit up a shocking scoreboard display.

All the Raiders could salvage was their 182-game scoring streak with a late Stabler to Branch touchdown. Final score: Seattle 27, Oakland 7.

Week 9 vs. San Diego

The following week found San Diego in Oakland for a Western Division rematch.

Aggressive linebacker Ted Hendricks forced a fumble that Mike McCoy picked off in midair. Then on a fake field goal, Dave Humm passed to Casper to keep the drive going. The Raiders rolled with van Eeghen and Whittington, utilizing blocking by Dalby, Mickey Marvin, Upshaw, Lawrence, and Shell.

But again, another thrilling San Diego–Oakland game would close in controversy.

On fourth down, Lester Hayes ended Charger hopes, but an official saw it differently than Raider players and John Madden, and San Diego had life. The Chargers' winning tally created more controversy when the receiver appeared to step out of bounds when making the catch.

Both 1978 finishes in this series would be long remembered. Final score: San Diego 27, Oakland 23.

Week 10 @ Kansas City

As pro football's winningest team, the Raiders created sellouts and did so again Kansas City's Arrowhead Stadium.

The Raiders were on the rebound and safety Jack Tatum turned an alert play into an Oakland plus. All-Pro Dave Casper had seven catches for 112 yards and Arthur Whittington rushed for 134 yards—the first Raider rookie to top 100 yards in a decade.

On the final play, Oakland captain Willie Brown and Lester Hayes ensured a 20–10 victory. With the victory, John Madden became the thirteenth head coach in NFL history to win 100 league games and only the second in modern times to achieve this remarkable feat in just ten seasons.

Week 11 @ Cincinnati

The Raiders were in Cincinnati for a Monday-night game, and their defense was punishing.

Kenny Stabler hit Raymond Chester for six and the Raiders were out to maintain an unsurpassed record of only one loss in nine years of Monday-night play. Colzie, Casper, Bradshaw, and van Eeghen added TDs totaling 34 points.

Phil Villapiano intercepted a Bengals pass to keep the Raiders in control, as Oakland raised their season record to 7–4, beating Cincinnati 34–21.

Week 12 vs. Detroit

A hot Detroit team, a short week, rain, and mud all failed to slow the Raiders.

Stabler threw to Branch, who was taken down at the one. The ball was knocked loose, and Mark van Eeghen recovered in the end zone for one of his three scores of the day. Casper scored the other touchdown while Phil Villapiano tackled Lions quarterback Gary Danielson in the end zone for a safety.

Next, Matuszak, McCoy, Hendricks, Hall, Tatum and the rest defeated the Lions by a score of 29–17.

Week 13 vs. Seattle

The only NFL division with four winning teams is the tough AFC West, so the Seattle–Oakland game was a crucial one between playoff contenders.

Otis Sistrunk and the Raiders defense had fire in their eyes. Big Charles Philyaw demolished plays and then Stabler went airborne for a 16–14 lead.

Another cliffhanger: with just two seconds left, a 46-yard field goal downed the Raiders and tightened the playoff race.

Final score: Seattle 17, Oakland 16.

Week 14 vs. Denver

A Sunday-night game against Denver was next with the division lead at stake.

On the first three possessions, the Raiders drove inside the Denver 20, but only got two field goals out of it. Oakland mistakes were Denver breaks as the Broncos closed in on the division title as Raiders fans saw their playoff hopes slipping out of reach. Final score: Denver 21, Oakland 6.

Week 15 @ Miami

In the season's 15th week, the Raiders traveled cross-country to Miami with a playoff berth still possible for the winner.

A Biletnikoff touchdown was Oakland's only score as their record dropped to 8–7—far below the level of excellence expected from Oakland. Final score: Miami 23, Oakland 6.

Week 16 vs. Minnesota

Before the final game of the season, Dave Casper received the Gorman as Most Inspirational Raider.

The Raiders dominated the playoff-bound Vikings for pride, respect, and tradition. Scores by Biletnikoff, Phillips, and van Eeghen, along with two field goals by Errol Mann, defeated the Vikings, 27–20.

It was John Madden's final win before retiring and Mark van Eegh-en's third consecutive 1,000-yard season.

The Raiders' will to win had now earned 14 consecutive winning seasons—a mark exceeded only once in NFL history.

1979 SEASON (9–7–0)

Week 1 @ Los Angeles

The team's twentieth season began against the Super Bowl-bound Rams. For new head coach Tom Flores, it was the first of four consecutive road games.

Punter Ray Guy and the Oakland kicking game cornered the Rams and rookie Jim Breech kicked his first Raider field goal aided by the sure-handed Dave Humm.

Defensive tackle Reggie Kinlaw, a twelfth-round draft choice who again proved Raider scouting prowess, blocked a punt to set up a touchdown as Ken Stabler hit Derrick Ramsey for six.

Pro Bowl performer Dave Pear, teamed with John Matuszak, spear-headed a rush that shut out the Rams the entire second half. All-Pro tight end Raymond Chester collected the winning score in a 24–17 Oakland victory.

Week 2 @ San Diego

The defense was without John Matuszak, the offense minus tackles Art Shell and Lindsey Mason (who missed the entire season), and Mickey Marvin went out during the game.

Against San Diego, speedster Joe Stewart helped propel the Raid-ers toward the 1979 NFL lead in kickoff returns. Wide receiver Rich Martini, one of eleven first-year players on the Oakland roster, recorded his first touchdown.

Dave Pear and Dave Browning pressured the Chargers with sup-port from linebackers Ted Hendricks, Monte Johnson, and Rod Mar-tin. Unfortunately for the Raiders, ten points weren't enough. Final score: San Diego 30, Oakland 10.

Week 3 @ Seattle

The Raiders were short on points in Seattle. A 12-yard pass from Stabler to Rich Martini and a field goal from Jim Breech was all the scoring that the Raiders would do that day. Final score: Seattle 27, Oakland 10.

Week 4 @ Kansas City

In Kansas City, the Raiders found themselves short on personnel. Out for the year were Morris Bradshaw and Joe Stewart, so the young players had to move to the forefront.

Rookie defensive end Willie Jones took rapid aim at team leadership in sacks. Rookie free agent Rufus Bess blocked the Chiefs' scoring try and came within inches of breaking loose himself.

Quarterback Jim Plunkett came in late and hit Raymond Chester deep to set up the Raiders' lone score, but Terry Robiskie was down for the season. Final score: Kansas City 25, Oakland 7.

Week 5 vs. Denver

After four road games, the Raiders finally opened at home against the Denver Broncos.

Short on experience but long on aggressiveness, Raiders rookies met the challenge, as Reggie Kinlaw alternated with Willie Jones to corral the Broncos.

The defense grew stronger as the game grew longer and Charles Philyaw, Willie Jones, Rod Martin, Mike Davis, Monte Johnson, and others sealed the verdict. Defensive coaches Charles Sumner, Willie Brown, Oliver Spencer, and Myrel Moore had their horses ready.

The Raiders' will to win still endured. Final score: Raiders 27, Denver 3.

The next game would be Miami on Monday night.

Week 6 vs. Miami

All-Pro tackle Art Shell was active again while Steve Sylvester checked in at center for the injured Dave Dalby.

In the third period, Art Shell, Gene Upshaw, Steve Sylvester, Dan Medlin, and Henry Lawrence gave Stabler time to find Chester for a score. The determined Raiders defense gave up only three points while scoring once.

Ted Hendricks proved that he had lost neither instinct nor talent in eleven pro seasons.

When the Dolphins threatened late, Reggie Kinlaw smothered Miami's scoring drive.

The 13–3 win evened the Raider record at 3–3.

Week 7 vs. Atlanta

Despite a short practice week, the Raider defense returned ready for the Falcons. A push by Jeff Barnes, Pat Toomay, Charles Philyaw, and John Matuszak gave cornerback Lester Hayes a chance to score his first Raider TD on a 51-yard interception.

The dominating silver and black thundered for 31 points in the second half alone. Mark van Eeghen scored a total of three TDs, while Clarence Hawkins and Larry Brunson scored one TD each for the Raiders and rolled for 50 points for the fifth time in team history. Final score: Oakland 50, Atlanta 19.

Point production was down, however, after the cross-country trip to tangle with the Jets.

Week 8 @ New York Jets

The defense faced a challenge from these longtime rivals. Rod Martin, Pat Toomay, and Phil Villapiano attacked with controlled fury. Second-year pro Mike Davis worked in combination with Monte Johnson and Henry Williams to record his second pro interception.

Despite 459 yards total offense, 25 first downs and two TDs— Stabler to Raymond Chester—the Raiders lost by 9. Final score: New York 28, Oakland 10.

Week 9 vs. San Diego

Primetime football and the Raiders—an unbeatable combination . . .

A national TV audience of fifty million looked on as the Raiders rose to challenge the Chargers.

Charles Phillips and Rod Martin blitzed quarterback Dan Fouts. When Fouts found time, Monte Jackson and Jack Tatum made certain he found little else.

A now-healthy Cliff Branch added another dimension to the varied Raiders passing game. Fullback Mark van Eeghen relentlessly banged away en route to becoming the number-two rusher in Oakland Raiders history.

A highpoint of the game was a kickoff return of 104 yards by Wisconsin rookie Ira Matthews.

Next came Booker Russell, a young player who learned quickly that a second effort is first nature to those in silver and black. Russell's third rushing touchdown of the game earned congratulations from teammate Todd Christensen. Final score: Oakland 45, Chargers 22.

Week 10 vs. San Francisco

In the Raiders' third game against NFC opponents, Oakland limited San Francisco to just 10 points.

For offensive position, the Raiders called on the skills of Larry Brunson, who became the NFL's number-one kickoff return man in 1979.

First-year fullback Derrick Jensen blasted up inside for Oakland while the Raiders' defense refused to yield to 49er runners with Hayes, Tatum, Hendricks, and Villapiano spearheading a fourth down stance.

The Raiders' total domination of NFC teams continued at a record pace. Final score: Oakland 23, San Francisco 10.

Week 11 @ Houston

The calm Texas sky above the Houston Astrodome could not conceal the fury within.

With Raider Mark van Eeghen out injured, heavy traffic concentrated on one fullback, Houston's All-Pro: Earl Campbell. Lester

Hayes, Mike Davis, and Jack Tatum zeroed in on #34, but Campbell was too tough to control.

Despite touchdowns from Chester and Casper, Oakland could not get enough points on the board.

The power and precision passing of quarterback Dan Pastorini, who hit for two long scores, were major factors in Oakland's loss. Final score: Houston 31, Oakland 17.

Week 12 vs. Kansas City

Back home to meet the Kansas City Chiefs, the Raiders would renew a Western Division rivalry that had thrilled fans for twenty seasons.

It would remain for Raider youth to rise to the occasion—quality youth in the form of rookie defender Reggie Kinlaw and in the performance of Arthur Whittington after missing seven games.

With protection by Dalby and van Eeghen, Stabler had time to go to second-year tight end Derrick Ramsey, van Eeghen, and Branch for scores, but when the gun sounded, the Raiders had lost by three. Final score: Kansas City 24, Oakland 21.

Next on the schedule was Denver on the road.

Week 13 @ Denver

There was snow and ice at Mile High Stadium, but Raiders running back Booker Russell stayed hot as he used blocks by Sylvester, Lawrence, Upshaw, and company to break loose for a 72-yard gain en route to his only 100-yard game of his career.

Stabler and tight end Dave Casper combined for one score and the Raiders battled to a 14–10 lead. Twice the Broncos threatened and twice rookie cornerback Henry Williams shut them down with interceptions. Final score: Oakland 14, Denver 10.

Week 14 @ New Orleans

The first Raiders visit to the Louisiana Superdome would provide the huge, national television audience another unforgettable showing of Raiders comeback courage.

For nearly three periods the Saints could do no wrong. After thirty-seven minutes, New Orleans ran up a seemingly insurmountable lead. What remained was totally incredible except to Raiders fans who knew that commitment to excellence, not miracles, key the silver and black.

Kinlaw handcuffed the Saints and the game plan of offensive coaches came alive.

After being down 35–14, the Raiders miraculously scored TDs by van Eeghen, Ramsey, and two from Cliff Branch. The Raiders came back to beat the Saints, 42–35.

The Raiders' Monday-night record now stood at only one loss in fifteen games.

Week 15 vs. Cleveland

Just six days later, the Raiders were again ready for battle. The enemy this time was the Cleveland Browns.

Browning, Toomay, Martin, and Jones led the defense to two interceptions and five sacks. A pass from Stabler to Branch and four field goals by Jim Breech insured victory. Final score: Oakland 19, Cleveland 14.

The win over Cleveland assured the Raiders a fifteenth consecutive winning season for the organization.

Week 16 vs. Seattle

As the 1979 season closed, Pro Bowler Raymond Chester was awarded Most Inspirational Raider.

Against Seattle, the driving battle to the playoffs continued as Lester Hayes picked off a pass and put up six for Oakland. Arthur Whittington fought his way to the end zone as the Raiders inched back, but even with a late score by van Eeghen, the Raiders ended six points from a chance for another year of playoff glory to add to the already unrivaled record of excellence. Final score: Seattle 29, Oakland 24.

Yet one loss could not alter the decades of greatness that had witnessed the Raiders' monumental climb to the top.

One man who so symbolized Raiders commitment to excellence was Jim Otto. Otto arrived in Oakland in 1960, the Raiders' first year, and started every game for fifteen seasons.

A keystone of so many outstanding Raider teams, Otto was a perennial giant among Raider giants, and twice won the Gorman Award as the player who best exemplified the pride and spirit of the organization.

"Double O" contributed much to the respect and national acclaim that came to these proud warriors in silver and black. Interior linemen often go unnoticed by the crowd, but Jim Otto won the recognition of his peers.

On August 2, 1980, Jim Otto was the first Raider enshrined in the Pro Football Hall of Fame.

His will to win spanned two glorious decades, and as a new decade began, this Raider commitment to excellence still burned fiercely as it has through these decades of destiny.

BEGINNING THE NEW DECADE ON A HIGH NOTE: SUPER BOWL XV

1980: ANOTHER INCREDIBLE SEASON AND SUPER BOWL XV

From 1967 through 1977, the Oakland Raiders won nine division titles, a Vince Lombardi trophy, and the reputation of being the most feared team in the NFL.

But by the end of the '70s, the silver and black were in decline. After not making the playoffs in '78 and '79, Oakland made major changes to compete for a title in 1980. Still, most experts picked them to finish last in the AFC West.

Even though fifteen new players joined the team, Oakland retained their trademark of "Just Win, Baby."

Veteran guard Gene Upshaw maintained his leadership role and rookie linebacker Matt Millen brought not only youth to the Raiders organization, but physical intensity.

Another new face was that of a former Heisman Trophy winner and number-one draft pick whose career in 1978 had hit rock bottom.

Stanford quarterback Jim Plunkett was drafted by the New England Patriots as the number-one pick of the 1971 NFL draft. The former Heisman Trophy winner spent five uneventful years with the Patriots and two more mediocre years with the 49ers before he was given a second chance with the Raiders.

"Talk about low points," said Plunkett. "Here I was a first-round draft choice just seven years earlier—out of football. Talk about depression. I didn't know what to do with myself. Maybe I should quit football altogether and seek employment elsewhere? It was a very difficult time in my life."

But Gene Upshaw and the rest of the Raiders knew Plunkett had talent.

"We knew he could play. I can remember him being a number-one pick out of Stanford. The Raiders go back to New England to play him in his first game and he beats us."

Jim still felt he could still play football.

"Even though I was down in the dumps and things weren't going well for me, I still knew I could play ball. All I needed was another opportunity."

They don't call Oakland "the league of lost souls" for nothing. And because of that, Plunkett got the chance to redeem himself with the Raiders.

"It's always a group that was seen as a renegade group—the halfway house of the NFL—guys who didn't fit anywhere else," said Upshaw. "And they always seemed to come to the Raiders and thrive. And it was a simple reason why it always seemed to work. Al Davis always gave you a chance to be you. We used to tell all the players, 'There ain't many stops after you leave here.'"

Plunkett felt comfortable with Al Davis.

"Everywhere you've gone you've been labeled as a savior. You've been brought in to help turn this team around. That wasn't the case with Oakland. Davis told me that he wanted me to sit back, watch and learn our offense, and get myself prepared."

Entering the 1980 season, Plunkett was the Raiders' backup behind Dan Pastorini, who was his high school rival in Northern California, and the man selected two spots after Plunkett in the 1971 draft.

"I had just about had it," said Jim. "Two years on the bench. Stabler was gone and they were now bringing in Pastorini—another strong-armed quarterback."

Even with his past struggles, Plunkett was not happy with being a bench warmer.

"He didn't like sitting on the bench," said Madden. "He wanted to get in a play. It's no fun to come to practice every day, work as hard as you work, and never get a chance to show it on Sunday and help your team win football games."

One player expected to help Oakland win right away was a six-two, 250-pound Penn State lineman turned linebacker Matt Millen. Oakland had selected him in the second round of the 1980 NFL draft.

While the team was revered throughout the league, Millen wasn't really familiar with the organization.

"I didn't know much about the Raiders. I knew them by reputation only. I knew they were a rogue outfit. When I arrived to Oakland there was a sign that hung above our old locker room that said:

Raiders Rules
Raiders Rule #1: Cheating Is Encouraged
Raiders Rule #2: See Rule #1

According to Gene Upshaw, the Raiders' rules were known only to the Raiders.

"It was something we said among ourselves when we would be out and away from the game. If we were playing golf, if we were playing shuffleboard—whatever was going on, the old saying was, 'If you're not cheating, you're not trying.'

"You laughed about it until you realized that what they were saying is, 'Find a way to get it done.' If someone is holding you, how do you make them stop? You need to talk to the official? Fine. You need to grab them by the throat? Great. You need to punch them in the throat—whatever you need to do, get it done. Is that cheating? Well, I read Raiders Rule #1. Is that cheating; no, actually it was not. I learned very early that every game has its own set of rules and every officiating crew calls them differently. Whatever those rules were that day, you learned them fast and then you learned how to skirt them."

Whether the Raiders cheated or not didn't matter. Few thought Oakland would win in 1980.

Matt Millen's hopes were not high for the 1980 season.

"I really didn't have very high expectations regarding Oakland because, the day I was drafted, I was quickly informed by the media that the Raiders weren't going to be very good that year."

But in 1980, the only surprise bigger than the Oakland Raiders would be the player who ended up leading them back to the Super Bowl.

A lineman in college, Matt Millen had six weeks in training camp to learn how to play middle linebacker. Millen made an impression on both his coaches and teammates almost immediately.

Gene Upshaw talks about Matt's intensity during training camp.

"Matt Millen in training camp . . . now that has to be one experience you could never forget! That was because Matt Millen thought that every day was game day; he thought every play was a game, and he thought they were voting for the Pro Bowl every time he came onto the field. The guy is coming in full speed, and we don't even have pads on, going right at Shell and myself. We're thinking, 'What's wrong with this guy? Where did he come from?'"

"Art and Gene took me under their wing the moment I got there," said Millen. "I was like their little puppy."

"The guy was nuts and he would have something called 'arm parties' where he would bring this bar into the room and he and a couple of other guys would do curls at night until they couldn't lift their arms," said Upshaw. "He would do this all during training camp!"

"Gene and Art would tell me to just be aggressive," said Millen. "You need to get that huddle straightened out over there. When I stepped into the huddle, they listened to me. They wanted somebody to take over. So, hey, I took over since no one else was going to."

While he was having a successful camp, Millen's ability to lead the defense faced an early obstacle.

"I was so proud to have a form-fitted mouthpiece. I brought it with me from Penn State and it fit in my mouth there perfectly. Kick 'em in the Head Ted Hendricks came walking over to me and said, 'You got that mouthpiece?' I said, 'Yeah.' He goes, 'Is that one of those form-fit mouthpieces?' 'Yeah, I got it at Penn State.' He goes, 'Let me see that thing.' I showed it to him and he threw it and it went flying. I said, 'What the hell are you doing?' He goes, 'I can't understand a damn thing you're saying. Don't wear any mouthpiece of any kind. Just yell it out!' That was the end of my form-fitting mouthpiece."

There were always guys who did crazy things but they just fit right in. They might be crazy somewhere else, but they weren't crazy for the Raiders.

John Matuszak had his own philosophy about the Raiders image.

"When you say I epitomize the Raiders, and then you say the Raiders aren't very well liked, I guess you are trying to say that the Raiders, as well as John Matuszak, have always been controversial."

Like the franchise he played for, Matt Millen was never afraid to tell it like it was.

"I didn't know anything about John Matuszak other than he was supposed to be nuts. And he didn't disappoint."

Matuszak had his own thoughts on the game of football.

"It's the closest thing to being a lion or a cheetah or a hawk that there is. It's the most beautiful but the most brutal game in the world."

The Raiders loved to have fun but they also knew how to work hard.

"Were they a bunch of guys who liked to have fun?" said Millen. "Absolutely! We had fun off the field and we had fun on the field. But the part that is missing is that we also worked hard. We were a hard-working group of guys who wanted to get better."

MADDEN'S REPLACEMENT

Oakland's coaching replacement for the Hall of Fame Madden was former Raiders assistant Tom Flores, whose low-key approach was a calming influence for the team.

Plunkett liked Flores's relaxed attitude.

"Tom was laid back and a matter-of-fact kind of guy. He sits back and watches everything and doesn't raise his voice very often."

Upshaw respected Flores.

"I think what Tom brought to the table was confidence and a quiet approach to the game. And we wanted to play for him. When Tom Flores brought us out on the field, you wanted to win for Tom Flores."

Flores's team opened the 1980 season with a new quarterback and six new starters on defense. It also had to contend with the scorching heat of Kansas City.

"It was brutal!" said Millen. "It was probably 110 degrees on the field. It was an Astroturf field and it was hot!"

"The heat was almost unbearable!" said Plunkett. "It burned the bottom of your feet!

"In the middle of the third quarter they had a beer commercial on. Everyone turned to look up at the video board when Ted Hendricks said, 'They're killin' me out here! They're killin' me! Somebody get rid of that fucking commercial!'"

Each day Millen was learning the Raider way. Play hard and have fun doing it. He began his NFL career by grabbing his first career interception. He also received a vital lesson in Raider etiquette.

"At Penn State we were instructed to address an official by saying, 'Excuse me, Mr. Official.' And then you asked the question. Now let's fast forward to the Raiders in my first game. I didn't know officials knew that kind of language. And I didn't know you could address them that way. I was literally in shock. Ted Hendricks started cussing out an official and the official turned back and started cussing back. I thought, 'Whatever happened to *Excuse me, Mr. Official?*'"

* * *

Dan Pastorini threw for 317 yards and two touchdowns as Oakland beat Kansas City in week one, 27–14. The revamped Raiders played like a contender, but it would take six weeks and another quarterback before they would finally become one.

During the season's first five weeks, Plunkett remained on the Oakland bench with no playing opportunity in sight.

"I was disappointed, but I still had a job to do. It's difficult to keep your edge and timing and keep focused on the chance that you will get in. I was just hoping for an opportunity to arise."

The Raiders play added to Plunkett's frustration. Oakland split their first four games as they struggled to adapt to Pastorini at quarterback.

"Dan had the bad habit of hitting his left hand with the ball before he actually threw it and we would think it was gone—but it wasn't," said Upshaw.

"They beat the piss out of him!" said Millen. "He would stand in there and see it coming and he would open himself up and get pounded. He came back the next week and did the same thing—and they got him and they broke him."

In Week 5, Pastorini suffered a broken leg against the Kansas City Chiefs, and Plunkett finally got his chance. In his first substantial action of the season, Plunkett did little to help the Raiders.

"I hadn't played in almost two and a half years," said Plunkett. "I did throw a couple of TDs but threw quite a few interceptions. We were behind and I was trying to get back into the football game. I was very disappointed."

The loss to Kansas City put the Raiders at 2–3. The Raiders were still confident, but could see their season slipping away.

"Losing was not something you got used to in Oakland," said Upshaw. "We got hammered, lost our quarterback, and now we were going into this unknown. But together we felt we still had enough talent to win this thing."

The team now turned to Plunkett, and nobody had any doubts that Jim could do the job.

"I was a little apprehensive, but in the back of my mind I knew I had to do well or I might be out of football again," said Plunkett.

Al Davis gave Jim the confidence he needed to hear.

"I told Plunkett that he was *part* of this team, not the *focus* of it. I told him that it's not important that you play well, but that we win."

"I kept telling myself to stay in the pocket and hold the ball to the last possible second and not run too soon," said Plunkett. "These were things I had to do in order to be successful."

With this, Jim revived the Raiders' offense.

With Plunkett in charge, Matt Millen and the rest of the team gained back their confidence.

"We took on the San Diego Chargers who were acknowledged as the best and highest scoring team in the NFL, and we whipped them. And what comes with a good whipping for a team that's struggling? It's called the great equalizer—*confidence*. And here I am as a young kid and I'm looking around the room and these guys are starting to believe that we have a chance. And so we finally start to show that we are starting to define ourselves—and Plunkett was our main guy.

"We had just beaten Dan Fouts and crew and now we were going to play the defending World Champions on Monday night. And with the Raiders I learned fast. When the lights turned off, we turned on.

"There was a lot of electricity. We were back in the Steel City on a Monday night. The criminal element was still there. You had the Oakland Raiders and the Pittsburgh Steelers. What an incredible rivalry!"

"We were down 17–7 early in the ballgame and had to claw and fight our way back in," said Plunkett. "On the next play, the Steelers went into a curtain defense that allowed Cliff Branch to be covered one on one. As soon as I saw it, I audibled to it, and there went Branch for a long touchdown."

Bradshaw never recovered.

"We put a beating on Terry Bradshaw," said Millen. "We knocked Terry down I can't tell you how many times. Terry was lying on the ground and I was talking to Jack Ham and said, 'Gee, I hope he's alright.' Jack says, 'What? Are you kidding me? It's Monday Night Football! He knows there's good camera time!'

"I think that was the game where we knew that we had a chance, because we just beat the defending Super Bowl Champions on Monday night in front of a national audience. And Pittsburgh needed that win."

The question that needed to be asked in terms of the 1980 Raiders was: Do you get confident because you're winning, or do you start winning because you're confident?

Behind Jim Plunkett, Oakland won six straight games. The man who was out of football just three seasons earlier was now the league's comeback story.

"It was a different area of the football team contributing to our victories week after week," said Plunkett. "Our defense for the first half of the season was literally giving up 27 to 28 points a game, and right after that Pittsburgh game, they cut that in half."

The Raiders took an 8–3 record into Philadelphia to take on the Eagles, the best team in the NFC.

Matt Millen, like the rest of us, despised the Eagles' home field.

"Veteran's Stadium was a dump. They had seams in the Astroturf, it was hard as a rock, but when it was cold outside, it was even worse."

Raiders defensive coordinator Charlie Sumner gave Millen special instructions for the Eagles' biggest weapon.

"Charlie told me, 'Harold Carmichael is six-eight and, the first time they run a deep end, you go hit him in the middle of the chest and don't worry about the flag. We'll handle the flag.' So the first time he ran that deep end, the ball was overthrown and I just tried to kill him. Hit him as hard as I could. I ended up hitting half of him and half of one of our guys. I think I hurt our guy."

The Eagles didn't hurt Plunkett—they just pressured him all day.

"They got eight sacks on me. They could have had more sacks. Art Shell felt I was dropping back too far. I was trying to give myself more time.

"When Philly scored their touchdown, one of our linebackers had Jaworski in his grasp. Jaworski ducked and slid over the top and made the play."

Final score: Eagles 10, Raiders 7. The Raiders were 8–4 and still had a shot at the playoffs, but other things were brewing with the organization. Al Davis was about to go up against Commissioner Pete Rozelle.

DAVIS VS. ROZELLE

"If I had to sum up the Oakland Raiders with only a couple of words, it would start with Al Davis," said Upshaw. "He is the Oakland Raiders. He is what the team is all about."

"He wanted to win as bad as anybody if not worse," said Plunkett.

Davis's combative style often put him at odds with the rest of the league.

Plunkett continued: "Ever since I joined the Raiders in 1978, there was always some controversy surrounding Mr. Davis and the organization."

After failing to extend the Raiders' lease in Oakland, Davis began preliminary plans to move his team to Los Angeles for the 1981 season.

Pete Rozelle made it clear to Al as to what needed to be done in order to move his team to another city.

"Al told me that he was seriously thinking about moving to Los Angeles. I said, 'Well, if you are, if you decide you want to pursue it further, let me know and I will schedule a league meeting and it will be reviewed.' He said, 'If I decide to move, I do not intend to ask for a league vote.' I said, 'That clearly was against the constitution and it would put us on opposite sides.'"

Upshaw was on Al's side.

"Al felt he should have the right, if his lease was up, to move to a better facility in another city. He sued the NFL and spent many years in court. I felt Al was right and that the Coliseum was not up to the same standards as some of the other stadiums in the NFL."

Davis was committed to his word.

"I've had three different owners, the commissioner, and league officials come to me and say if I were to stay in Oakland they will give me whatever I what. But I made a commitment and it's too late."

Rozelle differs with Davis.

"There were representatives from fourteen or fifteen teams who were at that meeting whose story will sharply contradict what Al Davis said."

* * *

While Oakland fans rallied to save their team, the Raiders were racing toward the playoffs. Oakland won three of their last four games to clinch their first playoff berth since 1977. The key to the Raiders' resurgence was "The Judge," cornerback Lester Hayes. Hayes, who led the league in 1980 with 13 interceptions, had four more called back because of penalties.

"Lester had a year in 1980 that was arguably the greatest year a corner has ever had," said Millen. "He just took the game over."

On the field, Hayes's play spoke volumes. But off the field he struggled with a speech impediment.

"Lester approached his stuttering like he did everything else. He attacked it straight on," said Millen. "He didn't make you feel uncomfortable with it because he knew that you knew he was struggling. He just stuck with it and he expected that you would stick with it too."

Hayes worked tirelessly to improve his speech and used Stickum to help his hands. He put Stickum everywhere and stuck to opposing players like glue.

"Of course, Stickum is no longer allowed in the NFL," said Upshaw. "But back then if you touched him, you would stick to him. That's why he got all those interceptions."

Matt Millen recalls a game with Houston where Lester left his mark.

"We were playing the Houston Oilers and they had a center by the name of Carl Mauck. They're getting ready to kick a field goal. They're in the huddle, Judge walks out with a big hunk of Stickum and slaps it on the ball nonchalantly and walks out. The Oilers come out and Carl reaches down and grabs the ball right on the Stickum. The veins pop right out of his neck. And he's like, 'That stuttering son of a bitch did something to the ball!' He was screaming at the officials and they had to calm him down. We came off the ball, Carl snapped it over his head, and I always wondered how much the Stickum had to do with that."

In that Wild Card playoff game against the Oilers, the Raiders drew first blood with a 47-yard field goal by Chris Bahr. Earl Campbell made the only score for Houston. The Raiders continued to roll with scores by Todd Christensen, Arthur Whittington, Lester Hayes and a second field goal by Chris Bahr. Oakland sacked former Raiders quarterback Kenny Stabler seven times and cruised to a 27–7 victory. In the fourth quarter, the Judge delivered his final verdict with an interception taken back for a touchdown.

DIVISIONAL PLAYOFFS: RAIDERS @ BROWNS

The Raiders would have to travel to Cleveland to play the Browns in the bitter cold in the divisional round. The ground was completely frozen and the locker room showers didn't work.

"It was freezing and our center, Dave Dalby, was in a T-shirt," said Plunkett. "Why? I'll never know.

"The wind was ferocious coming off the lake. There were 80 to 90 passes thrown during that game and only a few were completed against the wind."

In the first quarter, Cleveland's defensive back Ron Bolton intercepted a pass from Plunkett and ran it back 42 yards for the score. The Browns missed the PAT, but were still on top, 6–0. Cleveland took the lead in the third quarter and held it until the final nine minutes of the game, when Mark van Eeghen scored, which put Oakland up by two.

But Gene Upshaw was still a little nervous about a possible comeback from Cleveland's "Kardiac Kids."

"They were known as the Kardiac Kids—an offense that could move the ball down field and score within two minutes. And they started marching down the field again, and all we could do was stand there.

"I'm standing there thinking, 'We've come this far. We've fought this hard.' And I can tell you this: I had never felt that low in my life."

"Now they're going into the open end zone where the Dawg Pound was," said Millen. "We had already blocked one field goal going in there."

"And we look at their bench and we keep thinking that they are going to kick and we are going to lose," said Upshaw. "Well, they go back for one more pass. I just could not believe it. I don't think that anyone on our sidelines could believe it."

"I don't blame their play calling," said Plunkett. "You're taking a chance and their kicker Don Cockroft already had missed an extra point and they were afraid they were going to miss the field goal."

As the Browns' offense came out of the huddle and lined up for the play, nobody thought that quarterback Brian Sipe would chance throwing the ball . . . but he did.

The Raiders defensive back, "Mad Dog" Mike Davis, made the game-saving interception in the end zone on a play known as Red Right 88. Sipe's pass fluttered in the strong wind, and Davis stepped in front of receiver Ozzie Newsome to win the game.

What was ironic about that play was the fact that Davis could not catch the ball very well; but when it counted he made a phenomenal catch!

Gene Upshaw agrees about Mike's catching skills.

"Mike Davis was so bad that he couldn't catch a cold in Alaska barefooted. So you go from as low as you could possibly be and in one snap of the ball you go as high as you could possibly be. Also, I could not believe that Mike Davis actually caught the ball because I'm telling you, he had absolutely the worst hands in that secondary."

Final score: Oakland 14, Cleveland 12.

For the AFC Championship game, Oakland would travel from the Cleveland cold to the San Diego sun.

AFC CHAMPIONSHIP GAME RAIDERS @ CHARGERS

"Going into the Conference Championship, we knew that we would be playing our old rivals on their home field. But deep down inside, we knew that we were destined," said Upshaw. "We outplayed them the first time, so we approached this game with a lot of confidence."

Against the NFL's fourth-highest-scoring team, Plunkett went to the air early in the first quarter with a 65-yard pass to Raymond Chester. Following a Charlie Joiner pass from Dan Fouts to tie the score, Plunkett put the Raiders ahead with a 5-yard run to the end zone. On the next possession, Kenny King caught a 21-yard pass from Plunkett to take the lead to 21–7.

In the second quarter Mark van Eeghen rushed in for three yards to give Oakland a 28–7 lead, but San Diego responded with 17 unanswered points. The score was now Oakland 28, San Diego 24. Entering the fourth quarter, Oakland was worried.

Ted Hendricks grabbed Jim by his jersey.

"San Diego was getting back in the ballgame when Ted Hendricks grabbed me by the jersey, shook me and said, 'Keep scoring. We can stop them. All we have to do is hold on to the ball, control it, run out the clock and we're there.'"

And Oakland did just that.

"After Bahr's two field goals, we were just minutes away from a Super Bowl," said Millen, "an opportunity that we weren't going to let slip away."

"Our defensive back Burgess Owens and I were standing on the sideline and he'd say, 'How are we doing?' I said, 'We picked up six.' Two more first downs. One more first down and the game is ours.' He said, 'What happened?' I said, 'We're going to the Super Bowl!' And he was beside himself! 'New Orleans, here we come!'"

Final score: Oakland 34, San Diego 27.

SUPER BOWL XV

New Orleans during Super Bowl week was filled with distractions. For the Oakland Raiders, it was business as usual—even if business as usual meant breaking curfew for John Matuszak. Just ask Matt Millen.

"Did John show up late? Yeah. Was he late for practice? Yeah. Was he out on the town? Yeah. To John it was another regular season game. He was going to do that regardless."

According to Matuszak, things tightened up during the Super Bowl.

"Now this is a Super Bowl game, and things are a lot different when it comes to Super Bowl. A lot of things tighten up like the gluteus maximus tightening up. You can't even get a blade of grass up there—some people."

Matuszak was referring to Eagles coach Dick Vermeil. Vermeil publicly criticized John's off-field behavior and put strict team rules into effect.

"They could not go to Bourbon Street," said John. "They couldn't go into the French Quarter. We also heard that there were curfews and mandatory meetings at night. There was a tremendous amount of pressure on the Raiders because the Eagles were known for how they could not go and do things and have fun. We felt we had the burden of all the other teams to knock them off their perch."

"The first night Tom gave us no curfew and let us go out and get it out of our system, but a lot of the guys had large systems, and it took a few days to get it out of their systems," said Plunkett. Matuszak was one of those guys.

"The first night of curfew, there's no Matuszak," said Upshaw. "He staggers on the bus as we are leaving to go to the press conference. We asked, 'Tooz, where have you been.' He said, 'I was out.' And he looked like it.

"'Tooz, after all the discussions we had in practice and we all decided it's time to get serious and we have work to do—and you go out!' His response was, 'I went out to make sure that nobody else was out.' That was what he said and then he sat down. And that was that."

Tom Flores tolerated the late nights as long as the Raiders performed at practice. But Matt Millen got a little overexcited during those practices.

"Our practices were brutal! I got into a fight with Mickey Marvin. I tried to kill him. I head-butted him into oblivion. I was letting everything out. It felt so good to be on the field."

By game day, not even world events could shake the Raiders' focus.

"We drove to the Superdome and there was a big yellow ribbon around the Superdome," said Millen. "'What the heck is that up there for?' I asked. They said, 'The hostages are free!' I was so focused as to what was going on that I didn't have a clue what was going on in the world. Some would say that was great concentration; others would have said, 'The kid needs a little perspective.'

"But our job was to play one more football game—and to go to that game and not be prepared to play would have just been awful for what we had already accomplished. It wouldn't have meant anything."

"It was a such great feeling!" said Plunkett. I was so proud to run out on that field. It was like a storybook finish all coming to a head!"

"In some ways the Super Bowl was anticlimactic because the best team in football, we thought, were the San Diego Chargers," said Millen.

"I was ready the moment I stepped on that field," said Plunkett. "I still had something to prove to myself and to whomever else didn't believe in me."

In just three months, Jim Plunkett had gone from Heisman bust to Super Bowl savior. His three touchdown passes capped one of the greatest personal comebacks in NFL history.

"Jim Plunkett had a masterful game and Rod Martin had a game for the ages," said Millen. "He was everywhere. He had three interceptions. He played as good a Super Bowl as any defender has ever played. He did not get the MVP—Jim Plunkett got the honor—but Rod deserved it just as much."

Upshaw felt that Plunkett was due.

"I felt really good for Jim because he had paid his dues just like anyone else, but it meant a lot to him to be the guy that led us to that Super Bowl."

Plunkett finally got the monkey off his back.

"It was a great feeling. I finally accomplished something that everyone in the NFL wants to do."

With the game finally over, the only suspense that remained was whether the tension that remained between Rozelle and Davis would affect the presentation of the Vince Lombardi Trophy.

Al had a talk with his players prior to the presentation.

"I will never forget him telling us to be gentlemen and show respect in the locker room," said Upshaw.

Al's main purpose was to win. Tom Flores and his team only talked about football—nothing else.

"The relocations and legal actions were never allowed to become major distractions to our players and coaches," said Flores. "Al Davis would never let these things be distractions. The main purpose was for us to win. Everything else was secondary, and Al would take care of that in his own time. The team never talked about anything but football—winning football. This is a very courageous bunch of guys. They absolutely refused to believe anything but that they could win."

Flores addressed the squad and staff in the crowded Louisiana Superdome locker room after the win.

"We won the game. We were the best team. We deserve to be the World Champions, and I'm proud of you. I love it. This is the greatest moment of my life. I'm very proud of this bunch of guys."

The final word on this great season by the underdog Raiders belonged to the boss—to Al Davis—as he accepted the Super Bowl trophy from NFL Commissioner Pete Rozelle.

"You know when you look back on the glory of the Oakland Raiders, this was our finest hour . . . to Tom Flores, the coaches, and the great athletes, you were magnificent out there . . . take pride and be proud. Your commitment to excellence and your will to win will endure forever. You were magnificent!"

Matt Millen had a surreal moment after the team's victory.

"We won the Super Bowl. We all flew out back to Oakland. They were going to have a parade. I wanted to get home. I sat in my mom's living room and turned the news on, and there were my teammates in the parade. And I sat there and I thought, 'Was I even there? Did you even play that game?' Because it didn't seem real. Everything happened so fast and you don't really appreciate it. I really think that it should be mandatory for every team that wins the Super Bowl to take one day—players and coaches only—to go back to their facility, get a bunch of food, and sit down and watch the film together as a group so you could enjoy what you did. I think if you did that it would be awesome because that's the one time you don't have to worry about the next game. You did it—you finally did it."

Seventeen months after winning Super Bowl XV, the Raiders moved to Los Angeles. They returned to Oakland in 1995.

In 1983, Jim Plunkett led the Raiders to another championship in Super Bowl XVIII. He retired after the 1986 season.

OAKLAND RAIDERS OF THE 1970S IN THE PRO FOOTBALL HALL OF FAME

Name	Position(s)	Season	Inducted
Jim Otto	C	1960–74	1980
George Blanda	QB/K	1967–75	1981
Willie Brown	CB	1967–78	1984
Gene Upshaw	G	1967–81	1987
Fred Biletnikoff	WR	1965–78	1988
Art Shell	T	1968–82	1989
Ted Hendricks	LB	1975–83	1990
Al Davis	Owner	1963–2011	1992
Dave Casper	TE	1974–80, 84	2002
Bob Brown*	OT	1971–73	2004
John Madden	Coach	1969–78	2006
Ray Guy	P	1973–86	2014
Ron Wolf	Executive	1963–74, 79–89	2015

*Went into the Hall of Fame as a member of the Philadelphia Eagles

EPILOGUE

YOU EITHER LOVED THEM or hated them, but those Oakland Raiders of the 1970s under the guidance of Coach John Madden were an entertaining cast of characters in the guise of one of the greatest NFL teams of their era.

Throughout the decade of the 1970s, the Raiders won 71.5 percent of their games. They lost 38 games, one fewer than either the Steelers or Cowboys. Both Oakland and Pittsburgh played in six conference championship games in the '70s. They also produced ten players, one owner, and a head coach that would be enshrined in the Pro Football Hall of Fame.

It has been long argued that '70s quarterback Kenny Stabler and wide receiver Cliff Branch should also be enshrined in the Hall, as well as Coach Tom Flores, quarterback Jim Plunkett, and defensive back Lester Hayes. It's a compelling argument that needs to be reviewed by the HOF voting committee.

A total of twenty retired quarterbacks were named to the NFL's All Decade teams ranging from the 1930s through the 1990s. The only two quarterbacks *not* enshrined in Canton from those teams are Kenny Stabler and the Packers' Cecil Isbell, who played for Green Bay in the 1930s and 1940s.

But even with all of those Hall of Fame players, they only had one Super Bowl victory that decade. The Raiders enshrined are one more than that of the Steelers, who won four Super Bowls in the 1970s. It is also three more than the Cowboys, who appeared in a record five Super Bowls that decade, winning two.

With all that talent it's felt that they should have played in more Super Bowls than the Cowboys and won more than the Steelers . . . but that was not to be.

So the question remains: Were the Oakland Raiders of the 1970s a great team? Were they as great on the field—individually or collectively—as their image portrays?

That's for you, dear reader, to be the judge of.

REFERENCES

Books

America's Game, Michael MacCambridge, Anchor Books, 2004.

Badasses: The Legend of Snake, Foo, Dr. Death, and John Madden's Oakland Raiders, Peter Richmond, HarperCollins, 2010.

Blanda: Alive and Kicking—The Exclusive, Authorized Biography, Wells Twombly, Nash Publishing, 1972.

Crusin' with the Tooz, John Matuszak with Steve Delsohn, Franklin Watts, 1987.

The Garner Files, James Garner and Jon Winokur, Simon & Schuster, 2011.

The Good, the Bad & the Ugly, Steven Travers, Triumph Books, 2008.

Hey, Wait a Minute (I Wrote a Book!), John Madden with Dave Anderson, Villard, 1984.

Jim Otto: The Pain of Glory, Jim Otto with Dave Newhouse, Sports Publishing Inc., 1979.

Just Win, Baby, Glenn Dickey, Harcourt Brace Jovanovich, 1991.

The League: The Rise and Decline of the NFL, David Harris, Bantam, 1986.

Raiders Forever, John Lombardo, Contemporary Books, 2001.

Slick: The Silver and Black Life of Al Davis, Mark Ribowsky, Macmillan, 1991.

Snake, Ken Stabler and Berry Stainback, Doubleday, 1986.

Stadium Stories: The Oakland Raiders—Colorful Tales of the Silver and Black, Tom LaMarre, Globe Pequot Press, 2005.

Tales from the Oakland Raiders: A Collection of the Greatest Stories Ever Told, Tom Flores with Matt Fulks, Sports Publishing, 2003.

They Call Me Assassin, Jack Tatum with Bill Kushner, Everest House, 1979.

Periodicals

"Al Davis Isn't as Bad as He Thinks He Is," Gary Smith, *Inside Sports*, May 31, 1981.

"Raider Nation," Pat Toomay, ESPN.com.

Newspapers

Boston Globe
Dallas Morning News
New York Daily News
New York Times
Oakland Tribune

Internet

Dallas Morning News
"'70s Raiders had Hall of Fame talent, but were they great?"
by Rick Gosselin
www.dallasnews.com/incoming/20101019-70s-Raiders-had-Hall-of-9392.ece
November 3, 2010 (Accessed on April 2, 2015)

Denver Post
"Broncos RB Rob Lytle: Did he fumble against the Raiders? Well . . ."
by Terry Frei
http://blogs.denverpost.com/broncos/2013/09/22/broncos-lytle/21828/
September 22, 2013

ESPN
"Notorious Image Sticks with these Raiders"
by Jeffri Chadiha
http://sports.espn.go.com/espn/cheat/news/story?id=2957892
August 9, 2007 (Accessed on April 6, 2015)

NFL Deadspin
"The 1970s Oakland Raiders: Boozin' and Coozin' Through El Rancho"
by Peter Richmond
http://deadspin.com/5646039/the-1970s-oakland-raiders-boozin-
   and-coozin-through-el-rancho
September 23, 2010 (Accessed on May 3, 2015)

Sun-Sentinel
"Raiders' Camp Was Wild Affair"
by Charles Bricker
http://articles.sun-sentinel.com/2002-08-11/sports/0208100340_1_
   phil-villapiano-hells-angels-raiders-quarterback
August 11, 2002

DVDs

America's Game: The 1980 Oakland Raiders.
America's Game: The Immaculate Reception.
America's Game: The Story of the 1976 Raiders—The Super Bowl Champions.
A Football Life: Al Davis, NFL Network.
A Football Life: The Immaculate Reception, NFL Network
Raiders: The Complete History, NFL Productions, 2004.
Raiders Season Highlights: 1970–1979, NFL Films.
Rebels of Oakland: The A's, the Raiders, the '70s, HBO Studio Productions,
   2003.